SEXUAL ORIENTATION AND THE LAW

SEXUAL ORIENTATION AND THE LAW

The Editors of the
Harvard Law Review

HARVARD UNIVERSITY PRESS
CAMBRIDGE, MASSACHUSETTS
LONDON, ENGLAND
1990

This book is printed on acid-free paper, and its binding materials
have been chosen for strength and durability.

Library of Congress Cataloging-in-Publication Data

Sexual orientation and the law / Harvard law review.
        p.   cm.
     Includes bibliographical references.
     ISBN 0-674-80292-6 (alk. paper). — ISBN 0-674-80293-4
(pbk. alk. paper)
     1. Homosexuality — Law and legislation — United States.
2. Sex and law — United States.   I. Harvard law review.
KF4754.5.S492   1990
346.7301'3 — dc20
[347.30613]   89-24525
                                                              CIP

CONTENTS

"two women together is a work
nothing in civilization has made simple . . . ."

ADRIENNE RICH
THE DREAM OF A COMMON LANGUAGE 35 (1978)

"Great Alexander loved Hephaestion;
The conquering Hercules for Hylas wept,
And for Patroclus stern Achilles drooped.
And not kings only, but the wisest men:
The Roman Tully loved Octavius,
Grave Socrates, wild Alcibiades."

CHRISTOPHER MARLOWE
EDWARD THE SECOND (1640)

"Like all human behavior, homosexuality leads to make-believe, disequilibrium,
frustration, lies, or, on the contrary, it becomes the source of rewarding
experiences, in accordance with its manner of expression in actual living —
whether in bad faith, laziness, and falsity, or in lucidity, generosity, and
freedom."

SIMONE DE BEAUVOIR
THE SECOND SEX 473 (1952)

"Sooner or later, the massive gay population will indeed win their rights, as
other groups have already done. Sooner or later, the strife and anger and
hatred and violence against gay people will be put aside. What we seek now
is to leap over the many years and great turmoil that will take place by having
the person who represents these people speak out now."

HARVEY MILK
IN R. SHILTS, THE MAYOR OF CASTRO STREET:
THE LIFE AND TIMES OF HARVEY MILK 214 (1982)

I. INTRODUCTION

Sharply conflicting attitudes toward homosexuality[1] share an uneasy existence in today's society. This range of viewpoints is reflected in legislation, legal decisionmaking, and legal scholarship. Social — and therefore legal — attitudes vary along two dimensions. First, individuals hold different opinions on the relationship between same-sex intimacy or desire and an individual's identity. Although some view same-sex intimacy as actions separable from identity, most people today accept the concept of sexual orientation and believe that the gender of those to whom one is attracted is a function of personality and identity. Second, social attitudes vary depending on individuals' reactions to homosexuality. Views toward those labeled homosexual range from condemnation to pity to indifference to respect. This range also appears in the legal community. Although some courts[2] and commentators[3] are very sympathetic to claims by lesbians and gay

---

[1] Although sexual orientation denotes heterosexuality as well as homosexuality and bisexuality, sexual orientation only becomes an issue for those not in the majority. This Note, therefore, concentrates on same-sex sexual orientation. Estimates as to the number of lesbians and gay men differ depending on how those terms are defined. Many people who have had same-sex sexual experiences do not label themselves gay or lesbian, and others adopt the label without having had any same-sex sexual experiences. Although equating sexual orientation with sexual activity is both inaccurate and problematic, studies estimating the percentage of the population comprised of gay men and lesbians depend on such definitions. A recent study indicates that 20.3% of men have had at least one sexual encounter to orgasm with another man, and 6.7% have had such an encounter after age 19. *See* Fay, Turner, Klassen & Gagnon, *Prevalence and Patterns of Same-Gender Sexual Contact Among Men*, 243 SCIENCE 338, 341 table 2 (1989). Older studies on women report a lower frequency of same-sex sexual activity. *See* A. KINSEY, W. POMEROY, C. MARTIN & P. GEBHARD, SEXUAL BEHAVIOR IN THE HUMAN FEMALE 474–75 (1953) [hereinafter FEMALE SEXUAL BEHAVIOR] (finding that 13% of women had "overt contacts to the point of orgasm" with other females). The percentage of men and women who acknowledge psychological arousal by members of their gender is much larger. *See id.* at 452 (28% of women); A. KINSEY, W. POMEROY & C. MARTIN, SEXUAL BEHAVIOR IN THE HUMAN MALE 650 (1948) [hereinafter MALE SEXUAL BEHAVIOR] (50% of men). Gay women and men are found in all geographical areas, social classes, education levels, races, and religions. *See* Gonsiorek, *Mental Health: Introduction*, in HOMOSEXUALITY 61 (W. Paul, J. Weinrich, J. Gonsiorek & M. Hotvedt eds. 1982).

The range of gay or lesbian existence is much broader than merely sexual acts. Adrienne Rich uses

> the term *lesbian continuum* to include a range . . . of woman-identified experience, not simply the fact that a woman has had or consciously desired genital sexual experience with another woman. If we expand it . . . we begin to grasp breadths of female history and psychology which have lain out of reach of a consequence of limited, mostly clinical, definitions of *lesbianism*.

A. RICH, *Compulsory Heterosexuality and Lesbian Existence*, in BLOOD, BREAD AND POETRY: SELECTED PROSE 1979–1985, at 51–52 (1986) (emphasis in original).

[2] *See, e.g.*, Watkins v. United States Army, 847 F.2d 1329 (9th Cir.), *reh'g granted en banc*, 847 F.2d 1362 (9th Cir. 1988); High Tech Gays v. Defense Indus. Sec. Clearance Office, 668 F. Supp. 1361 (N.D. Cal. 1987).

[3] *See, e.g.*, L. TRIBE, AMERICAN CONSTITUTIONAL LAW § 16-33, at 1616 (2d ed. 1988); Michelman, *Law's Republic*, 97 YALE L.J. 1493 (1988).

men for equal treatment, a substantial portion of the legal community retains negative views of those with minority sexual orientations.[4]

Differing views along these two dimensions — whether sexual orientation is part of identity and whether gay men and lesbians are viewed positively, negatively or neutrally — combine to create four competing conceptions of homosexuality.[5] The "sin" conception views homosexual acts as immoral and wrong; it generally does not ascribe to the view of homosexuality as an intrinsic part of identity. The "illness" viewpoint similarly sees homosexuality negatively; this framework, however, sees it as part of the affected individual's personality, albeit a potentially curable component. The "neutral difference" approach, like the illness approach, embraces the concept of sexual orientation as identity but views it merely as a difference that should not be a basis for discriminatory treatment. Finally, the "social construct" conception rejects categorizing individuals by sexual orientation and views same-sex acts and relationships as not materially different from opposite-sex ones. The vocabulary one uses in discussing sexual orientation issues, and even the fact that one chooses to discuss them, necessarily implicates one of these four viewpoints.[6]

The sin conception of same-sex sexual activity prevailed in the colonies and in the United States before the late nineteenth century.[7] During this period, the modern concepts of heterosexuality and homosexuality did not exist;[8] rather, almost all nonprocreative or nonmarital sexual activities were considered immoral and made criminal.[9]

---

[4] These attitudes not only result in the denial of claims brought by lesbians and gay men but also cause many legal issues concerning gay men and lesbians to be trivialized and ignored. For example, cases dealing with these issues often remain unpublished and legal scholars addressing sexual orientation issues often face stigmatization by their academic peers. *See* Rivera, *Our Straight-Laced Judges: The Legal Position of Homosexual Persons in the United States*, 30 HASTINGS L.J. 799, 805 (1979).

[5] This Note refers to "sexual orientation," "homosexuality," and "gay men and lesbians" for simplicity although those who view same-sex attractions and eroticism merely as acts rather than as part of identity would use a more complicated vocabulary.

[6] For example, use of the term "homosexual," with its scientific connotation, is typical of the sickness viewpoint. Most adherents to the neutral difference conception, in contrast, prefer the nonpejorative terms "gay" or "gay and lesbian." Some, particularly those who see sexual orientation as a social construct, use "gay" only as an adjective, viewing the use of the word as a noun as implying that being gay is the most important characteristic of the individuals so described. "Sexual orientation" implies that the gender of an individual's partner is part of that individual's identity and not a matter of choice whereas "sexual preference" does not. This Note will use the term "gay men and lesbians" because it is preferred by most of those whom it describes.

[7] *See* J. KATZ, GAY/LESBIAN ALMANAC 31–48 (1983).

[8] *See* D'Emilio, *Making and Unmaking Minorities: The Tensions Between Gay Politics and History*, 14 N.Y.U. REV. L. & SOC. CHANGE 915, 917 (1986); Goldstein, *History, Homosexuality, and Political Values: Searching for the Hidden Determinants of* Bowers v. Hardwick, 97 YALE L.J. 1073, 1087 (1988). The terms "homosexual" and "heterosexual" and the concepts behind them were not popular in the United States until the 1920's. *See* J. KATZ, *supra* note 7, at 16.

[9] *See* J. KATZ, *supra* note 7, at 29–65; Law, *Homosexuality and the Social Meaning of*

Yet those who transgressed the society's sexual moral code were not stigmatized as long as they repented.[10] Furthermore, sharp distinctions were not drawn between same-sex sexual activity and other forms of sin; rather, sodomy "represented a capacity for sin inherent in everyone."[11]

This conception of all nonmarital or nonprocreative sexual acts as sinful is reflective of the largely homogeneous society in which the family was the basic economic and social unit.[12] The homogeneity of society also explains the absence of distinction between homosexual and heterosexual sexual orientation. The idea that some members of a community might be "different" and have different sexual orientations was less intuitive in such a society than the contrary notion that all members of the community were equally capable of moral transgression.[13]

The absence of a concept of sexual orientation is particularly vivid in nineteenth-century society's treatment of relationships between women. During this time, deeply-felt, intimate relationships between women were seen as normal and acceptable.[14] These relationships were "both sensual and platonic";[15] they were never labeled "lesbian"[16] but rather were seen as complementary to the woman's relationship with her husband and family.[17] Because men and women lived and worked in different spheres, relationships between women developed naturally.[18]

Gender, 1988 WIS. L. REV. 187, 199. However, sexual acts between two women were generally not criminalized because the laws only sought to deter "the unnatural spilling of seed, the biblical sin of Onan." J. D'EMILIO & E. FREEDMAN, INTIMATE MATTERS: A HISTORY OF SEXUALITY IN AMERICA 122 (1988); *see also* Law, *supra*, at 202 n.75 ("The traditional common law and religious condemnation of homosexuality did not encompass women.").

[10] *See* J. D'EMILIO & E. FREEDMAN, *supra* note 9, at 15.

[11] D'Emilio, *supra* note 8, at 917.

[12] *See* Law, *supra* note 9, at 199.

[13] *See id.*

[14] *See* L. FADERMAN, SURPASSING THE LOVE OF MEN: ROMANTIC FRIENDSHIP AND LOVE BETWEEN WOMEN FROM THE RENAISSANCE TO THE PRESENT 157 (1981); Smith-Rosenberg, *The Female World of Love and Ritual: Relations Between Women in Nineteenth-Century America*, 1 SIGNS 1, 9, 27 (1975); A. RICH, *Vesuvius at Home: The Power of Emily Dickinson*, in ON LIES, SECRETS AND SILENCE: SELECTED PROSE 1966–1978, at 162–63 (1979).

[15] Smith-Rosenberg, *supra* note 14, at 4.

[16] Indeed, most people never imagined that relationships between two women could be sexual. *See* P. BLUMSTEIN & P. SCHWARTZ, AMERICAN COUPLES 40 (1983); *see also* Law, *supra* note 9, at 202 ("Lesbians were censured by silence; sexual acts between two women were unimaginable."). This view was also a reflection of the common belief that women were asexual. *See* D. GREENBERG, THE CONSTRUCTION OF HOMOSEXUALITY 376–77 (1988).

[17] *See* P. BLUMSTEIN & P. SCHWARTZ, *supra* note 16, at 41; P. CONRAD & J. SCHNEIDER, DEVIANCE AND MEDICALIZATION 173 (1980) ("As long as women's behavior did not interfere with carrying, bearing, and rearing of children, it received comparatively little attention."); D. WEST, HOMOSEXUALITY RE-EXAMINED 177 (1977) ("In male-dominated societies, . . . lesbian activities . . . seem to have been treated with an amused tolerance, so long as they did not interfere with masculine satisfactions.").

[18] *See* Smith-Rosenberg, *supra* note 14, at 9–13; L. FADERMAN, *supra* note 14, at 157–58.

Although the conception of homosexual acts, and more generally "the homosexual lifestyle,"[19] as sinful is much less prevalent today, it has been a powerful influence throughout the twentieth century. Before the rise of the neutral difference conception in the 1970's, the sin conception exerted considerable influence on judicial decisionmaking. For example, in 1969, the Court of Claims based its refusal to reinstate a dismissed gay civil servant on the finding that "[a]ny schoolboy knows that a homosexual act is immoral, indecent, lewd, and obscene."[20] Although the immorality viewpoint has present-day supporters,[21] judges less frequently rely explicitly on this conception.[22]

The illness view, which also sees homosexual activity as wrong and deviant, maintains that deviant sexual acts are symptoms of a sickness. In contrast to the sin conception, the sickness view sees the desire to engage in homosexual activity as inhering in the individual's identity. The concept of homosexual and heterosexual individuals emerged during the late nineteenth and mid-twentieth centuries,[23] as science and medicine replaced religion as the major influences in society. The medical and psychiatric professions invented the term "homosexuality"[24] and began to study the illness it described.[25]

During this period, much of the literature on homosexuality focused on means of curing the disease.[26] Although the conception of homosexuality as a disease made criminal condemnation less defensible, it also led to institutionalization of and psychological and medical experimentation on gay men and lesbians.[27] Furthermore, the concept of homosexual persons as a distinct group led to differentiation among

---

[19] *See* J. FALWELL, LISTEN, AMERICA! 186 (1980).

[20] Schlegel v. United States, 416 F.2d 1372, 1378 (Ct. Cl. 1969).

[21] *See, e.g.*, Bowers v. Hardwick, 478 U.S. 186, 197 (1986) (Burger, C.J., concurring) ("To hold that the act of homosexual sodomy is somehow protected as a fundamental right would be to cast aside millennia of moral teaching."). In fact, this viewpoint witnessed a resurgence in the late 1970's due to the efforts of the Moral Majority and the New Right. These groups seek to restore the heterosexual, patriarchal family, and view homosexuality as a threat to their vision of an ideal society. *See, e.g.*, A. BRYANT, THE ANITA BRYANT STORY 53–55 (1977); J. FALWELL, *supra* note 19, at 181–86.

[22] *See, e.g.*, Constant A. v. Paul C.A., 344 Pa. Super. 49, 54, 496 A.2d 1, 3 (1985) (terming "gratuitous" the trial court's "finding concerning the moral nature" of a mother's lesbian relationship).

[23] *See, e.g.*, 1 M. FOUCAULT, THE HISTORY OF SEXUALITY 43 (R. Hurley trans. 1978) (placing the birth of the "psychological, psychiatric, medical category of homosexuality" in 1870); V. BULLOUGH, HOMOSEXUALITY: A HISTORY 7 (1979).

[24] *See* Goldstein, *supra* note 8, at 1088 (noting that the word homosexual "was coined in the nineteenth century to express the new idea that a person's immanent and essential nature is revealed by the gender of his desired sex partner").

[25] *See* P. BLUMSTEIN & P. SCHWARTZ, *supra* note 16, at 41–42.

[26] *See* J. D'EMILIO, SEXUAL POLITICS, SEXUAL COMMUNITIES: THE MAKING OF A HOMOSEXUAL MINORITY IN THE UNITED STATES, 1940–1970, at 17 (1983).

[27] *See id.* at 18; J. KATZ, *supra* note 7, at 131.

various immoral sexual activities. Although all states had sodomy statutes criminalizing both male/male and male/female acts, over time these were enforced primarily against gay men.[28]

The third conception of homosexuality, that of neutral difference, could not emerge until both the concept of homosexuality and a group of people who defined themselves as homosexual came into existence.[29] Although developments in the medical and psychiatric professions led to the creation of a concept of the "homosexual" individual, it was social and economic changes that inspired the formation of gay communities. The rise of industrial capitalism and the accompanying movement of individuals to large urban centers in the late nineteenth century decreased the importance of family units in determining morality and law.[30] In addition, some barriers to women's economic independence were reduced, allowing women to live apart from men and pursue relationships only with women.[31] These changes allowed individuals to choose to have same-sex relationships instead of marrying.[32] Between the 1870's and 1930's, gay and lesbian communities appeared in American cities[33] and continued to grow during and after World War II.[34] In 1948 and 1953, Kinsey's groundbreaking studies[35] of human sexuality were released, causing mainstream American society to realize that homosexual activity was much more prevalent than generally thought.[36]

The 1950's witnessed both the increase of anti-gay sentiment and official harassment[37] and the formation of precursors to the contemporary gay and lesbian rights movement. Relatively secret "homophile" organizations, such as the Mattachine Society, held meetings in major urban centers and published magazines aimed at informing gay

---

[28] See infra p. 16.

[29] See J. D'EMILIO, supra note 26, at 1–5; J. D'EMILIO & E. FREEDMAN, supra note 9, at 288 ("The infiltration of psychiatric and psychoanalytic concepts into popular culture contributed to this process of labeling homosexual desire even as they cast the shadow of morbidity over gay relationships.").

[30] See J. BOSWELL, CHRISTIANITY, SOCIAL TOLERANCE AND HOMOSEXUALITY 35 (1980).

[31] See V. BULLOUGH, supra note 23, at 118. Because women were still barred from many occupations, the phenomenon of "passing women" became more common. These women dressed and worked as men, and entered into relationships, often marriages, with other women. By living as men, these women were able to escape the limitations of women's roles. See generally J. KATZ, supra note 7, at 209–79 (documenting the lives of passing women between 1782 and 1920); Musician's Death at 74 Reveals He Was a Woman, N.Y. Times, Feb. 2, 1989, at A18, col. 1.

[32] See J. D'EMILIO, supra note 26, at 11; D. GREENBERG, supra note 16, at 355.

[33] See J. D'EMILIO, supra note 26, at 11–13.

[34] See id. at 23–39.

[35] MALE SEXUAL BEHAVIOR, supra note 1; FEMALE SEXUAL BEHAVIOR, supra note 1.

[36] See J. D'EMILIO, supra note 26, at 37. The Kinsey authors rejected classifications in terms of normal and abnormal. See MALE SEXUAL BEHAVIOR, supra note 1, at 201.

[37] See J. D'EMILIO, supra note 26, at 42.

men and lesbians.[38] In 1955, lesbians formed the Daughters of Bilitis
to promote their interests separately.[39] These groups rejected the view
of homosexuality as wrong or sick, and instead viewed lesbians and
gay men as an oppressed minority whose civil rights deserved protection.[40] The neutral difference model gained momentum in the late
1960's with the birth of the contemporary gay and lesbian[41] rights
movement.[42] The women's movement's attack on traditional gender
roles, increased openness about and lessened taboos on sexuality, and
the "culture of protest" in the 1960's all contributed to the spread of
"gay liberation."[43] Mental health professionals also revised their views
on homosexuality during the early 1970's and ceased to characterize
homosexuality as an illness.[44]

Many legal developments reflect the neutral difference model's
view that homosexuals either deserve legal protection or should not
be legally penalized for their sexual orientation.[45] In 1962, the Amer-

---

[38] *See* P. CONRAD & J. SCHNEIDER, *supra* note 17, at 200–01; Licata, *The Homosexual
Rights Movement in the United States*, in HISTORICAL PERSPECTIVES ON HOMOSEXUALITY 168–
70 (J. Licata & R. Petersen eds. 1980). The publication of magazines by these groups led to
legal conflict when the Los Angeles Postmaster withdrew the October 1954 issue of the magazine
One from the mail. In *One, Inc. v. Olesen*, 355 U.S. 371 (1958), the Supreme Court required
the Postmaster to deliver the magazine, summarily reversing the Ninth Circuit's decision in
favor of the Postmaster.

[39] *See* V. BULLOUGH, *supra* note 23, at 72. For more about the Daughters of Bilitis, see D.
MARTIN & P. LYON, LESBIAN/WOMAN 219–55 (1972).

[40] *See* J. D'EMILIO, *supra* note 26, at 65–66.

[41] Although gay men and lesbians have joined together to fight discrimination, it would be
a mistake to suggest that the histories, experiences, and beliefs of all members of the two groups
are identical. *See* A. RICH, *supra* note 1, at 52–53; Licata, *supra* note 38, at 171. Some lesbians
find themselves more closely aligned with feminists than with the "gay movement." *See id.* at
180–81; V. BULLOUGH, *supra* note 23, at 117. Other lesbians, however, reject the mainstream
feminist movement as heterosexist and anti-gay. *See* D. MARTIN & P. LYON, *supra* note 39, at
266–67; *see also* R. MORGAN, GOING TOO FAR 7 (1978) (discussing the lesbian/nonlesbian rift
in the women's movement). A lesbian separatist movement also developed as the gay movement
grew. *See generally* FOR LESBIANS ONLY: A SEPARATIST ANTHOLOGY (S.L. Hoagland & J.
Penelope eds. 1988).

[42] The Stonewall Bar riot in the early hours of June 28, 1969, in response to police harassment
following Judy Garland's burial, is generally considered to be the start of the gay and lesbian
rights movement. *See* M. BRONSKI, CULTURE CLASH: THE MAKING OF GAY SENSIBILITY 2
(1984). Important gay and lesbian activist organizations such as the Gay Liberation Front and
the Gay Activist Alliance, were formed after Stonewall. *See* P. CONRAD & J. SCHNEIDER, *supra*
note 17, at 202; *see also* V. BULLOUGH, *supra* note 23, at 76; Voeller, *Society and the Gay
Movement*, in HOMOSEXUAL BEHAVIOR 243 (J. Marmor ed. 1980) (reporting that by 1972 twelve
hundred lesbian and gay groups had formed in the United States).

[43] *See* J. D'EMILIO & E. FREEDMAN, *supra* note 9, at 321.

[44] In 1973, the American Psychiatric Association removed homosexuality from its list of
psychiatric disorders. *See* R. BAYER, HOMOSEXUALITY AND AMERICAN PSYCHIATRY 137 (1987).
In 1975, the American Public Health Association and the American Psychological Association
passed similar resolutions. *See* Law, *supra* note 9, at 214 n.131.

[45] Adherents of the illness approach often also favor legal reform on gay and lesbian issues.
They see homosexuality as not freely chosen, and therefore requiring sympathy and understand-

ican Law Institute issued its Model Penal Code recommending de-criminalization of consensual private same-sex activities between adults.[46] In the late 1960's and early 1970's, gay and lesbian plaintiffs began to challenge successfully federal civil service dismissals,[47] gay bar liquor license revocations,[48] and other anti-gay state actions.[49] Legislative changes also reflected the shift toward a civil rights con-ception of sexual orientation. Since then, half the states have repealed sodomy statutes[50] and anti-discrimination legislation is in force in the state of Wisconsin and over sixty cities and counties.[51]

The fourth approach views sexual orientation as a social con-struct.[52] Under this approach, the gender of those to whom an in-dividual is attracted becomes important only if society attaches im-portance to it. Not all societies share the American conception of sexual orientation.[53] In the United States, the institutionalization of gender roles and heterosexuality causes the label "homosexual" to be placed upon individuals as a mark of difference.[54] The label "homo-sexual" stands in sharp contrast to the term "heterosexual" and cre-

---

ing rather than discrimination. *See, e.g.,* R. KRONEMEYER, OVERCOMING HOMOSEXUALITY 9 (1980). Those within the neutral difference framework ground arguments for the legal protection of gay men and lesbians in the immutability of homosexuality, *see, e.g.,* R. MOHR, GAYS/JUSTICE 39–40 (1988), or argue from the proposition that sexual orientation is intrinsic to personhood. *See, e.g.,* Note, *The Constitutional Status of Sexual Orientation: Homosexuality as a Suspect Classification,* 98 HARV. L. REV. 1285, 1300–05 (1985).

[46] *See* MODEL PENAL CODE § 213.2 note on status of section (Proposed Official Draft 1962).

[47] *See infra* p. 44.

[48] *See, e.g.,* One Eleven Wines & Liquors Inc., v. Division of Alcoholic Beverage Control, 50 N.J. 329, 235 A.2d 12 (1967).

[49] *See infra* pp. 156–57.

[50] *See infra* p. 9.

[51] *See infra* pp. 157–58.

[52] *See* J. KATZ, *supra* note 7, at 7 ("All homosexuality is situational, influenced and given meaning and character by its location in time and social space.").

[53] *See* J. BOSWELL, *supra* note 30, at 41 n.1. Similarly, not all societies have condemned same-sex relationships or sexual conduct. In some societies, such behavior was or is widely tolerated. *See, e.g.,* Goldstein, *supra* note 8, at 1087 (noting that some sexual practices between men were widely accepted in ancient Greece and Rome, and in medieval Europe); *see also* Carrier, *Homosexual Behavior in Cross-Cultural Perspective,* in HOMOSEXUAL BEHAVIOR, *supra* note 42, at 108–12 (stating that in some areas, such as Mexico, Southern Europe and Morocco, stigmatization of men who engage in same-sex sexual activity is limited to those who play the passive role). *See generally* D. WEST, *supra* note 17, at 132–36 (reviewing the anthropological research involving homosexual practices in nonwestern societies). In others, same-sex sexual conduct is or was institutionalized. *See, e.g.,* J. MONEY, GAY, STRAIGHT, AND IN-BETWEEN: THE SEXOLOGY OF EROTIC ORIENTATION 10–11 (1988) (discussing tribal practices in Sumatra, Papua New Guinea, and Melanesia).

[54] *See* Arriola, *Sexual Identity and the Constitution: Homosexual Persons as a Discrete and Insular Minority,* 10 Women's Rts. L. Rep. (Rutgers Univ.) 143, 156 (1988) ("[G]ay people emerge as a social minority only in the context of a heterosexually-dominant culture."); Rubenfeld, *The Right of Privacy,* 102 HARV. L. REV. 737, 780 (1989).

ates difference by forcing individuals to choose exclusively between their same- and opposite-sex attractions — in effect, to choose to be "deviant" or "normal," as society has defined those terms.[55] Labeling individuals based on the gender of their sexual partners reinforces prejudice by making sexual orientation appear fundamental to their identity.[56] Adherents to the social construct conception reject the civil rights model of neutral difference, and argue that basing legal protections for gay men and lesbians on the fundamental difference of their sexual orientation reinforces the very repression sought to be removed.[57]

The four conceptions of sexual orientation — as sin, sickness, neutral difference, and social construct — inform much of the law and policy concerning gay men and lesbians. One or more of these views underlies the statutes, regulations, and case law discussed in this Note.

The past few years have brought increased attention to legal issues involving gay men and lesbians. In 1986, the Supreme Court in *Bowers v. Hardwick*[58] upheld a Georgia sodomy statute as applied to oral sex between two men. The Acquired Immune Deficiency Syndrome (AIDS) epidemic and its disproportionate impact on gay and bisexual men[59] also have brought gay and lesbian issues into mainstream American media. The epidemic has increased discrimination against both gay men and lesbians,[60] even though lesbians are at a much lower risk than heterosexuals of contracting the disease,[61] and despite the increasing number of heterosexuals with AIDS.[62] AIDS

---

[55] Although bisexuals do exist, they are pressured by both society in general and the gay and lesbian community to choose to be either exclusively heterosexual or exclusively homosexual.

[56] *See* D'Emilio, *supra* note 8, at 920 ("[C]entral to the oppression of lesbians and gay men, and to society's ability to shape and enforce it, are the homosexual and heterosexual categories themselves.").

[57] As Jed Rubenfeld states:

To protect the rights of 'the homosexual' would of course be a victory; doing so, however, because homosexuality is essential to a person's identity is no liberation, but simply the flip side of the same rigidification of sexual identities by which our society simultaneously inculcates sexual roles, normalizes sexual conduct, and vilifies 'faggots.'

Rubenfeld, *supra* note 54, at 781.

[58] 478 U.S. 186 (1986).

[59] A majority of persons with AIDS are bisexual or gay men. *See* Altman, *Who's Stricken and How: AIDS Pattern Is Shifting*, N.Y. Times, Feb. 5, 1989, at 1, col. 1.

[60] *See* D. GREENBERG, *supra* note 16, at 478 (reporting the results of a survey finding that one-third of Americans have less favorable attitudes toward lesbians and gay men because of AIDS). Anti-gay people have claimed that AIDS is God's punishment for deviant sexual conduct. *See id.* at 478–79.

[61] *See* Mueller, *The Epidemiology of the Human Immunodeficiency Virus Infection*, 14 LAW, MED. & HEALTH CARE 250, 256 (1986) ("At present, there is no evidence of transmission between lesbians."); *see also* Arriola, *supra* note 54, at 171 (reporting that much of the general public assumes that lesbians are in a high risk group).

[62] *See* Altman, *supra* note 59, at 1, col. 1.

itself, however, is not solely a gay issue; it is a medical problem for everyone.[63]

This Note examines the legal problems faced by gay men and lesbians. Part II examines the interaction between gay men and lesbians and the criminal justice system. Part III discusses sexual orientation discrimination in public and private employment. Part IV addresses the first amendment issues posed by gay and lesbian students and teachers in public schools and universities. Part V analyzes the legal problems faced by men and women in same-sex relationships. Part VI explores the rights of gay and lesbian parents to custody and visitation of their children as well as the ability of gay men and lesbians to become adoptive or foster parents and the legal difficulties associated with having children of their own. Part VII examines a variety of other contexts in which gay men and lesbians face discrimination, including immigration, insurance, and incorporation of gay rights organizations, and also discusses legislation enacted by some cities and states to prevent sexual orientation discrimination.

II. GAY MEN AND LESBIANS AND THE CRIMINAL JUSTICE SYSTEM

A. The Criminalization of Same-Sex Sexual Activity

1. Sodomy Statutes. — Despite efforts by the gay- and lesbian-rights movement to obtain reform,[1] sodomy remains a crime in twenty-four states and the District of Columbia.[2] These statutes vary

---

[63] AIDS will not, therefore, be discussed in this Note except insofar as it has increased anti-gay discrimination, *see* note 64, *infra* p. 127; *infra* pp. 70, 153–56, and violence, *see infra* p. 31.

[1] *See generally* J. D'EMILIO, SEXUAL POLITICS, SEXUAL COMMUNITIES: THE MAKING OF A HOMOSEXUAL MINORITY IN THE UNITED STATES 1940–1970 (1983) (documenting the history of the gay and lesbian legal rights movement).

[2] *See* ALA. CODE § 13A-6-65(a)(3) (1982); ARIZ. REV. STAT. ANN. §§ 13-1411 to -1412 (Supp. 1988); ARK. STAT. ANN. § 5-14-122 (1987); D.C. CODE ANN. § 22-3502 (1981); FLA. STAT. § 800.02 (1987); GA. CODE ANN. § 16-6-2 (1988); IDAHO CODE § 18-6605 (1987); KAN. STAT. ANN. § 21-3505 (Supp. 1987); KY. REV. STAT. ANN. § 510.100 (Michie/Bobbs-Merrill 1985); LA. REV. STAT. ANN. § 14:89 (West 1986); MD. CODE ANN. art. 27, §§ 553–554 (1987); MICH. COMP. LAWS §§ 750.158, 750.338-.338(b) (1979); MINN. STAT. § 609.293 (1988); MISS. CODE ANN. § 97-29-59 (1972); MO. REV. STAT. § 566.090 (1986); MONT. CODE ANN. §§ 45-2-101, 45-5-505 (1987); NEV. REV. STAT. § 201.190 (1987); N.C. GEN. STAT. § 14-177 (1986); OKLA. STAT. tit. 21, § 886 (1981); R.I. GEN. LAWS § 11-10-1 (1986); S.C. CODE ANN. § 16-15-120 (Law. Co-op. 1985); TENN. CODE ANN. § 39-2-612 (1982); TEX. PENAL CODE ANN. §§ 21.01 (1), 21.06 (Vernon 1989); UTAH CODE ANN. § 76-5-403 (Supp. 1988); VA. CODE ANN. § 18-2-361 (1988). Massachusetts also has a sodomy statute criminalizing anal sex, *see* MASS. GEN. L. ch. 272, § 34 (1986) (prohibiting "the abominable and detestable crime against nature"), but the statute was arguably invalidated as applied to private consensual conduct by Commonwealth v. Balthazar, 366 Mass. 298, 302, 318 N.E.2d 478, 481 (1974), which found a companion statute criminalizing "lewd and lascivious acts" unconstitutional as applied to private, consensual adult behavior. Although the above statutes do not uniformly use the term "sodomy" to describe the

in the specific acts proscribed and the classes of persons explicitly affected. Most sodomy statutes prohibit oral-genital and anal-genital contact, although some state courts have construed their statutes not to apply to oral acts.[3] Many of the statutes prohibit "unnatural and lascivious acts" or "crimes against nature," rather than naming the specific acts themselves. In these states, judicial construction determines what acts are specifically prohibited.[4] Seven states prohibit only sodomy between persons of the same gender.[5] Among states proscribing both heterosexual and homosexual sodomy, at least one distinguishes between married and unmarried persons.[6]

Consenting adults are generally not prosecuted for nonpublic violations of sodomy statutes.[7] Prosecutors primarily employ such statutes as a lesser charge against defendants accused of rape or aggravated assault.[8] Although rarely enforced against private, consensual

---

prohibited behavior, for convenience, "sodomy" will be used throughout this section to refer to oral and/or anal sex. Some states prohibit oral-genital and anal-genital contact under separate statutes. See infra note 3.

[3] See, e.g., State v. Potts, 75 Ariz. 211, 213, 254 P.2d 1023, 1024 (1953) (holding that oral-genital contact is not an "infamous crime against nature"). However, states with sodomy statutes construed not to apply to oral sex generally also have statutes proscribing "lewd and lascivious acts" or "sexual misconduct" that include oral-genital contact. See, e.g., State v. Pickett, 121 Ariz. 142, 146, 589 P.2d 16, 20 (1978); ARIZ. REV. STAT. ANN. § 13-1412 (Supp. 1988).

[4] Despite sodomy statutes' use of such open-ended terms, courts have almost uniformly upheld the statutes against vagueness challenges. See Rose v. Locke, 423 U.S. 48 (1975) (per curiam) (upholding TENN. CODE ANN. § 39-2-612 (1980), which prohibits "crimes against nature"); Wainwright v. Stone, 414 U.S. 21 (1973) (per curiam) (upholding FLA. STAT. § 800.02 (1987), which prohibits "the abominable and detestable crime against nature"). But see Balthazar v. Superior Court, 573 F.2d 698 (1st Cir. 1978) (finding Massachusetts statute prohibiting "unnatural and lascivious acts" unconstitutionally vague as applied to acts of fellatio and oral-anal contact).

[5] See ARK. STAT. ANN. § 5-14-122 (1982); KAN. STAT. ANN. § 21-3505 (Supp. 1987); KY. REV. STAT. ANN. § 510.100 (Michie/Bobbs-Merrill 1985); MO. REV. STAT. § 566.090(3) (1986); MONT. CODE ANN. § 45-2-101 (1987); NEV. REV. STAT. § 201.190(2) (1987); TEX. PENAL CODE ANN. § 21.06 (Vernon 1989). Sodomy statutes in other states may prohibit only same-sex sodomy due to judicial invalidation of the statutes as applied to opposite-sex, but not to same-sex sodomy. See, e.g., Post v. State, 715 P.2d 1105 (Okla. Crim. App.) (finding application of Oklahoma sodomy statute to private, consensual, opposite-sex sodomy unconstitutional but not reaching the question of the statute's validity as applied to same-sex sodomy), cert. denied, 479 U.S. 890 (1986).

[6] See ALA. CODE § 13A-6-60 (1982).

[7] See R. MOHR, GAYS/JUSTICE 51 n.9 (1988). Although rare, arrests and prosecutions for sodomy are not unheard of, as Bowers v. Hardwick, 478 U.S. 186 (1986), demonstrates. Even without further prosecution, the mere arrest for same-sex sodomy may result in publicity. See, e.g., Matthews, The Louisiana Constitution's Declaration of Rights: Post-Hardwick Protection for Sexual Privacy?, 62 TUL. L. REV. 767, 804 n.208 (1988) (citing testimony by John Anthony D'Emilio). Given the lack of legal protection from discrimination for gay men and lesbians, see infra pp. 65–66, 120–22, 151–53, such publicity can prove highly damaging.

[8] See, e.g., Stover v. State, 256 Ga. 515, 350 S.E.2d 577 (1986); State v. Blue, 225 Kan. 576, 592 P.2d 897 (1979); Post, 715 P.2d at 1106. The laws are also used to prosecute men for raping men when rape statutes criminalize only the rape of women. See R. MOHR, supra note

same-sex conduct,[9] these statutes are frequently invoked to justify other types of discrimination against lesbians and gay men on the ground that they are presumed to violate these statutes.[10] This discrimination occurs despite the fact that not all gay men and lesbians engage in sodomy,[11] just as not all heterosexuals engage in sodomy. Sodomy statutes also provide a basis for the enforcement of laws against the solicitation of same-sex sexual activity.[12]

(a) Federal Constitutional Challenges to Sodomy Statutes. — (i) The Right to Privacy and Bowers v. Hardwick. — In Bowers v. Hardwick,[13] the Supreme Court upheld against a constitutional challenge the application of Georgia's sodomy statute[14] to consensual

---

7, at 51 n.9. However, changing the elements and evidentiary burdens of proof for nonconsensual crimes would more effectively combat violent sexual assault, see generally S. ESTRICH, REAL RAPE 92–104 (1987) (advocating negligence liability for rape), while avoiding the stigmatization of gay men and lesbians.

[9] See R. MOHR, supra note 7, at 52–53. However, military regulations prohibiting sodomy, see UNIFORM CODE OF MILITARY JUSTICE, ch. 47, art. 10, § 925 (codified at 10 U.S.C. § 925 (1983)) (prohibiting both same- and opposite-sex sodomy), are enforced against military personnel, some of whom are currently in prison for private, consensual, same-sex sexual conduct, see Lewin, Gay Groups Suggest Marines Selectively Prosecute Women, N.Y. Times, Dec. 4, 1988, at 34, col. 1.; Bull, Lesbian Purge by Marines Continues, Gay Community News, Mar. 12–18, 1989, at 2. Section 925 of the Uniform Code of Military Justice has been upheld against constitutional challenge as applied to private, consensual, same-sex sodomy between enlisted personnel. See Hatheway v. Secretary of the Army, 641 F.2d 1376, 1382 (9th Cir.), cert. denied, 454 U.S. 869 (1981). That women are discharged from military service for same-sex sexual conduct ten times more frequently than men suggests that the prohibitions may be selectively enforced against women. See Lewin, supra, at 34, col. 1.

[10] See, e.g., Mississippi Gay Alliance v. Goudelock, 536 F.2d 1073, 1075–76 (5th Cir. 1976) (invoking state sodomy statute and newspaper's right to choose not to be involved in criminal activity to justify newspaper's refusal to print advertisements for gay counseling and legal aid), cert. denied, 430 U.S. 982 (1977); Appeal in Pima City Juvenile Action B-10489, 151 Ariz. 335, 340, 727 P.2d 830, 835 (Ct. App. 1986) (invoking sodomy statute as pertinent to finding bisexual man "nonacceptable to adopt children").

[11] By defining gay people as persons who commit sodomy, see, e.g., Gay Activists v. Lomenzo, 66 Misc. 2d 456, 458, 320 N.Y.S.2d 994, 997 (Sup. Ct. 1971) (noting that "in order to be a homosexual, the prohibited act must have at some time been committed, or at least presently contemplated"), rev'd sub nom. Owles v. Lomenzo, 38 A.D.2d 981, 329 N.Y.S.2d 181 (App. Div. 1973), aff'd sub nom. Gay Activitists Alliance v. Lomenzo, 31 N.Y.2d 965, 293 N.E.2d 255, 341 N.Y.S.2d 108 (1973); Head v. Newton, 596 S.W.2d 209 (Tex. Ct. App. 1980) (finding the statement that someone is "queer" slanderous per se because it imputes the crime of sodomy), courts overemphasize the importance of certain types of homosexual sex and devalue love and companionship in a homosexual relationship. The assumption that sodomy is more essential to homosexuality than it is to heterosexuality ignores the fact that a gay man or lesbian need not be celibate to avoid violating the statutes, as most statutes do not prohibit genital-hand contact. But see MO. REV. STAT. § 566.010(2) (1986); MONT. CODE ANN. § 45-2-101 (1987).

[12] See R. MOHR, supra note 7, at 54–55.

[13] 478 U.S. 186 (1986).

[14] The statute provides that: "A person commits the offense of sodomy when he performs or submits to any sexual act involving the sex organs of one person and the mouth or anus of another." GA. CODE ANN. § 16-6-2 (1988).

same-sex sodomy. Justice White,[15] framing the issue in terms of the existence of a fundamental privacy right to engage in homosexual sodomy, found that no such right existed.[16] Justice White read *Griswold v. Connecticut*[17] and its progeny[18] as encompassing only those privacy rights integral to procreative choice and family autonomy,[19] and concluded that the recognition of a fundamental right requires that the right be either "deeply rooted in this nation's history and tradition"[20] or implicit in the concept of ordered liberty.[21] Finding homosexual sodomy unprotected under either standard,[22] the Court engaged in a highly deferential analysis of the state interest involved, and found a rational relationship between the statute and the state's interest in regulating morality.[23]

Justices Blackmun and Stevens each filed a dissenting opinion.[24] Justice Blackmun criticized the majority opinion's focus on the particular act rather than the underlying right to freedom from government intrusion.[25] Justice Blackmun found that private consensual sodomy is protected under the right to privacy as a decision properly left to individuals and as involving places afforded privacy regardless of the particular activities taking place there.[26] According to Justice Blackmun, a fair reading of the Court's prior privacy cases discloses a commitment to individual autonomy in matters of personal choice — a principle that should apply with full force to the decision to engage in sodomy.[27] Justice Blackmun also criticized the majority's state-interest analysis, and concluded that Georgia's interest in en-

---

[15] Chief Justice Burger and Justices Powell, Rehnquist, and O'Connor joined Justice White's majority opinion. Chief Justice Burger and Justice Powell also filed separate concurring opinions.

[16] 478 U.S. at 190.

[17] 381 U.S. 479 (1965). In *Griswold*, the Court struck down a statute prohibiting the use of contraceptives by married couples. Justice Douglas, writing for the majority, recognized a constitutional right to privacy based on the "penumbras" of certain provisions of the Bill of Rights. *See id.* at 484.

[18] Eisenstadt v. Baird, 405 U.S. 438 (1972), held that the right to privacy protects the distribution of contraceptives to unmarried couples; Roe v. Wade, 410 U.S. 113 (1973), held that the right to privacy protects a woman's right to decide to have an abortion in the first trimester of pregnancy.

[19] *See* 478 U.S. at 191. Justice White's formulation defines "family" according to traditional mainstream culture.

[20] *Id.* at 192 (quoting Moore v. City of East Cleveland, 431 U.S. 494, 503 (1977)).

[21] *See id.* at 191–92 (citing Palko v. Connecticut, 302 U.S. 319, 325–26 (1937)).

[22] *See id.*

[23] *See id.* at 196.

[24] Justices Brennan, Marshall, and Stevens joined Justice Blackmun's dissenting opinion; Justices Brennan and Marshall joined Justice Stevens' dissenting opinion.

[25] *See* 478 U.S. at 199 (Blackmun, J., dissenting).

[26] *See id.* at 204.

[27] *See id.* at 204–08.

forcing private morality could not sustain the statute.[28] Both Justices Blackmun and Stevens criticized the majority for analyzing the Georgia statute as if it applied only to homosexuals.[29]

⌒ The majority's analysis of the right at stake in *Hardwick* solely in terms of marriage, procreation, and the family departs from the privacy doctrine established in the Court's prior cases.[30] Had the majority examined the regulated conduct in *Hardwick* at the same level of generality employed in previous privacy decisions, it would have found constitutional protection for private, consensual, same-sex sodomy. Although *Griswold* and *Eisenstadt v. Baird*[31] involved procreative freedom, these decisions cannot be limited to procreative matters. If constitutional protection extended only to procreative decisions, the government could constitutionally restrict the use of contraceptives because couples could simply abstain from sexual relations. The constitutional protection of private, consensual, nonprocreative sex established by the right to privacy does not depend on any relation to marriage, procreation, and the family. *Stanley v. Georgia*[32] ruled that the right to privacy allows an individual to view pornography in the privacy of his home.[33] *Roe v. Wade*[34] held that the right to privacy encompasses a woman's right to decide not to use her body to procreate. In both cases, the Court protected a person's conduct regardless of his or her family status because of the centrality of sexual freedom to individual autonomy and identity.[35]

---

[28] *See id.* at 211–12.

[29] *See id.* at 200–01, 203 n.2 (criticizing the Court for ignoring the statute's facial applicability to heterosexual sodomy and thus avoiding the equal protection problem of selective application); *id.* at 214–20 (Stevens, J., dissenting) (arguing that the Constitution does not permit the statute to reach heterosexual sodomy and that its selective application to homosexual sodomy cannot be justified).

[30] Commentators have been virtually unanimous in their criticism of *Hardwick*'s reading of the Court's privacy jurisprudence. *See, e.g.,* L. TRIBE, AMERICAN CONSTITUTIONAL LAW § 15-21, at 1422–35 (2d ed. 1988); Conkle, *The Second Death of Substantive Due Process*, 62 IND. L.J. 215 (1987); Stoddard, Bowers v. Hardwick: *Precedent by Personal Predilection*, 54 U. CHI. L. REV. 648 (1987); *The Supreme Court, 1985 Term—Leading Cases*, 100 HARV. L. REV. 100, 210-20 (1986).

[31] 405 U.S. 438 (1972). Although *Eisenstadt* was decided on equal protection grounds, the extension to unmarried persons of the freedom from government restrictions on access to contraceptives implicitly guarantees unmarried persons the same right to privacy that *Griswold* provided for married persons.

[32] 394 U.S. 557 (1969).

[33] The *Hardwick* majority interpreted *Stanley* as "firmly grounded in the first amendment." 478 U.S. at 195. Until *Hardwick*, *Stanley* had been consistently read by the Court as a privacy case. *See* L. TRIBE, *supra* note 30, § 15-21, at 1426 & n.41.

[34] 410 U.S. 113 (1973).

[35] *See* L. TRIBE, *supra* note 30, § 15-21, at 1423–24. As Professor Richards stated:

Traditional moral condemnation of homosexuality has eroded the intimate resources and imaginative, emotional, and intellectual freedom through which homosexuals can con-

Having relied on a cramped reading of the Court's privacy decisions to locate homosexual sodomy outside the categories of protected activity, the majority applied its "history and tradition" test in an arbitrary manner to conclude that privacy protection should not encompass same-sex sodomy. First, the majority, choosing the eighteenth and nineteenth centuries as its historical benchmark, selectively examined history to find condemnation of homosexuality. Had the Court explored earlier or later periods, it would have found ambiguity or social tolerance.[36]

Second, requiring that the specific activity conform to traditional values and historical teachings in order to receive constitutional protection is inconsistent with the Court's privacy jurisprudence. For example, had such an approach been taken in *Griswold* and *Eisenstadt*, the Court likely would have found the use of contraceptives (even within marriage) condemned historically and therefore unprotected.[37] The only distinction between the activity protected in the Court's previous privacy cases and the behavior found unprotected in *Hardwick* is an unpersuasive one — a majoritarian consensus against homosexual sodomy. Moreover, the Court's previous privacy cases do not rely entirely on history and tradition but also consider the burden on individuals[38] and the strength of the state interests involved.[39] The burden imposed on individuals by sodomy statutes is comparable to that imposed on pregnant women in *Roe v. Wade*, and the state interests justifying the regulation of abortion are far more compelling than those justifying the regulation of sodomy.[40]

---

struct a personal and ethical life in the only way that generates value in living. That erosion of moral independence is not at the periphery of the historical meaning of the protection of constitutional privacy as an unenumerated right; it is at its very core.

Richards, *Constitutional Legitimacy and Constitutional Privacy*, 61 N.Y.U. L. REV. 800, 853 (1986). For an alternative approach to privacy focusing on the affirmative consequences of state actions rather than on the fundamentality of the act proscribed, see Rubenfeld, *The Right of Privacy*, 102 HARV. L. REV. 737 (1989). Rubenfeld's formulation would also invalidate sodomy statutes, as they intrude pervasively on personal life choices. *See id.* at 799–802.

[36] *See* Goldstein, *History, Homosexuality, and Political Values: Searching for the Hidden Determinants of* Bowers v. Hardwick, 97 YALE L.J. 1073, 1081–91 (1988); *see also* J. BOSWELL, CHRISTIANITY, SOCIAL TOLERANCE, AND HOMOSEXUALITY (1980) (detailing and analyzing the lack of uniformity in historical prohibitions on homosexuality). Moreover, the tradition relied on by the majority does not justify singling out same-sex sodomy for special treatment, *see* J. D'EMILIO & E. FREEDMAN, INTIMATE MATTERS 30 (1988), nor do the historical prohibitions apply to oral sex, *see* Vieira, Hardwick *and the Right of Privacy*, 55 U. CHI. L. REV. 1181, 1184 (1988).

[37] *See, e.g.*, Law, *Homosexuality and the Social Meaning of Gender*, 1988 WIS. L. REV. 187, 198–201 & n.70 (contextualizing historical prohibitions of sodomy in the broader social condemnation of nonprocreative sex); *see also* R. MOHR, *supra* note 7, at 77 (noting that history does not uniformly uphold marriage as a sacred social institution).

[38] *See, e.g.*, Roe v. Wade, 410 U.S. 113, 153 (1973).

[39] *See, e.g., id.* at 162–64.

[40] *See* Vieira, *supra* note 36, at 1184–85.

If the Court had, consistent with its privacy jurisprudence, framed the issue at stake in *Hardwick* more broadly, it would have concluded that Georgia's sodomy statute implicated the right to privacy. Had the Court recognized that the criminalization of private, consensual, adult intimacy between persons of the same sex implicates a fundamental right to privacy, the state interest in advancing morality would not have supported the statute.[41]

Given its reliance on history, *Hardwick* should not extend beyond its facts to apply to other types of same-sex sexual activity that have not been the subject of historical prohibitions. However, the Missouri Supreme Court has invoked *Hardwick*'s privacy rationale to uphold a Missouri statute prohibiting contact between the genitals of one person and the hand of another person of the same sex.[42] This sweeping prohibition of "deviate sexual misconduct" exceeds the offense of sodomy as defined by the historic condemnation considered so important by Justice White in *Hardwick*.[43] Moreover, because the historical prohibitions relied on only condemn male homosexual sodomy, *Hardwick* should not apply to sodomy between lesbians.[44]

(ii) Equal Protection Challenges to Same-Sex Sodomy Statutes. — Although *Hardwick* established that there is no fundamental right to engage in private, consensual, same-sex sodomy, it left open other constitutional challenges to state sodomy statutes.[45] The fourteenth amendment's equal protection clause provides the most promising basis for such a challenge.[46]

Statutes that criminalize sodomy between persons of the same sex, but not between a man and a woman, discriminate against persons

---

[41] *See infra* pp. 18–19.

[42] *See* State v. Walsh, 713 S.W.2d 508 (Mo. 1986). However, another lower court has limited *Hardwick* to sodomy. *See* High Tech Gays v. Defense Indus. Sec. Clearance Office, 668 F. Supp. 1361, 1368–69 (N.D. Cal. 1987).

[43] *See Walsh*, 713 S.W.2d at 514 (Blackmar, J., dissenting). The respondent in *Walsh* was actually convicted for touching an officer's genitalia over layers of clothing. *See id.* at 514 (Wellivar, J., dissenting).

[44] *See, e.g.*, Thompson v. Aldredge, 187 Ga. 467, 200 S.E. 799 (1939) (construing Georgia's sodomy statute to permit sexual conduct between women but not heterosexual sodomy); J. D'EMILIO & E. FREEDMAN, *supra* note 36, at 122 (noting that historically, sodomy laws only applied to men because of the biblical injunction against "unnatural spilling of seed").

[45] *See Hardwick*, 478 U.S. at 196 & n.8.

[46] Under equal protection analysis, laws or regulations that employ suspect classifications — race, national origin, and alienage — are strictly scrutinized. *See* City of Cleburne v. Cleburne Living Center, Inc., 473 U.S. 432, 440 (1985). Under strict scrutiny, the classification must be necessary to achieve a compelling government interest. *See, e.g.*, Palmore v. Sidoti, 466 U.S. 429, 432–33 (1984). Quasi-suspect classifications include gender and illegitimacy, *see Cleburne*, 473 U.S. at 441, and trigger intermediate scrutiny, which requires a substantial relationship between the classification and an important government interest. *See* Craig v. Boren, 429 U.S. 190, 197 (1976). Classifications that are not suspect or quasi-suspect and do not implicate fundamental interests need only serve a legitimate state interest and be reasonably related to the pursuit of such interest. *See* L. TRIBE, *supra* note 30, § 16-2, at 1440–41.

with a gay or lesbian sexual orientation. Although litigants and courts have assumed that such statutes classify based on sexual preference,[47] the statutes actually prevent all persons from engaging in same-sex sodomy, regardless of sexual orientation.[48] However, the absence of a facial classification based on sexual orientation does not insulate the statutes from equal protection scrutiny. Facially neutral statutes that disproportionately and adversely harm a minority violate equal protection if the legislature intended such a result.[49] Same-sex sodomy statutes burden gay men and lesbians far more than they burden non-gay persons.\ Moreover, because the disparate impact on gay men and lesbians was foreseeable and intended,[50] courts should continue to treat statutes forbidding only same-sex sodomy as expressly based on sexual orientation.

In light of the history of persecution and invidious discrimination aimed at gay men and lesbians, classifications based on sexual preference deserve strict scrutiny.[51] In contexts other than challenges to sodomy statutes, some courts have recognized homosexuality as a suspect or quasi-suspect classsification.[52] To date, however, courts evaluating equal protection challenges to sodomy statutes have rejected heightened scrutiny and have upheld the statutes under rational basis analysis.[53]

Sodomy statutes that criminalize only acts between persons of the same sex also discriminate on the basis of gender. Because the statutes permit a woman to engage in sodomy with a man, but prohibit a man from engaging in the same acts with a man, an act's criminality

---

[47] *See, e.g.,* State v. Walsh, 713 S.W.2d 508, 510 (Mo. 1986). The willingness of courts to characterize such statutes as classifying based on sexual preference probably stems from the perception that persons are either heterosexual or homosexual, and from the tendency to view homosexuality solely as a sexual phenomenon.

[48] This classification differs from those in military and employment cases, where the classification facially discriminates based on sexual preference. *See infra* pp. 44–45.

[49] *See* McClesky v. Kemp, 481 U.S. 279, 299 (1987); Washington v. Davis, 426 U.S. 229, 241–42 (1976).

[50] The state of Texas, for example, defended its sodomy statute on the basis of an abhorrence of homosexuality. *See* Baker v. Wade, 553 F. Supp. 1121, 1145 (N.D. Tex. 1982), *rev'd,* 769 F.2d 289 (5th Cir. 1985) (en banc), *cert. denied,* 478 U.S. 1022 (1986).

[51] *See infra* pp. 1564–72. *Hardwick* does not foreclose a determination that gay men and lesbians comprise a suspect class for equal protection purposes. *See* Sunstein, *Sexual Orientation and the Constitution,* 55 U. CHI. L. REV. 1161, 1164–70 (1988). *But see* Watkins v. United States Army, 847 F.2d 1329, 1353–58 (Reinhardt, J., dissenting).

[52] *See, e.g.,* Watkins v. U.S. Army, 847 F.2d 1329, 1349 (concluding that analysis of the relevant factors and the principles underlying the equal protection clause require defining gay men and lesbians as a suspect class), *reh'g en banc ordered,* 847 F.2d 1362 (9th Cir. 1988); High Tech Gays v. Defense Indus. Sec. Clearance Office, 668 F. Supp. 1361, 1368–69 (N.D. Cal. 1987) (ruling that gay men and lesbians comprise a quasi-suspect class entitled to heightened scrutiny under the equal protection clause); *infra* p. 56.

[53] *See, e.g.,* Baker v. Wade, 769 F.2d 289, 292 (5th Cir. 1985) (en banc), *cert. denied,* 478 U.S. 1022 (1986); State v. Walsh, 713 S.W.2d 508 (Mo. 1986).

is determined solely by the actor's gender. Proponents of same-sex sodomy statutes have argued that because the statutes prohibit both sexes from engaging in same-sex sodomy, they treat both sexes equally.[54] The Supreme Court rejected this "separate but equal" reasoning in the school segregation context, concluding that laws prohibiting both races from mixing with each other violate equal protection.[55] The miscegenation cases extended the Court's rejection of the separate but equal rationale to interracial marriage, and held that a statute that defines conduct by a particular characteristic is not neutral with respect to that characteristic.[56] Because same-sex sodomy statutes define the prohibited conduct by reference to gender, these statutes are gender-discriminatory rather than gender-neutral.[57]

Not only do these statutes classify based on gender, but the classification also reinforces stereotypical sex roles,[58] and therefore may not be sustained as a "benign" classification.[59] The prohibition of same-sex sodomy reinforces a dichotomous view of gender in which differences between men and women are so significant that same-sex sexual conduct violates the roles assigned to each gender through cultural indoctrination.[60] The very characterization of sodomy as a "crime against nature" implies that men and women were created to

---

[54] See Walsh, 713 S.W.2d at 510.

[55] See Brown v. Board of Educ., 347 U.S. 483 (1954). Rejecting the argument that any stigma from separate facilities is subjective and not inherent, the Court recognized the social implications of the separate treatment in a society that accords one race dominant status over the other. See id. at 494–95. Similarly, such a gender classification reinforces the dichotomous nature of culturally constructed gender roles that, in a society that privileges a traditional male role, contributes to the oppression of women.

[56] See, e.g., Loving v. Virginia, 388 U.S. 1 (1967); McLaughlin v. Florida, 379 U.S. 184 (1964). For a more detailed examination of the parallels between miscegenation and sodomy laws, see Note, The Miscegenation Analogy: Sodomy Law as Sex Discrimination, 98 YALE L.J. 145 (1988).

[57] One cannot distinguish gender discrimination under these sodomy statutes from the race discrimination wrought by segregation and miscegenation laws based on "biological difference." The physical acts themselves — anal and oral sex — are the same whether between a man and a woman or two persons of the same sex; the difference is in the cultural significance attached to the gender of the participants.

[58] See Law, supra note 37, at 187 (arguing that the legal marginalization of homosexual relationships is attributable to the fact that these relationships challenge traditional institutions premised on gender inequality and differentiation).

[59] Although gender classifications adopted for the remedial reason of redressing past discrimination have been sustained as benign, see Califano v. Webster, 430 U.S. 313 (1977) (per curiam), gender classifications based on sexist stereotyping and traditional gender roles have been invalidated, see Weinberger v. Wiesenfeld, 420 U.S. 636, 648–49 (1975).

[60] See Law, supra note 37, at 197–206; Note, Custody Denials to Parents in Same-Sex Relationships: An Equal Protection Analysis, 102 HARV. L. REV. 617, 627–30 (1989); Note, supra note 56, at 158–60. The popularity of the "sexual inversion" theory — explaining homosexuality as an inversion of gender identity — in the nineteenth century illustrates the centrality of gender to the stigma attached to homosexuality. See J. D'EMILIO & E. FREEDMAN, supra note 36, at 226.

fulfill their respective procreative roles, and that their sexual options should be restricted accordingly. The acceptance of same-sex intimacy would threaten these notions of masculinity and femininity upon which traditional gender roles are based.[61] A prohibition on same-sex sodomy also reinforces stereotypical gender roles, as stigmatizing homosexuality contributes to the bifurcation of male and female identities.[62] In a society with a history of legal and economic subordination of women, the preservation of traditional gender roles disproportionately disadvantages women.[63] The tendency of same-sex sodomy statutes to perpetuate traditional gender roles demonstrates that their classificatory structure is not benign, but rather discriminates based on gender and requires heightened scrutiny.[64]

Once a court acknowledges that a same-sex sodomy statute employs a quasi-suspect or suspect classification, the state interests advanced to support the statute will not survive heightened scrutiny. The primary state justification for punishing same-sex sodomy and not opposite-sex sodomy is a moral interest in deterring homosexual activity.[65] The Court in *Griswold* struck down a regulation establishing procreation as the only purpose of marital sex.[66] Consequently, *Griswold* forecloses the use of the criminal law for the sole purpose of effecting a particular sexual norm.[67] Moreover, a desire to deter homosexuality is motivated by a belief that gay men and lesbians are inferior to non-gay persons.[68] However, a moral interest based on

---

[61] *See* Taylor, *Conceptions of Masculinity and Femininity as a Basis for Stereotypes of Male and Female Homosexuals*, 9 J. HOMOSEXUALITY 37, 50 (1983) ("[T]hose who value traditional sex roles devalue homosexuals because they perceive them to be role deviants, and those who do not value the roles so highly do not care.").

[62] *See* Rubenfeld, *supra* note 35, at 800 ("Indeed it is difficult to separate our society's inculcation of a heterosexual identity from the simultaneous inculcation of a dichotomized complementarity of roles to be borne by men and women.").

[63] *See* Stanton v. Stanton, 421 U.S. 7, 14–15 (1975) (noting that traditional gender roles subordinate women by assuming that "the female [is] destined solely for the home and the rearing of the family, and [that] only the male [is qualified] for the marketplace . . . of ideas").

[64] The fact that these statutes also disadvantage gay men, both by justifying other forms of discrimination, *see supra* pp. 10–11, and by perpetuating gender roles that stigmatize gay men as not "masculine," *see* Arriola, *Sexual Identity and the Constitution: Homosexual Persons as a Discrete and Insular Minority*, 10 Women's Rts. L. Rep. (Rutgers Univ.) 143, 166–67 (1988), does not make them any less gender discriminatory. Much of the Court's gender discrimination jurisprudence derives from claims by men that they were victimized by gender classifications that only secondarily harmed women by perpetuating stereotypical gender roles. *See, e.g.*, Orr v. Orr, 440 U.S. 268, 279–80 (1979) (invalidating a statute requiring men but not women to pay alimony, based on its tendency to perpetuate stereotypical views of gender).

[65] *See supra* note 50. Georgia also defended its statute based on "traditional Judeo-Christian values" against homosexuality. *See Hardwick*, 478 U.S. at 211 (Blackmun, J., dissenting).

[66] *See supra* note 17.

[67] *See* Richards, *supra* note 35, at 836–37.

[68] The state's moral interest in deterring homosexuality is inextricable from prejudice against gay men and lesbians. In this regard, a heterosexist "morality" serves as the basis for denying

prejudice toward persons within a suspect or quasi-suspect class does not rise to the level of an important state interest.[69] Because the maintenance of traditional gender roles underlies the moral condemnation of homosexuality,[70] a moral interest in deterring homosexuality cannot support same-sex sodomy statutes.[71]

Non-moralistic rationales also fail heightened scrutiny. Arguments that gay men disproportionately molest children have been discredited,[72] as have claims that anti-sodomy laws strengthen heterosexual marriage.[73] The state's interest in the protection of public health also fails to survive heightened scrutiny. Although the disproportionately high incidence of AIDS among gay men might support a state's argument that an important government health interest is at stake,[74] lesbians as a group have almost no risk of contracting the disease through sexual contact.[75] Even if sodomy statutes were more nar-

---

gay men and lesbians legal rights today in the same way that a racist "morality" was invoked to justify racial segregation based on nineteenth-century theories of race differences. See id. at 854.

[69] See Loving v. Virginia, 388 U.S. 1, 11 (1967). In fact, because the moral interest in deterring homosexuality is so intertwined with group prejudice, such a state interest may be illegitimate even under a rational basis test. See City of Cleburne v. Cleburne Living Center, Inc., 473 U.S. 432 (1985) (rejecting prejudice against mentally retarded adults as a legitimate state justification). For an argument that sectarian interests in promoting a particular view of morality should always be regarded as constitutionally dubious, see Richards, cited above in note 35, at 845–48. Cf. J. Locke, A Letter Concerning Toleration 36, 39–40 (P. Romanell 2d ed. 1955) (1681) (defining the limits of legitimate state power in terms of "civil interests").

[70] See supra note 61. The relationship between gender stereotyping and moral opposition to homosexuality is perhaps best illustrated by the opponents of gay liberation. See, e.g., J. Falwell, Listen America! 183 (1980) ("In the Christian home the father is . . . to be the head over his wife and children . . . . In the Christian home the woman is to be submissive . . . . Homosexuality is Satan's diabolical attack upon the family, God's order in Creation.").

[71] See, e.g., Mississippi Univ. for Women v. Hogan, 458 U.S. 718, 725–76 (1982) (requiring "reasoned analysis rather than . . . the mechanical application of traditional, often inaccurate, assumptions about the proper roles of men and women" to determine whether a substantial relationship exists between a legitimate and important state interest and legislative means to justify a gender discriminatory statute).

[72] See R. Geiser, Hidden Victims: The Sexual Abuse of Children 75 (1979). Because no commentators have asserted a correlation between lesbianism and child molestation, no research has been conducted to disprove such a claim.

[73] Cf. Geis, Reported Consequences of Decriminalization of Consensual Adult Homosexuality in Seven States, 1 J. Homosexuality 419 (1976) (noting that the decriminalization of sodomy has had no effect on the amount of private homosexual behavior).

[74] However, members of the gay community have modified their sexual practices to a remarkable degree to reduce the risk of contracting AIDS. See Martin, The Impact of AIDS on Gay Male Sexual Behavior in New York City, 77 Am. J. Pub. Health 578, 581 (1987); Winkelstein, Padian, Wiley, Lang, Anderson & Levy, The San Francisco Men's Health Study: III. Reduction in Human Immunodeficiency Virus Transmission Among Homosexual/Bisexual Men, 1982–86, 77 Am. J. Pub. Health 685, 687–88 (1987).

[75] See Meuller, The Epidemiology of the Human Immunodeficiency Virus Infection, 14 Law, Med. & Health Care 250, 256 (1986) ("At present there is no evidence of [HIV] transmission between lesbians.").

rowly tailored to prohibit only same-sex sodomy between males, they would still be grossly overinclusive, as not all prohibited acts carry a high risk of transmission,[76] and the risks depend on the acts themselves rather than the gender of the participants. In addition to being overinclusive and underinclusive, same-sex sodomy statutes are not the least restrictive means of controlling AIDS.[77]

Same-sex sodomy statutes are also subject to facial challenge under rational basis analysis. Although courts have upheld same-sex sodomy statutes under rational basis review based on a state interest in regulating morality,[78] a more substantive rational basis test, as the Supreme Court has adopted in other contexts,[79] would produce a different result. Disfavored groups cannot be penalized because of their disfavored status.[80] Statutes employing classifications based solely on prejudice against a particular class of persons have been struck down under rational basis review.[81] Similarly, same-sex sodomy statutes should be invalidated under rational basis review, as they are premised upon social disapprobation of gay men and lesbians.[82] Public health concerns also fail to support the statutes under a substantive rational basis review, as the risk of transmitting diseases through sexual contact inheres in the act itself, and does not depend on the gender of the participants.[83]

---

[76] See Padian, Marquis, Francis, Anderson, Rutherford, O'Malley & Winkelstein, *Male-to-Female Transmission of Human Immunodeficiency Virus*, 258 J. A.M.A. 788, 789 (1987) (noting that oral sex appears not to have accounted for any reported cases of transmission). *But see* Tofani, *Doubt Cast on 2 Safe-Sex Practices*, Philadelphia Inquirer, Nov. 28, 1987, at 1A, col. 1 (describing a European medical study suggesting that persons may be able to contract HIV through oral sex).

[77] See, e.g., Sullivan & Field, *AIDS and the Coercive Power of the State*, 23 HARV. C.R.-C.L. L. REV. 139, 182–89 (1988) (favoring disclosure requirements and precautions over more restrictive alternatives, but ultimately finding any use of the criminal law to deter AIDS overly intrusive). Education and tort suits against persons transmitting AIDS through sexual conduct are other viable alternatives for deterring AIDS transmission. *See id.* at 192–93.

[78] See, e.g., Bowers v. Hardwick, 478 U.S. 186 (1986); Baker v. Wade, 769 F.2d 289, 292 (5th Cir. 1985) (en banc), *cert. denied*, 106 S. Ct. 3337 (1986).

[79] See, e.g., City of Cleburne v. Cleburne Living Center, Inc., 473 U.S. 432 (1985); Hooper v. Bernalillo County Assessor, 472 U.S. 612 (1985); Zobel v. Williams, 457 U.S. 55 (1982); United States Dep't of Agric. v. Moreno, 413 U.S. 528 (1973).

[80] See *Moreno*, 413 U.S. at 534 ("'[E]qual protection of the laws' . . . must at the very least mean that a bare congressional desire to harm a politically unpopular group cannot constitute a *legitimate* governmental interest." (emphasis in original)).

[81] See *Cleburne*, 473 U.S. at 447–50 (rejecting irrational prejudice against the mentally retarded as a legitimate state interest for denying a permit for the operation of a group home for mentally retarded adults).

[82] See *supra* note 70.

[83] See *supra* note 76. A legislature would have no conceivable rational basis for criminalizing sexual activity between lesbians, the lowest AIDS-risk group, and not criminalizing sexual activity between opposite-sex couples, which carries a much higher risk of transmission. *See supra* note 75. Moreover, because same-sex sodomy statutes were enacted before the onset of AIDS, the prevention of this disease could not have been the basis for the statutory classification.

Cases employing rational basis analysis to strike down sodomy statutes distinguishing between married and unmarried persons provide strong precedent for litigants challenging same-sex sodomy statutes under rational basis review.[84] New York's highest court, in *People v. Onofre*,[85] found that no rational relationship existed between the statute's marital classification and the purported state interest of strengthening the institution of marriage.[86] The court also rejected the enforcement of moral or theological values as a function of the criminal law, and distinguished between private and public morality as a subject for regulation.[87] Under the reasoning of *Onofre*, it is irrational to prohibit only same-sex sodomy, as the distinction between same- and opposite-sex sodomy does not preserve the institution of marriage, and distinctions based purely on the morality of private sexual conduct cannot justify according differential treatment under the criminal law.[88]

(iii) Equal Protection Challenges to Facially Neutral Sodomy Statutes. — Arguably, the combination of disparate impact with discriminatory legislative purpose subjects even facially neutral sodomy statutes to the equal protection challenges discussed above,[89] as the impetus and effect of these statutes are primarily to discourage same-sex sodomy.[90] Statutes that criminalize sodomy between unmarried

---

[84] *See* People v. Onofre, 51 N.Y.2d 476, 415 N.E.2d 936, 434 N.Y.S.2d 947 (1980), *cert. denied*, 451 U.S. 987 (1981); Commonwealth v. Bonadio, 490 Pa. 91, 415 A.2d 47 (1980). *But cf.* State v. Poe, 40 N.C. App. 385, 387, 252 S.E.2d 843, 835 (holding that the state can prohibit sodomy between unmarried persons without prohibiting the same acts between married persons), *cert. denied*, 298 N.C. 303, 259 S.E.2d 304 (1979). Other courts have construed such statutes as applicable to both married and unmarried persons in order to avoid such equal protection challenges. *See* Neville v. State, 290 Md. 364, 373, 430 A.2d 570, 579 (1981).

[85] 51 N.Y.2d 476, 415 N.E.2d 936, 434 N.Y.S.2d 947 (1980), *cert. denied*, 451 U.S. 987 (1981).

[86] *See id.* at 490, 415 N.E.2d at 941, 434 N.Y.S.2d at 952. Finding it irrational to require that one group behave more morally than the other, the Pennsylvania Supreme Court also held unconstitutional the state sodomy statute's classification between married and unmarried persons. *See Bonadio*, 490 Pa. 91, 415 A.2d 47 (1980). This reasoning could also defeat same-sex sodomy statutes, if, as the traditional prohibitions suggest, *see supra* notes 36–37, the stigma of immorality attaches to the acts themselves rather than the gender of the participants.

[87] *See Onofre*, 51 N.Y.2d at 488 n.3, 415 N.E.2d at 940 n.3, 434 N.Y.S.2d at 951 n.3. Other state courts, while not expressly declaring their sodomy statutes unconstitutional, have indicated that the regulation of private consensual sodomy is not a legitimate state interest. *See* Commonwealth v. Balthazar, 366 Mass. 298, 318 N.E.2d 478 (1974).

[88] *See Onofre*, 51 N.Y.2d at 488 n.3, 415 N.E.2d at 940 n.3, 434 N.Y.S.2d at 951 n.3. Arguably, judicial scrutiny should be more stringent where the state imposes morality through the criminal law. *See* Poe v. Ullman, 367 U.S. 497, 547 (1961) (Harlan, J., dissenting).

[89] *See* Washington v. Davis, 426 U.S. 229 (1976).

[90] Georgia, for example, justified its facially neutral statute based on its "interest in prosecuting homosexual activity." *Hardwick*, 478 U.S. at 203 n.2 (Blackmun, J., dissenting); *see also* Note, *supra* note 56, at 152–53 (arguing that animus toward gays as the motivating factor for even facially neutral statutes renders such statutes constitutionally equivalent to those prohibiting only same-sex sodomy).

persons but not between married persons[91] may have been especially
motivated by a desire to disadvantage same-sex couples, given the
prohibition on same-sex marriage.[92]

Alternatively, facially neutral sodomy statutes are subject to an
equal protection challenge based on a *Griswold/Eisenstadt* line of
analysis, which first establishes the right of married couples to engage
in sodomy, and then extends that right to other couples through the
equal protection clause.[93] Courts considering the issue have found
that a right to engage in private consensual sodomy inheres in the
marital relationship.[94] Moreover, the most plausible reading of *Griswold* requires that married couples have the right to engage in sodomy.
Griswold established a fundamental right to engage in nonprocreative
sex within the marital relationship.[95] Courts can distinguish sodomy
from nonprocreative intercourse only by prescribing a particular view
of sexual morality for married couples. *Griswold* foreclosed such a
distinction, however, by refusing to recognize private sexual morality
— in the form of the preservation of an exclusively procreative function of sex — as a legitimate justification for an intrusion into marital
bedrooms.[96]

Once the right of married couples to engage in sodomy is recognized, *Eisenstadt* supports the extension of that right to all unmarried
couples.[97] If married couples have a fundamental right to engage in

---

[91] At least one state prohibits only sodomy committed outside the marital relationship. *See*
ALA. CODE §§ 13A-6-60, 13A-6-65 (1982). Other states may apply the statutes only to unmarried
persons because of *Griswold*'s protection of marital intimacy. *See, e.g.*, State v. Poe, 40 N.C.
App. 385, 252 S.E.2d 304 (assuming, without deciding, that *Griswold* prohibits the application
of North Carolina's sodomy statute to married persons, and upholding the statute as applied to
unmarried persons), *cert. denied*, 298 N.C. 303, 259 S.E.2d 304 (1979).

[92] No state permits marriage between same-sex partners. *See infra* p. 96. Moreover, given
the likelihood that *Griswold* protects sodomy within the marital relationship, *see infra* note 94
and accompanying text, the prohibition on same-sex marriage justifies treating even statutes
facially applicable to all acts of sodomy as if they singled out same-sex sodomy, *see* Note, *supra*
note 56, at 152–53.

[93] Gay litigants may encounter difficulty in the first stage of this argument, however, as
standing requirements could prohibit them from asserting the rights of married persons. *See*
Gordon v. State, 257 Ga. 439, 360 S.E.2d 253 (1987).

[94] *See* Cotner v. Henry, 394 F.2d 873 (7th Cir.), *cert. denied*, 393 U.S. 847 (1968); Buchanan
v. Batchelor, 308 F. Supp. 729 (N.D. Tex. 1970), *vacated on other grounds*, 401 U.S. 989
(1971); *see also Hardwick*, 478 U.S. at 218 n.10 (Stevens, J., dissenting) (noting that Georgia's
Attorney General conceded the unconstitutionality of the sodomy statute as applied to married
couples).

[95] *See Griswold*, 381 U.S. 479 (1965); *supra* p. 18.

[96] *See supra* text accompanying note 67.

[97] *See* Eisenstadt v. Baird, 405 U.S. 438, 453 (1972). Once such a privacy right is recognized
for married couples, *Hardwick* does not foreclose the extension of a fundamental right to sexual
privacy to same-sex couples through the equal protection clause. The finding that no fundamental right exists to engage in same-sex sodomy, and that morality serves as a rational basis
for its criminalization, does not answer the question of why the right to privacy would protect
opposite-sex sodomy, but not same-sex sodomy. *See* Sunstein, *supra* note 51, at 1166.

sodomy, equal protection requires that the fundamental right be applied evenhandedly.[98] *Eisenstadt* invalidated a statute respecting the privacy of married, but not unmarried persons, with regard to access to contraception, because it was both underinclusive and overbroad.[99] Similarly, a fundamental right to privacy for married couples to engage in sodomy, but not for unmarried couples, should not survive equal protection scrutiny under *Eisenstadt*'s analysis.[100] Not only do prejudice and the desire to harm same-sex couples fail as legitimate state interests,[101] but under *Eisenstadt* a particular view of sexual morality will not sustain against the right to privacy a criminal statute prohibiting certain sexual conduct only when engaged in by certain individuals.

Selective enforcement provides an additional basis for invalidation of sodomy statutes. (Given the evidence that sodomy statutes criminalizing private consensual sodomy are enforced almost exclusively against persons engaging in same-sex sodomy,[102] statutes that facially apply to both same-sex and opposite-sex partners should be invalidated under the equal protection clause based on selective enforcement.[103])In fact, the breadth of these statutory prohibitions renders evenhanded enforcement of the law virtually impossible.[104] However, selective enforcement claims are highly fact-dependent,[105] and must include proof of intentional or purposeful discriminatory enforcement

---

[98] Although courts have split in their interpretation of the right to privacy as applied to heterosexual sodomy between unmarried persons, *compare* Schochet v. State, 75 Md. App. 314, 541 A.2d 183 (Ct. Spec. App. 1988) (holding that the right to privacy does not include consensual adult heterosexual activity between unmarried persons) *with* Post v. State, 715 P.2d 1105, 1109–10 (Okla. Crim. App.) (finding that the right to privacy includes private, consensual sodomy between unmarried adult heterosexuals), *cert. denied*, 479 U.S. 890 (1986), unmarried persons need not have an independent right to engage in sodomy to be entitled to protection under the right if it is extended to married couples.

[99] *See* 405 U.S. at 447–52. *Eisenstadt* clearly required more than a mere rational relationship between the classification and the alleged state interest to justify a statute's differential treatment of a similarly situated group with a fundamental right to engage in such conduct.

[100] As Justice Jackson said in his concurring opinion in *Eisenstadt*: "[N]othing opens the door to arbitrary action so effectively as to allow . . . officials to pick and choose only a few to whom they will apply legislation and thus to escape the political retribution that might be visited upon them if larger numbers were affected . . . ." *Id.* at 454 (Jackson, J., concurring) (quoting Railway Express Agency v. New York, 336 U.S. 106, 112–13 (1949)).

[101] *See* United States Dep't of Agric. v. Moreno, 413 U.S. 528, 534 (1973) ("[A] bare . . . desire to harm a politically unpopular group cannot constitute a *legitimate* governmental interest." (emphasis in original)); *supra* note 69.

[102] *See* Pearson, *The Right of Privacy and Other Constitutional Challenges to Sodomy Statutes*, 15 U. Tol. L. Rev. 811, 846 & n.228 (1984).

[103] *See* Yick Wo v. Hopkins, 118 U.S. 356, 373–74 (1886).

[104] *See* Bowers v. Hardwick, 478 U.S. 186, 220 (1986) (Stevens, J., dissenting).

[105] *See, e.g.*, Gordon v. State, 257 Ga. 439, 360 S.E.2d 253 (1987) (rejecting a gay defendant's selective enforcement challenge to Georgia's sodomy statute, as the record failed to establish the manner of the statute's enforcement).

to succeed.[106] In addition, such claims have been rejected where the selective administration bears a substantial relation to an important governmental interest.[107]

   (b) State Constitutional Challenges. — Twenty states provide explicit privacy guarantees in their state constitutions.[108] Of these, twelve[109] currently criminalize private consensual sodomy. Numerous other states have judicially recognized an implicit right to privacy from other provisions within their state constitutions, similar to the Supreme Court's recognition of a right to privacy from the "penumbra" of explicitly guaranteed rights.[110] Some lower state courts have invalidated sodomy statutes on state constitutional grounds.[111] In the aftermath of *Hardwick*, state constitutional challenges to sodomy statutes may become more frequent.[112]

---

[106] *See, e.g.*, Stewart v. United States, 364 A.2d 1205, 1208 (D.C. App. 1976) (rejecting a selective enforcement challenge to a facially neutral sodomy statute because the evidence did not justify a finding of intentional or purposeful discriminatory enforcement against homosexuals).

[107] *See, e.g.*, Hatheway v. Secretary of the Army, 641 F.2d 1376, 1382 (9th Cir.) (upholding discriminatory enforcement of the Uniform Code of Military Justice against homosexuals, given a prior finding that homosexual conduct among enlisted personnel "bears a substantial relationship to the important government interest" of "maintaining a strong military force"), *cert. denied*, 454 U.S. 869 (1981). However, given the deference afforded military policies, selective enforcement in a civilian context would encounter greater judicial scrutiny.

[108] ALA. CONST. art. I, § 5 (right against unreasonable searches and seizures); ALASKA CONST. art. I, § 22 (right of privacy); ARIZ. CONST. art. II, § 8 (right not to be disturbed in private affairs without authority of law); ARK. CONST. art. II, § 29 (enumeration of rights of people not exclusive of other rights); CAL. CONST. art. I, § 1 (right of privacy); FLA. CONST. art. I, § 23 (right of privacy); HAW. CONST. art. I, § 6 (right of privacy); IDAHO CONST. art. I, § 17 (right against unreasonable searches and seizures); ILL. CONST. art. I, § 6 (right against unreasonable searches, seizures, invasions of privacy, and interceptions); KY. CONST., § 1 (inherent and inalienable rights); LA. CONST. art. I, § 5 (right of privacy); MD. CONST., art. XXVI (right to use of search warrants); MONT. CONST. art. II, § 10 (right of privacy); NEV. CONST. art. I, §§ 18, 20 (right against unreasonable seizure and search and rights retained by the people); OHIO CONST. art. I, § 14 (right against unreasonable searches and seizures); R.I. CONST. art. I, § 6 (right against unreasonable searches and seizures); S.C. CONST. art. I, § 10 (right against unreasonable searches and seizures, invasions of privacy); WASH. CONST. art. I, § 7 (right against invasions of private affairs or the home); W. VA. CONST. art. III, § 6 (right against unreasonable searches and seizures); WYO. CONST. art. I, § 4 (right against unreasonable searches and seizures). However, where the privacy right is attached to prohibitions on unreasonable searches and seizures, courts have been reluctant to extend their state constitutional right to the general right of privacy protected in the Constitution. *See* Note, *The Use of the State Constitutional Right to Privacy To Defeat State Sodomy Laws*, 14 N.Y.U. REV. L. & SOC. CHANGE 973, 980 (1986) (authored by Nan Feyler) [hereinafter Note, *State Constitutional Right*].

[109] Alabama, Arizona, Arkansas, Florida, Idaho, Kentucky, Louisiana, Maryland, Montana, Nevada, Rhode Island, and South Carolina all criminalize sodomy. *See supra* note 2.

[110] *See* Note, *State Constitutional Right*, *supra* note 108, at 980 & n.75.

[111] *See, e.g.*, Kentucky v. Wasson, No. 86M859, slip op. at 2 (Fayette Dist. Ct. Oct. 31, 1986) (holding that the state sodomy statute violates the right to privacy in the Kentucky constitution).

[112] The Court in *Hardwick* expressly stated that its holding did not affect state constitutional challenges. *See* 478 U.S. at 190.

State courts can define state privacy guarantees more broadly than *Hardwick* defined the federal privacy right by basing the right on individual integrity rather than family or procreative autonomy. State constitutional interpretation need not simply mirror the interpretation of similar federal constitutional provisions,[113] as state constitutions are generally broader and more comprehensive than the federal Constitution.[114] Justifications for state divergence from federal interpretation of rights include: perceived flaws in the federal doctrine; institutional differences between the federal and state governments; and state-specific factors favoring broader coverage.[115]

The first factor, perceived flaws in the federal doctrine, weighs heavily in favor of the interpretation of state constitutional privacy rights to include protection of same-sex sodomy, regardless of whether the state privacy guarantee is explicit or implicit. Because many believe that the Supreme Court has adopted an overly restrictive approach to the right to privacy, as evidenced by the extensive criticism of *Hardwick*,[116] state courts should feel free to depart from the Supreme Court's current interpretation of the federal privacy right in analyzing their own constitutions.[117]

The second consideration, institutional differences between the state and federal governments, also supports a more expansive interpretation of the right to privacy than *Hardwick* recognized. Respect for the values of federalism and deference to the traditional state role in regulating public morality in part motivated Justice White's conservative construction of constitutional privacy rights in *Hardwick*.[118] The different conceptions of states rights and judicial deference to

---

[113] *See Developments in the Law — The Interpretation of State Constitutional Rights*, 95 HARV. L. REV. 1324, 1356–66 (1982) [hereinafter *Developments*].

[114] *See id.* at 1355. State courts interpreting state constitutional provisions are not limited to Supreme Court constructions of even identically phrased federal constitutional provisions. *See* Brennan, *State Constitutions and the Protection of Individual Rights*, 90 HARV. L. REV. 489, 502 (1977); *Developments, supra* note 113, at 1334–35.

[115] *See Developments, supra* note 113, at 1359–62.

[116] *See supra* note 30.

[117] State courts have criticized Supreme Court holdings construing rights restrictively in order to justify divergent interpretation of a textually similar state constitutional right. *See Developments, supra* note 113, at 1442 nn.69–70. State courts have even criticized and departed from federal holdings after having previously declared their state right coextensive with its federal counterpart. *See* State v. Miyasaki, 62 Haw. 269, 279–80, 614 P.2d 915, 921 (1980); State v. Benoit, 417 A.2d 895, 901 (R.I. 1980).

[118] *See Hardwick*, 478 U.S. at 190. Although it is unclear whether Justice White's reluctance to extend unenumerated constitutional rights stemmed from concerns about states' rights or separation of powers, even if his primary concern was deference to the Georgia legislature, differences between the state and federal constitutions justify less deference to legislatures in interpreting state constitutions, which are more easily amended. Differences between state and federal judges also justify less deference to legislatures by state courts, as state judges are frequently elected and more responsive to popular will than federal judges, who are appointed for life. *See Developments, supra* note 113, at 1351–52.

legislatures operative in state and federal courts justify state court departure from federal doctrine.[119]

The third consideration, state-specific factors, also counsels for an interpretation of state constitutional rights independent from the federal doctrine. The most persuasive state-specific consideration is a textual difference between the federal and state constitutions. When state constitutions explicitly contain privacy provisions, *Hardwick* should not automatically govern the state court's analysis; Justice White's refusal to extend the right to privacy to homosexual sodomy rested in part on his reluctance to recognize unenumerated constitutional rights.[120] Even when a state's constitution does not enumerate a right to privacy, state-specific factors may still influence state interpretation and justify a departure from the federal interpretation. Distinctive features of a state's history, the attitudes of the citizenry, or the legislative history surrounding the constitution's adoption should have a bearing on the interpretaton of a state constitutional provision. For example, the existence of an ordinance within the state's jurisdiction prohibiting sexual orientation discrimination may demonstrate a different tradition and public policy from those relied on in *Hardwick* to justify restricting the right of privacy to consensual, heterosexual activity.[121]

(c) Legislative Action. — In the post-*Hardwick* era, legislative action appears to be the best prospect for eliminating the persecution of individuals engaging in homosexual sodomy. However, legislative repeal has proven to be a long and arduous process.[122] Twenty-three states have legislatively decriminalized sodomy, beginning with Illinois in 1961.[123] Successful strategies for sodomy decriminalization have varied,[124] with legislative action sharply diminishing in the 1980's in partial response to widespread fear of AIDS and its association with homosexual activity. In the current political climate, with its emphasis

---

[119] *See, e.g.*, Alderwood Assocs. v. Washington Envtl. Council, 96 Wash. 2d 230, 238–39, 242, 635 P.2d 108, 113, 115 (1981) (en banc) (plurality opinion) (noting that the Supreme Court's development of the state action doctrine is dictated by conservative pressures peculiar to its federal constitutional role, and that the doctrine is hence not binding at the state constitutional level).

[120] *See Hardwick*, 478 U.S. at 194–95.

[121] *See infra* pp. 72, 157–58.

[122] *See* Mathews, *Antisodomy Laws Targeted for Repeal After High Court Ruling*, Washington Post, Feb. 4, 1987, at A-16, col. 1. In the 1980's, only Wisconsin has repealed its sodomy statute absent judicial invalidation. *See* WIS. STAT. ANN. § 944.17 (West 1982 & Supp. 1988).

[123] *See* Note, *State Constitutional Right, supra* note 108, at 979 & nn.51–53. New York and Pennsylvania effected decriminalization of sodomy through judicial invalidation of their state statutes. *See supra* notes 85–86 and accompanying text.

[124] Although in many states, judicial invalidation of sodomy statutes facilitated legislative reform, *see* State v. Pilcher, 242 N.W.2d 348, 359 (Iowa 1976); State v. Saunders, 75 N.J. 200, 219, 381 A.2d 333, 342 (1977), in Wisconsin, an anti-discrimination law preceded penal reform by one year. *See infra* WIS. STAT. ANN. § 111.31–.395 (West 1988).

on traditional family values bolstered by lingering hysteria surrounding AIDS, state decriminalization of sodomy will be difficult at best.

2. *Solicitation Statutes.* — *(a) Enforcement Challenges.* — In practice, loitering and solicitation statutes, not sodomy laws, provide the primary means of regulating homosexual activity.[125] Courts have construed such statutes to prohibit the solicitation of illegal sexual activity in order to avoid vagueness challenges.[126] Consequently, the solicitation of noncommercial, consensual same-sex sexual activity is a crime in many jurisdictions.[127]

The use of plainclothes police officers to enforce the solicitation statutes has precipitated complaints of illegal entrapment.[128] Defendants can invoke entrapment as a defense to prosecution under the solicitation statutes when the criminal design originates with the government officials who induce the solicitation in order to make an arrest.[129] However, no entrapment occurs when the defendant has the intent and design to commit the crime, and the officer, in good faith, merely furnishes the opportunity or encourages the defendant to perpetrate the crime that originated in the defendant's own mind.[130]

Discriminatory enforcement of solicitation statutes also violates the equal protection clause.[131] When police officers frequent gay bars to

---

[125] *See* Corstvet v. Boger, 757 F.2d 223, 225 (10th Cir. 1985); R. MOHR, *supra* note 7, at 54–55; Project, *The Consenting Adult Homosexual and the Law: An Empirical Study of Enforcement and Administration in Los Angeles County*, 13 UCLA L. REV. 643, 691 & n.30 (1966). Like sodomy statutes, the enforcement of solicitation statutes can cause severe disruption in the lives of gay men and lesbians. *See, e.g., Corstvet*, 757 F.2d at 223 (affirming a state university's dismissal of a professor arrested for soliciting sexual activities in student union restroom).

[126] *See, e.g.*, Riley v. United States, 298 A.2d 228, 231 (D.C. 1972), *cert. denied*, 414 U.S. 840 (1973); Pedersen v. City of Richmond, 219 Va. 1061, 1066, 254 S.E.2d 95, 98 (1979).

[127] *See* ALA. CODE § 13A-11-9 (1982); ARIZ. REV. STAT. ANN. § 13-2905 (1978 & Supp. 1988); ARK. STAT. ANN. § 5-71-213 (1987); DEL. CODE ANN. tit. 11, § 1321 (1987); D.C. CODE ANN. § 22-2701 (1981 & Supp. 1988); GA. CODE ANN. § 16-6-15 (1988); KAN. STAT. ANN. § 21-4108 (1981); MD. ANN. CODE art. 27, § 15 (1987 & Supp. 1988); NEV. REV. STAT. ANN. § 207.030 (Michie 1986); R.I. GEN. LAWS §§ 11-34-8, 11-34-8.1 (1981 & Supp. 1988); WIS. STAT. ANN. § 947.02 (West 1982). In states without solicitation statutes, persons can still be convicted for homosexual solicitation as an attempt to violate the sodomy statute. *See* State v. Walsh, 713 S.W.2d 508 (Mo. 1986).

[128] *See* Rittenour v. District of Columbia, 163 A.2d 558 (D.C. 1960) (reversing a conviction for commission of a "lewd, obscene, or indecent act" where police decoy phoned the defendant, went to his home, and led the defendant to believe that the decoy was a homosexual); R. MOHR, *supra* note 7, at 54 & n.18; Project, *supra* note 125, at 704 & n.114. Even if prosecutors do not prosecute many gay persons under existing solicitation statutes, plainclothes police officers continue to harass many persons suspected of making homosexual propositions. *See* E.C. BOGGAN, M. HAFT, C. LISTER, J. RUPP & T. STODDARD, THE RIGHTS OF GAY PEOPLE 113 (1983).

[129] *See* Sorrells v. United States, 287 U.S. 435, 452 (1932).

[130] *See* Sherman v. United States, 356 U.S. 369, 372–73 (1958) ("[A] line must be drawn between the trap for the unwary innocent and the trap for the unwary criminal.").

[131] *See* Yick Wo v. Hopkins, 118 U.S. 356, 373–74 (1886) (holding a facially valid law "applied and administered by public authority with an evil eye and unequal hand, so as

make arrests under the solicitation statutes, but do not make similar efforts in heterosexual bars, a gay, lesbian, or bisexual defendant may claim discriminatory enforcement. However, courts require proof of intentionally discriminatory enforcement, rather than mere lax law enforcement or the existence of violators who go unpunished.[132] Consequently, such claims are difficult to prove.

(b) *Facial Challenges.* — Solicitation statutes can be challenged facially as unconstitutional abridgements of speech. Because a spoken request to engage in same-sex sexual activity is speech rather than conduct, courts must either distinguish homosexual solicitation from protected speech, or identify state interests that outweigh the harms of regulating protected speech in order to uphold prohibitions on homosexual solicitation.

A statute that by judicial construction prohibits only the solicitation of illegal acts does not violate the first amendment, as the incitement of illegal activity is unprotected speech.[133] Solicitation as a crime has its roots in the common law, which held that solicitation to commit any criminal act was a crime in and of itself.[134] The validity of a solicitation statute depends to a large extent on the constitutionality of that state's sodomy statute and the legality of private, consensual, same-sex sodomy. Where sodomy is no longer a crime, courts have invalidated statutes prohibiting the solicitation of such acts, or have construed the statutes to apply only to the solicitation of acts that remain illegal.[135] Other courts and commentators have argued, however, that despite the legality of the act solicited, first amendment protection should not extend to such solicitation.[136]

---

practically to make unjust and illegal discriminations between persons in similar circumstances," to be "within the prohibition of the Constitution").

[132] *Cf.* United States v. Cozart, 321 A.2d 342 (D.C. 1974) (rejecting a male defendant's equal protection challenge that gay men bear the brunt of the sodomy statute's enforcement while lesbians go unpunished).

[133] *See* Brandenburg v. Ohio, 395 U.S. 444 (1969); Pryor v. Municipal Court, 25 Cal. 3d 238, 254, 599 P.2d 636, 646, 158 Cal. Rptr. 330, 339–40 (1979).

[134] *See* W. CLARK & W. MARSHALL, A TREATISE ON THE LAW OF CRIMES 219 (7th ed. 1967).

[135] *See* Pryor v. Municipal Court, 25 Cal. 3d 238, 253–54, 599 P.2d 636, 645–46, 158 Cal. Rptr. 330, 339 (1979); Commonwealth v. Sefranka, 382 Mass. 108, 118, 414 N.E.2d 602, 606 (1980); People v. Uplinger, 58 N.Y.2d 936, 937, 447 N.E.2d 62, 63, 460 N.Y.S.2d 514, 515 (1983), *cert. denied*, 467 U.S. 246 (1984).

[136] *See Pryor*, 25 Cal. 3d at 259, 599 P.2d at 649, 158 Cal. Rptr. at 342–43 (Clark, J., concurring in part and dissenting in part) (arguing that because the state could outlaw sodomy, the statute prohibiting solicitation is valid); *Uplinger*, 58 N.Y.2d at 942, 945–56, 447 N.E.2d at 65, 67, 460 N.Y.S.2d at 518, 520 (Jasen, J., dissenting) (finding that the state interest in protecting public sensibilities justifies the solicitation statute, and noting that such solicitation involves more than pure speech); State v. Phipps, 58 Ohio St. 2d 271, 278–79, 389 N.E.2d 1128, 1134 (1979) (upholding a statute prohibiting the solicitation of deviate sexual conduct, in spite of the legality of sodomy, as applied to a solicitor who knew of or was reckless as to any offensiveness to the solicitee); MODEL PENAL CODE § 251.3 comment (Official Draft and Revised

One rationale for denying first amendment protection to solicitation for noncriminal, same-sex, sexual conduct is that the state could prohibit such conduct, even if it has chosen not to.[137] This rationale is used to justify proscriptions on the solicitation of prostitution in the absence of a statute criminalizing prostitution.[138] However, these cases rely on a categorization of the regulated speech as commercial advertising of a trade that the state could proscribe entirely, and is therefore unprotected speech. This conclusion rests upon the lower value accorded commercial speech.[139] Consequently, this analysis should not apply to the solicitation of noncommercial, same-sex, sexual conduct.

Another rationale for eliminating homosexual solicitation from protected speech relies on the fighting words doctrine.[140] At least one court has employed this doctrine to uphold the constitutionality of a statute criminalizing the solicitation of homosexual sex. In *State v. Phipps*,[141] the Ohio Supreme Court construed its solicitation statute to apply only to "fighting words," where the offender knows or is reckless as to possible offensiveness to the solicitee, or where the very utterance of the solicitation inflicts injury. The court presumed that such solicitations "are likely to provoke the average person to retaliation and thereby cause a breach of the peace."[142] The court's willingness to accept violence as the likely response of the "average person" to a homosexual solicitation characterizes solicitation as necessarily "reckless," and therefore proscribed by the statute. This analysis sharply contradicts Supreme Court cases that have narrowed the fighting words exception to only the most urgent of situations.[143] Even if the requisite showing of probable violence could be made in this context, courts should still reject the characterization of homosexual solicitation as provoking the average person to violence. This characterization frames the "average person" in a traditional, hetero-

---

Comments 1980) (distinguishing loitering and solicitation statutes — aimed at protecting the public from offensive conduct — from sodomy statutes regulating private morality, and concluding that the former, and not the latter, should be criminal).

[137] See *Pryor*, 25 Cal. 3d at 259, 599 P.2d at 649, 158 Cal. Rptr. at 342–43 (Clark, J., concurring in part and dissenting in part).

[138] See Wood v. United States, 498 A.2d 1140 (D.C. 1985); United States v. Moses, 339 A.2d 46, 53 (D.C. 1975), *cert. denied*, 426 U.S. 920 (1976).

[139] See Virginia State Bd. of Pharmacy v. Virginia Citizens Consumer Council, Inc., 425 U.S. 748 (1976).

[140] This doctrine exempts from first amendment protection speech consisting of words that, by their very utterance, inflict injury or tend to incite an immediate breach of the peace. *See* Chaplinsky v. New Hampshire, 315 U.S. 568 (1942). The doctrine was later refined in Cohen v. California, 403 U.S. 15, 22–23 (1972), which distinguished merely offensive language from "fighting words," and accorded only the latter first amendment protection.

[141] 58 Ohio St. 2d 271, 389 N.E.2d 1128 (1979).

[142] *Id.* at 278, 389 N.E.2d at 1134.

[143] *See, e.g.*, Gooding v. Wilson, 405 U.S. 518, 522 (1972).

sexual, male-dominant role and legitimates anti-gay violence by placing the burden on gay persons to avoid a violent heterosexual response to their sexual orientation.

An alternative basis for removing homosexual solicitation from the realm of protected speech is to construe such solicitation as speech plus conduct, rather than pure speech.[144] However, the fact that speech proposes that some conduct take place does not transform pure speech into speech plus conduct, as virtually all speech advocates conduct at some level. Homosexual solicitation is no more speech plus conduct than is a request for participation in some political event.

Because homosexual solicitation does not fall within any of the established exceptions to speech, solicitation statutes must be analyzed as viewpoint-specific restrictions[145] regulating the content of protected speech rather than the manner in which it is expressed.[146] Because such statutes severely restrict the ability of the speaker to convey the message by only permitting the restricted speech in non-public places, they cannot be regarded as reasonable time, place, and manner restrictions.[147] Statutes prohibiting the solicitation of homosexual but not heterosexual sex endorse a particular form of sexuality while censoring an alternative preference. Even statutes that facially prohibit the solicitation of both opposite- and same-sex sodomy are viewpoint-specific; they favor one view of sexual morality — that sodomy is immoral or that sex should have the potential for procreation — over an alternative view that individuals should be free to engage in the private, consensual sexual practices of their choice.

Protection of public sensibilities is not a sufficient state interest to justify content-specific restrictions of speech.[148] Justifying restrictions of speech based on public offensiveness, defined by the prevailing view of morality, would violate the very essence of the first amendment — that individuals should have the autonomy to express even unpopular views.[149]

---

[144] *See* People v. Uplinger, 58 N.Y.2d 936, 942, 447 N.E.2d 62, 65, 460 N.Y.S.2d 514, 518 (1983) (Jasen, J., dissenting) (noting that although solicitation may be verbal in nature, "it . . . involves conduct which is greater than speech alone"), *cert. denied*, 467 U.S. 246 (1984).

[145] *See* L. TRIBE, *supra* note 30, § 12-3, at 794–804.

[146] *See* District of Columbia v. Garcia, 335 A.2d 217, 223 (D.C.) (noting that the statute prohibits all public solicitation to commit sodomy, regardless of the inoffensiveness of the language used), *cert. denied*, 423 U.S. 894 (1975).

[147] *See* Schneider v. State, 308 U.S. 147 (1939) (holding a municipal ordinance forbidding persons rightfully on a public street from handing literature to those willing to receive it violative of first amendment protections).

[148] *See* Cohen v. California, 403 U.S. 15 (1971); United States v. O'Brien, 391 U.S. 367, 377 (1968) (requiring "an important or substantial government interest . . . unrelated to the suppression of free expression" to justify a viewpoint-specific restriction on speech).

[149] *See* Richards, *Free Speech and Obscenity Law: Toward a Moral Theory of the First Amendment*, 123 U. PA. L. REV. 45, 62 (1974).

B. Gay Men and Lesbians as Victims
in the Criminal Justice System

The criminal justice system's inequitable treatment of gay men and lesbians perpetuates a vicious cycle of anti-gay violence and abuse. Judicial practices and jury biases mitigate the deterrence of anti-gay crimes by reducing penalties for those violations. Police insensitivity toward gay people makes gay and lesbian victims less likely to report crimes against them, which in turn decreases the capacity of the criminal justice system to punish and deter anti-gay crimes. This section examines anti-gay crimes, police harassment of gay people, and judicial lenience toward defendants whose victims are gay men and lesbians.

I. Bias Crimes[150] *Against Gay Men and Lesbians.* — Acts of violence against gay men and lesbians illustrate society's intolerance of non-heterosexual lifestyles and exacerbate the oppression of gay men and lesbians as a group. According to a recent study commissioned by the National Institute of Justice, gay men and lesbians are probably victimized more often than any other minority group.[151] In a 1984 study by the National Gay and Lesbian Task Force, one in five gay men and nearly one in ten lesbians reported being physically assaulted because of their sexual orientation.[152] Moreover, perhaps as a result of the AIDS epidemic,[153] anti-gay violence appears to be increasing.[154]

Bias crimes are more socially invidious than crimes not motivated by group hatred because of their tendency to perpetuate prejudice and victimize an entire class of persons. Anti-gay violence resembles racial violence in that both serve to intimidate and disempower their victims and others like them. Due to the pervasive social disparagement of

---

[150] Bias crimes, or hate violence, are "words or actions designed to intimidate an individual because of his or her race, religion, national origin, or sexual preference." P. Finn & T. McNeil, The Response of the Criminal Justice System to Bias Crime: An Exploratory Review 1 (1987) (on file at Harvard Law School Library).

[151] *See* P. Finn & T. McNeil, *supra* note 150, at 2. The National Gay and Lesbian Task Force (NGLTF) has defined "anti-gay" violence as violence "directed against persons or their property *because*: 1) they are lesbian or gay or perceived to be so; 2) they are associated with or advocate on behalf of gay and lesbian people." K. Berrill, Anti-Gay Violence: Causes, Consequences, Responses 2 (1986) (on file at Harvard Law School Library).

[152] *See* K. Berrill, *supra* note 151, at 3. Studies show that gay men face a disproportionately greater risk of being victims of bias crime than lesbians. *See* National Gay & Lesbian Task Force, Anti-Gay Violence, Victimization & Defamation in 1987, at 9 (1987) [hereinafter Anti-Gay Violence] (on file at Harvard Law School Library).

[153] *See* Anti-Gay Violence, *supra* note 152, at 8 (noting that 15% of all anti-gay incidents reported to the NGLTF "involved verbal reference to AIDS by the perpetrators or were directed against persons with AIDS"). Anti-gay propaganda from right-wing political groups also incites anti-gay violence. *See* D. GREENBERG, THE CONSTRUCTION OF HOMOSEXUALITY 467 (1988).

[154] *See* Anti-Gay Violence, *supra* note 152, at 2.

homosexuality and the continued legality of many forms of anti-gay discrimination, many gay and lesbian victims are reluctant to report acts of violence against them, perhaps out of a fear that their sexual orientation will be exposed.[155] A history of conflict between law enforcement officials and the gay and lesbian community has contributed to the under-reporting of anti-gay crimes. Law enforcement authorities often devote great attention to the enforcement of public sex and loitering laws against same-sex sexual conduct and solicitation.[156] Gay men and lesbians also have been subjected to unprovoked violence by police officers, as well as other forms of police harassment.[157] As a result of their reluctance to report crimes, and their distrust of the criminal justice system, gay men and lesbians are more attractive victims for perpetrators of bias crime.[158]

2. *Sexual Orientation and Criminal Defenses.* — Courts often allow perpetrators of anti-gay violence to claim that their violent actions stem from a psychological disorder known as homosexual panic. Homosexual panic is premised on the theory that a person with latent homosexual tendencies will have an extreme and uncontrollably violent reaction when confronted with a homosexual proposition.[159] Although no appellate court has explicitly upheld homosex-

---

[155] Surveys of various communities indicate that from 76% to 82% of anti-gay attacks go unreported. *See* K. Berrill, *supra* note 151, at 6. Crimes against gay people also tend to be characteristically more violent and heinous than crimes against non-gay persons, *see* Miller & Humphreys, *Lifestyles & Violence: Homosexual Victims of Assault & Murder,* 3 QUALITATIVE SOC. 169, 179–80 (1980), perhaps as a result of the greater likelihood that such crimes will go unreported and unpunished.

[156] *See, e.g.,* People v. Kalchik, 160 Mich. App. 40, 407 N.W.2d 627 (1987) (finding that police use of videotaping equipment in men's restroom stalls to enforce public sex laws violated the defendant's reasonable expectation of privacy and was conducted pursuant to an invalid search warrant); Bull, *Fruit Picked in Jersey Rest Stop,* Gay Community News, Jan. 22–28, 1987, at 1, col. 1 (noting the use of police entrapment techniques in arrests of gay men in men's restroom for "lewd behavior"); *supra* p. 27. For an historical account of police harassment of gay men and lesbians in New York City, see Rosen, *Police Harassment of Homosexual Women and Men in New York City 1960–1980,* 12 COL. HUM. RTS. L. REV. 159 (1980–1981).

[157] *See* Anti-Gay Violence, *supra* note 152, at 17–18; Report of the Governor's Task Force on Gay Issues, Discrimination on the Basis of Sexual Orientation 140–46 (1986) (reporting anecdotal evidence of police abuse and harassment of gay men and lesbians in New York) (on file at Harvard Law School Library). In a 1984 survey of gay men and lesbians in eight cities, 23% of the gay men and 13% of the lesbians surveyed reported police abuse due to their sexual orientation. *See* K. Berrill, *supra* note 151, at 7.

[158] Victimologists have labeled this phenomenon "derivative deviance," referring to the victimization of stigmatized persons because of their inability to avail themselves of the protections of civil society without the threat of being discredited. *See generally* Harry, *Derivative Deviance: The Cases of Extortion, Fag-Bashing, and Shakedown of Gay Men,* 19 CRIMINOLOGY 546 (1982).

[159] Proponents of the homosexual panic theory apply it to latent homosexuals who react violently, while in a disassociative mental state, triggered by an encounter that confronts them with their own homosexuality. *See* D. WEST, HOMOSEXUALITY RE-EXAMINED 202–03 (4th ed. 1977). Critics of the theory attribute the reaction to cultural rather than psychological factors,

ual panic as a basis for acquitting a defendant, the defense has nevertheless served as an unstated basis for acquittals in homicide cases involving gay victims.[160] Even where defendants accused of committing violence against gay persons do not raise homosexual panic as a defense, the admission of evidence of a victim's homosexuality often results in undue lenience towards such defendants.

(a) Homosexual Panic as a Mental Defect. — (i) Homosexual Panic as an Insanity Defense. — When a defendant raises an insanity defense[161] based on homosexual panic, courts will submit the defense to the jury.[162] In fact, a defendant may be able to bring a writ of habeas corpus in federal court to overturn a state court conviction where the defendant raised an insanity defense based on homosexual panic and the state court excluded evidence of a victim's homosexuality.[163] However, the acceptance of homosexual panic as a legiti-

---

and argue that it stems from insecurities about one's masculinity rather than homoerotic tendencies. *See* J. MARMOR, HOMOSEXUAL BEHAVIOR 15 (1980).

[160] *See* Finn, *Bias Crime: Difficult To Define, Difficult To Prosecute*, CRIM. JUST., Summer 1988, at 19, 47; *Does Gay Pass Justify a Murder?*, Montrose Voice, Apr. 1, 1983, at 14, col. 1; P. Finn & T. McNeil, *supra* note 150, at 34–35. Some courts, however, have refused to acquit defendants on the basis of the gay panic defense. *See* Commonwealth v. Carr, No. CC-385-88 (Pa. Ct. of C.P., Adams County, Apr. 3, 1989), cited in 1988 LESBIAN/GAY L. NOTES 64; State v. Bell, No. 88-1-00158-0 (Super. Ct. of Wash., Pierce County, Sept. 28, 1988), cited in 1988 LESBIAN/GAY L. NOTES 64.

[161] The standards for insanity vary by jurisdiction, and the persuasiveness of homosexual panic as an insanity defense will depend on the particular test adopted. A majority of American jurisdictions follow the *M'Naghten* test, which absolves a defendant of criminal responsibility if he or she suffered from a mental defect when committing the act, such that he or she either did not know the nature and quality of the act or did not know of its wrongfulness. *See* 1 W. LaFAVE & A. SCOTT, SUBSTANTIVE CRIMINAL LAW § 4.2, at 436 (1986). A few jurisdictions following the *M'Naghten* test have supplemented it with the "irresistible impulse" rule, which also negates culpability if the mental defect prevented the defendant from controlling his or her conduct. *See id.* at 449–50. A significant minority of jurisdictions have adopted the Model Penal Code's "substantial capacity" standard, which defines a mental disease or defect as lacking the substantial capacity to appreciate the wrongfulness of the allegedly criminal conduct or to conform the conduct to the requirements of law. *See* MODEL PENAL CODE § 4.01, at 61–62 (1985).

[162] *See, e.g.*, State v. Thornton, 532 S.W.2d 37, 44–45 (Mo. Ct. App. 1975). The mere presence of some evidence of homosexual panic, however, does not require an insanity defense to be interposed. *See* Commonwealth v. Doucette, 391 Mass. 443, 458–59, 462 N.E.2d 1084, 1097 (1984).

[163] *See* Parisie v. Greer, 705 F.2d 882 (7th Cir.) (en banc) (relying on a mixture of jurisdictional and merit-based grounds to affirm the district court's dismissal of the defendant's habeas corpus petition), *cert. denied*, 464 U.S. 950 (1983). The only two judges reaching the constitutional implications of the homosexual panic defense arrived at different conclusions. *Compare Parisie*, 705 F.2d at 893 (Posner, J., concurring) (arguing that whether or not the state recognizes a homosexual panic defense, the Constitution does not require a state to "defame the murderer's victim as a homosexual" where the state court determines that the evidence does not meet that state's requirements for reputation evidence) *with Parisie*, 705 F.2d at 899–902 (Swygert, J., concurring in part and dissenting in part) (arguing that the sixth amendment requires the admission of evidence of the victim's homosexuality, either as a character trait or medical condition, to demonstrate the victim's propensity for making an advance towards the defendant).

mate insanity defense encounters theoretical, evidentiary, and socio-logical problems.

The classification of homosexual panic as a mental defect or form of insanity is theoretically problematic because it attributes a defendant's mental illness to his or her sexual orientation. Homophobia differs from recognized mental illnesses because it is a product of culturally imposed values rather than abnormal psychological traits.[164] Homosexual panic should therefore not be accepted as a mental defect negating or reducing individual culpability. Moreover, given the American Psychiatric Association's declassification of homosexuality as a mental illness,[165] it is unclear why someone who is latently gay or lesbian should be classified as mentally disturbed when someone who has openly chosen a gay lifestyle is not.[166]

Homosexual panic as a legal defense also encounters evidentiary problems of proof. The premise of homosexual panic — that latent homosexuality is provable — implicates fundamental assumptions about human sexuality that are themselves unproven. Many researchers depict sexual orientation as a continuum in which persons are neither entirely homosexual nor entirely heterosexual, but fall somewhere in between.[167] Under this paradigm, all persons not acting on their homosexual impulses could be classified as "latently homosexual"; thus, any person committing an act of anti-gay violence could assert a homosexual panic defense. Even if the judiciary does not adopt such an expansive view of sexual orientation, proof of latent homosexuality is highly manipulable by defendants.

By relying upon a normative determination that fear and hatred of gay people as a group is determined by a person's mental state, rather than volitional choice, the defense also has adverse implications for controlling anti-gay violence.[168] Recognizing homosexual panic as a mental disease or defect diminishes individual responsibility for the consequences of bias and prejudice,[169] and accepts such behavior as unchangeable and unavoidable, thereby encouraging its reoccurrence.

---

[164] See D. GREENBERG, supra note 153, at 463 n.39 (criticizing the classification of homophobia as a mental illness).

[165] See R. BAYER, HOMOSEXUALITY AND AMERICAN PSYCHIATRY 137 (1987).

[166] In Parisie, psychiatric testimony based the defense on the defendant's reaction to his own reciprocation of the victim's advances, rather than to the advances themselves. See Parisie v. Greer, 671 F.2d 1011, 1016 (7th Cir. 1982), rev'd per curiam, 705 F.2d 882 (7th Cir.) (en banc), cert. denied, 464 U.S. 950 (1983). This formulation identifies latent homosexuality, rather than homophobia, as the mental problem.

[167] See, e.g., A. KINSEY, W. POMEROY & C. MARTIN, SEXUAL BEHAVIOR IN THE HUMAN MALE 638 (1948).

[168] Even where the defense is unsuccessful, the prejudicial impact of evidence of a gay advance on the part of the victim can affect the result. See infra p. 36.

[169] Although, in theory, the defense requires proof of the defendant's latent homosexuality,

(ii) Homosexual Panic as a Diminished Capacity Defense. — Of the jurisdictions that recognize the diminished capacity defense,[170] most accept the defense to mitigate the offense by negating an element of the crime charged.[171] Case law concerning the use of homosexual panic as a diminished capacity defense is extremely sparse. However, no court recognizing the partial defense of diminished capacity has barred evidence of homosexual panic as a matter of law or because homosexual panic rests on an unsupported and untenable psychological theory. The above-mentioned theoretical, evidentiary, and sociological problems with recognizing homosexual panic as a mental disease apply equally to the use of homosexual panic to prove diminished responsibility resulting from a mental defect.

Courts accepting homosexual panic as a diminished capacity defense should only use it to negate the premeditation or deliberation requirements of first degree murder, and not to reduce murder to manslaughter. Very few jurisdictions allow diminished capacity to decrease murder to manslaughter[172] because voluntary manslaughter requires objectively reasonable provocation.[173] Those jurisdictions that do mitigate murder to manslaughter based on diminished capacity strike a balance between the goals of ensuring moral culpability and preserving minimum standards of conduct in favor of individualistic

---

it is not used to account for societal homophobia. The decision to excuse a defendant for his or her homophobia does not depend upon a determination that the defendant's homophobia is societally induced. Moreover, the criminal justice system refuses to mitigate the culpability of defendants who, as a result of societal repression, react violently and in a generalized manner against other repressed persons, or even perceived oppressors. Violence motivated by racial hatred, for example, is no more excusable because its perpetrator happens to be a member of a victimized racial minority.

[170] Fewer than half of the states accept a diminished capacity defense, *see* 1 W. LaFave & A. Scott, *supra* note 161, § 4.7, at 522 n.2, and the popularity of the defense seems to be declining. *See* State v. Wilcox, 70 Ohio St. 2d 182, 436 N.E.2d 523 (1982). For an argument against the defense, see 2 Encyclopedia of Crime and Justice 612–16 (S. Kadish ed. 1983) [hereinafter Encyclopedia].

[171] *See* 1 W. LaFave & A. Scott, *supra* note 161, § 4.7, at 524–25. This is also the variety of the defense adopted by the Model Penal Code. *See* Model Penal Code § 4.02 (1985). For an alternative version, permitting the jury to decrease a proven offense to a lesser included offense whenever the jury finds the defendant's culpability diminished by mental capacity, see 2 Encyclopedia, *supra* note 170, at 612–16, which notes that no American jurisdiction has explicitly adopted this version; and Model Penal Code § 210.3 & comment, at 67–69 (Official Draft and Revised Comments 1980), which describes this alternative use of diminished capacity and notes that California appears to follow it.

[172] *See* Model Penal Code § 210.3 & comment, at 70–71 & n.77 (Official Draft and Revised Comments 1980); *see also* 1 W. LaFave & A. Scott, *supra* note 161, § 4.7, at 526 (arguing that diminished capacity has no place in the decision to mitigate murder to heat-of-passion voluntary manslaughter).

[173] *See* Model Penal Code § 210.3 & comment, at 70–72 (Official Draft and Revised Comments 1980); 1 W. LaFave & A. Scott, *supra* note 161, § 4.7, at 526.

subjectivity. The cost of that balance is that abnormal individuals have fewer incentives to behave normally.[174] However, the social balance should be struck differently where the diminished capacity defense is based on homosexual panic because the use of such a defense to reduce murder to manslaughter will tend to perpetuate the victimization of all gay men and lesbians, and not just isolated individuals.

   (b) Evidence of a Victim's Homosexuality. — Even absent any psychiatric evidence of homosexual panic, the introduction of evidence of a victim's homosexuality can inflame and prejudice juries and judges.[175] Courts have permitted defendants to introduce evidence of the victim's homosexuality to support claims of self-defense to a homosexual advance by the victim.[176] The "gay advance defense" has resulted in reductions in sentences for convicted defendants,[177] mitigation in the degree of offense for which a defendant is convicted,[178] and acquittals.[179]

---

   [174] *See* MODEL PENAL CODE § 210.3 & comment, at 71 (Official Draft and Revised Comments 1980).

   [175] *See* Moore, *Justice Is Not Blind for Gays*, San Diego Union, Jan. 10, 1989, at B7, col. 3 (quoting presiding judge who described a jury's acquittal of a man accused of murdering a gay man as "shocking" and "absolutely inappropriate"); *Panel To Examine Remarks by Judge on Homosexuals*, N.Y. Times, Dec. 21, 1988, at A16, col. 5 (quoting a Texas judge who sentenced a defendant to 30 years instead of the maximum term of life for killing two gay men, as saying that he would "put prostitutes and gays at about the same level," and that he would be "hard put to give somebody life for killing a prostitute"); *Gays Say Murderer Set Free*, Kalamazoo News, Feb. 14–20, 1986, at 1, col. 3 (noting community and judicial outrage at jury's acquittal of a man accused of beating to death a gay man); Valente, *Gays Call for Resignation of Judge Who Sentenced Teen-Agers*, Washington Post, May 19, 1984, at B1, col. 1; *see also* Parisie v. Greer, 705 F.2d 882, 893 (7th Cir.) (per curiam) (Posner, J., concurring) (characterizing testimony as to a victim's homosexuality as "defam[ation]"), *cert. denied*, 464 U.S. 950 (1983).

   [176] Such proof can assume highly intrusive forms. *See, e.g.*, Russell v. State, 522 So. 2d 969, 970–71 (Fla. Dist. Ct. App. 1988) (noting the trial court's decision to admit evidence that the victim had AIDS as corroborative of the victim's homosexuality and relevant to proving the victim's gay advance).

   [177] *See* Gilvin v. State, 418 So. 2d 996, 999–1000 (Fla. 1982) (Boyd, J., concurring in part and dissenting in part) (dissenting from the court's reversal of the trial court's imposition of the death penalty over the jury's life sentence where the defendant's only justification for the crime was the victim's homosexual advances toward him, and stating that "[o]ne can only speculate about the reason for the recommendation").

   [178] *See* State v. Oliver, No. 49613 (Ohio Ct. App. Oct. 17, 1985) (LEXIS, States library, Ohio file) (reversing trial court's finding that homosexual advance could not as a matter of law constitute provocation reasonably sufficient to incite the use of deadly force). On retrial, the defendant in *State v. Oliver* claimed self-defense to a gay advance, and was acquitted by the jury, to the dismay of the presiding judge. *See* Moore, *supra* note 175, at B7, cols. 2–3.

   [179] *See* Rangel, *Brooklyn Youth Acquitted in Slaying of Catholic Priest*, N.Y. Times, Feb. 5, 1987, at B3, col. 3; *Gays Say Murderer Set Free*, Kalamazoo News, Feb. 14–20, 1986, at 1, col. 3; *Does a Gay Pass Justify a Murder?*, Montrose Voice, Apr. 1, 1983, at 14, col. 1.

The gay advance defense has also been invoked to reduce murder to manslaughter[180] by showing heat of passion, and to prove self-defense as an affirmative defense to homicide.[181] However, a gay advance should not qualify as heat of passion under accepted standards. A reduction of murder to voluntary manslaughter requires a defendant to have acted in the heat of passion caused by provocation sufficient to cause a reasonable person in similar circumstances to lose his or her normal self-control.[182] Merely experiencing fear or hatred of gay people in response to a homosexual overture should not suffice to provoke a reasonable person to lose his or her self-control and resort to deadly force.[183]

The use of the gay advance defense to show self-defense is similarly flawed. The self-defense standard requires defendants to have acted based on a reasonable fear, given their objective circumstances, regardless of their particular mental abnormalities or value systems.[184] Even when the fear is reasonable, defendants must use reasonable force, given the circumstances.[185] A defendant's violent response to a nonviolent gay advance is unreasonable and thus does not satisfy the standard.

---

[180] *See supra* note 178.

[181] *See* Califia & Kulieke, *"Justifiable" Homicide? Verdict in Calif. Gay Slaying Sparks Protest*, Advocate, May 12, 1983, at 12, col. 1 (giving examples of cases where the gay advance defense was raised to show self-defense).

[182] *See* 1 W. LaFave & A. Scott, *supra* note 161, § 4.7, at 526 (stating that heat of passion "by its very nature presumes a person without serious mental and emotional defects"). The Model Penal Code follows a more subjective heat of passion standard, reducing murder to manslaughter when "committed under the influence of extreme mental or emotional disturbance for which there is a reasonable explanation or excuse," the reasonableness of which is "determined from the viewpoint of a person in the actor's situation under the circumstances as he believes them to be." Model Penal Code § 210.3 (1985). However, even this more subjective formula does not justify acceptance of homosexual panic as a mitigating circumstance, as "the question is whether the actor's loss of self-control can be understood in terms that arouse sympathy in the ordinary citizen." *Id.* comment, at 63. Courts should not reinforce anti-gay prejudices held by ordinary citizens.

[183] The type and extent of provocation sufficient to cause a loss of control in the reasonable person should change with the times. *See* 2 W. LaFave & A. Scott, *supra* note 161, § 7.10, at 256.

[184] *See* 1 *id.* § 5.7, at 653–54. Although the Model Penal Code standard for self-defense only requires that "the actor believe[s] that such force is immediately necessary for [self-protection against] unlawful force," Model Penal Code § 3.04 (1985), in order to use deadly force, the actor must believe that such force is necessary to prevent his or her own death, serious bodily injury, or forced sexual intercourse; a reckless or negligent determination of necessity subjects the actor to prosecution for the offense of recklessness or negligence under § 3.09. *See id.* § 3.09 & explanatory note. The requirement that the determination not be negligent subjects the actor to a reasonableness standard. Only a few jurisdictions follow the Model Penal Code approach. *See* 1 W. LaFave & A. Scott, *supra* note 161, § 5.7, at 655 & n.31.

[185] *See* 1 W. LaFave & A. Scott, *supra* note 161, § 5.7, at 652.

Some courts have admitted evidence of a victim's homosexuality as relevant reputation evidence where the defendant has alleged self-defense in response to an attempted homosexual rape.[186] Although a victim's homosexuality may appear relevant to whether the victim attempted to homosexually rape the defendant, the effect on the jury may be more prejudicial than probative. Evidence of a man's homosexuality does not demonstrate his propensity to rape another man any more than evidence of a man's heterosexuality demonstrates his propensity to rape a woman.[187] Rape is an act of violence, not sexual gratification, and, in fact, many men who rape other men identify themselves as heterosexual.[188] Because of its prejudicial impact, evidence of a victim's sexual preference should not be admissible unless it is essential to prove a victim's previous use of force in sexual encounters.[189]

3. Toward a Criminal Justice System More Responsive to Gay and Lesbian Victims. — Only recently have federal agencies devoted attention to the problem of anti-gay violence. In addition to a National Institute of Justice study,[190] both Houses of Congress are likely to pass the Hate Crime Statistics Act, which would require the Attorney General to collect national data on crimes motivated by a victim's race, religion, sexual orientation, or ethnicity.[191] Although the Act

---

[186] *See, e.g.*, State v. Carter, No. 82CA22 (Ohio Ct. App. Mar. 18, 1983) (LEXIS, States library, Ohio file); Williamson v. State, 692 P.2d 965 (Alaska Ct. App. 1984). *But see* State v. Oliver, No. 49613 (Ohio Ct. App. Oct. 17, 1985) (LEXIS, States library, Ohio file) (refusing to admit evidence of the victim's homosexuality where the victim's character had not been properly placed at issue, and finding no relationship between the victim's homosexual activities and any violent propensity).

[187] In fact, placing a homicide victim's sexuality at issue to prove self-defense is quite like placing a woman's sexual promiscuity at issue to show consent to rape — a practice now prohibited in some jurisdictions by rape shield laws. *See* Brown, *Blaming the Victim: The Admissibility of Sexual History in Homicides*, 16 FORDHAM URB. L.J. 263 (1988).

[188] *See* W. WOODEN & J. PARKER, MEN BEHIND BARS 224 (1982) (noting that heterosexual and bisexual inmates primarily instigate sexual violence in prison).

[189] In addition, legislatures should enact legislation similar to the rape shield laws to exclude evidence of a victim's sexual orientation in homicide cases. The San Fransisco District Attorney has suggested legislative reform similar to the rape shield laws to exclude evidence of a homicide victim's sexual orientation. *See* Smith, *Dealing with Anti-Gay Violence*, BAY AREA REPORTER, Nov. 3, 1983, at 1, 11; *cf.* Brown, *supra* note 187, at 265 (advocating the exclusion of evidence of a homicide victim's sexual history).

[190] *See* P. Finn & T. McNeil, *supra* note 150. Additionally, Congress appropriated funds for a comprehensive follow-up report on bias crimes to provide guidelines for state and local criminal justice agencies. *See* 134 CONG. REC. H8297, H8306 (daily ed. Sept. 26, 1988).

[191] *See* 135 CONG. REC. S1563 (daily ed. Feb. 22, 1989) (reprinting the Hate Crime Statistics Act). The House of Representatives passed the Hate Crime Statistics Act in 1988, and a similar bill passed the Senate Judiciary Committee, but did not receive further action before adjournment. *See* 135 CONG. REC. E464 (daily ed. Feb. 22, 1989). The bill was recently reintroduced in the House of Representatives, *see id.*, and the Senate, as S. 419, *see id.* at S1563 (daily ed. Feb. 22, 1989).

explicitly declines to create any substantive rights for victims,[192] the collection of data could assist law enforcement and criminal justice agencies in devising effective programs to control bias crime. In the absence of a federal statute providing heightened penalties for crimes motivated by anti-gay biases, federal civil rights statutes should be interpreted to apply to acts motivated by the victim's sexual orientation.[193] Federal prosecution and the availability of private civil causes of action could effectively address anti-gay bias crimes.[194]

The state legislative response to anti-gay bias crimes has been somewhat more tepid. Of the many states that have specifically criminalized offenses motivated by bias,[195] only California specifies sexual orientation as a prohibited motivation.[196] California also authorizes the attorney general, district attorneys, and victims themselves to seek injunctions against the perpetrators of anti-gay violence in order to deter reoccurrence.[197] Of the states that have statutes mandating

---

[192] S. 419(3) specifically disclaims the creation of any right of action based on sexual orientation discrimination. *See id.* at S1562.

[193] *See* 18 U.S.C. § 241 (1982) (proscribing conspiracies against the rights of individuals); 42 U.S.C. § 1985(3) (1982) (prohibiting conspiracies to interfere with civil rights). For an argument that these statutes should apply to racially motivated bias crimes, see Comment, *Racially-Motivated Violence and Intimidation: Inadequate State Enforcement and Federal Civil Rights Remedies*, 75 J. CRIM. L. & CRIMINOLOGY 103 (1984). Authority exists to support the use of congressional power under § 5 of the fourteenth amendment to reach entirely private action. *See* United States v. Guest, 383 U.S. 745, 761–62 (1966) (Clark, J., concurring); *id.* at 774–86 (Brennan, J., concurring in part and dissenting in part); Action v. Gannon, 450 F.2d 1227 (8th Cir. 1971). The constitutional acts entitled to protection under the statutes include both fourteenth amendment and due process rights. *See* United States v. Price, 383 U.S. 787 (1966); *Guest*, 383 U.S. 745. Consequently, because the equal protection clause protects gay men and lesbians against the deprivation of their rights, either under a theory of gender or sexual orientation discrimination, *see supra* notes 47–64 and accompanying text, § 241 should apply to the perpetrators of anti-gay bias crimes. Although § 1985(3) does not reach wholly private conspiracies against the fourteenth amendment, *see* United Bhd. of Carpenters, Local 610 v. Scott, 436 U.S. 825 (1983), a non-racial, class-based animus to deny equal protection may be actionable under § 1985(3), *see* Griffin v. Breckenridge, 403 U.S. 88, 102 (1971). Consequently, § 1985(3) should include actions by state officials or attempts "to influence the activity of the State," *Scott*, 463 U.S. at 830, motivated by anti-gay prejudice.

[194] *See* Comment, *supra* note 193, at 105 (advocating the combination of federal prosecution and civil remedies with increased state legislation and enforcement as the most effective approach to combating racial violence).

[195] Many states criminalize specific acts of intimidation. *See* P. Finn & T. McNeil, *supra* note 150, at 7–8. At least three states have statutes generally proscribing interference with a person's civil rights. *See id.* at 8. Seven states and some localities have statutes providing civil causes of action by individuals whose civil rights have been violated. *See id.* At least one state statute provides for injunctive relief against violations of state and federal rights to be brought by the Attorney General on the victim's behalf. *See* MASS. GEN. LAWS ANN. ch. 265, § 37 (West Supp. 1989); *id.* ch. 12, § 11H (West 1986). The Massachusetts Attorney General has interpreted that state's statute to include deprivations of rights based on sexual orientation. *See* Gay Community News, Nov. 20–26, 1988, at 2, col. 3.

[196] *See* CAL. PENAL CODE §§ 422.6–.7 (West 1985).

[197] *See* CAL. PENAL CODE § 52.1 (West Supp. 1989). However, nonstatutory, common-law

the collection of bias-crime-related data,[198] only Connecticut authorizes the collection of statistics on all crimes motivated by bigotry and bias.[199] Lower courts have upheld bias crime statutes against constitutional challenges based on the first amendment and the equal protection clause.[200] Although the impact of bias crime statutes on the level of hate violence is difficult to assess due to the reporting problems inherent in bias crime, anecdotal evidence in at least one study suggests that such statutes may deter bias crimes.[201]

Local law enforcement efforts are crucial to controlling anti-gay violence. Such efforts should include the coordination of police department and gay community relations groups,[202] as well as the development of model training programs to teach officers to recognize and respond to anti-gay violence[203] and to interview gay and lesbian victims with sensitivity.[204] Although political and administrative considerations may deter many police administrators from singling out bias crimes,[205] the police departments in several cities have made special efforts to investigate bias crimes against gay men and lesbians.[206] Despite efforts by district attorneys in some jurisdictions to target bias crimes, prosecutors often lag behind police departments in responding to these crimes.[207] Prosecutors can lessen the likelihood that offenders will be given lenient sentences, especially where juveniles are involved, by pressing for fines and community service rather than by plea bargaining such offenses.[208]

---

remedies against the perpetrators of anti-gay bias crimes may be limited. *See* Coon v. Joseph, 192 Cal. App. 3d 1269, 1272, 1275–76, 237 Cal. Rptr. 873, 874, 877 (1987) (refusing to allow a plaintiff to recover for emotional distress based on an intentional assault on his gay partner because gay relationships were declared insufficiently "close" as a matter of law).

[198] *See* CONN. GEN. STAT. ANN. § P.A. 87-279 (West 1988 Appendix Pamphlet); MD. ANN. CODE art. 88B, §§ 9-10 (1985).

[199] *See* CONN. GEN. STAT. ANN. § P.A. 87-279 (West 1988 Appendix Pamphlet).

[200] *See* People v. Grupe, 141 Misc. 2d 6, 532 N.Y.S.2d 815 (N.Y. Crim. Ct. 1988); People v. Dinan, 118 Misc. 2d 857, 461 N.Y.S.2d 724 (Long Beach City Ct. 1983), *appeal denied*, 64 N.Y.2d 650, 474 N.E.2d 264 (1984).

[201] *See* P. Finn & T. McNeil, *supra* note 150, at 36 (noting reported effectiveness of the Massachusetts Civil Rights Act).

[202] The district attorney of Manhattan, New York has appointed a liaison between law enforcement officials and the gay community. *See* Nichols, *YLD Studies Anti-Gay Violence*, 14 BARRISTER, Summer 1987, at 19.

[203] *See* Pitt, *Police Anti-Bias Decoy Unit Is Scaling Back Operations*, N.Y. Times, Sept. 20, 1988, at B1, col. 4; *id.* at B2, col. 6.

[204] *See* K. Berrill, *supra* note 151, at 15.

[205] *See* P. Finn & T. McNeil, *supra* note 150, at 24.

[206] *See id.* at 7.

[207] *See id.*

[208] *See* Finn, *supra* note 160, at 48. Civil injunctions can also ensure that juvenile offenders, who are less likely to be sentenced for a first violation, will receive greater punishment for a repeated incident. *See id.* at 47.

Gay and lesbian victims of police harassment can vindicate their rights by bringing civil actions for violation of their constitutional rights under 42 U.S.C. § 1983[209] and for deprivation of their rights to equal protection of the laws under 42 U.S.C. § 1985.[210] In *Cyr v. Walls*,[211] the district court refused to grant the defendants' motion to dismiss the plaintiffs' section 1983 and 1985 claims of police harassment of patrons of gay bars and members of a church dedicated to serving the gay community. However, the court noted that, in light of the state's prohibition against same-sex sodomy, the plaintiffs might have difficulty proving that police surveillance and harassment efforts violated their constitutional rights.[212] The argument that police surveillance of gay social and political groups is justified by the propensity of those groups to violate the sodomy statutes mistakenly equates homosexuality with the act of sodomy, and falsely assumes that the object of any group of people dedicated to gay rights is to facilitate the commission of sexual acts.[213] An effective remedy for police harassment of gay men and lesbians — one that does not place any unnecessary burdens on gay litigants by mistakenly treating them as potential violators of the sodomy statutes — could help deter police abuse and promote better relations between law enforcement and the gay and lesbian community. Such a climate would increase the probability that gay men and lesbians would report anti-gay bias crimes, and enhance the capacity of law enforcement to control such crimes.

C. Gay Men and Lesbians as Criminal Defendants

1. Evidentiary Questions and Prosecutorial Conduct. — Gay and lesbian defendants also experience prejudice in the criminal justice system due to their sexual orientation.[214] Although evidence of a defendant's homosexuality is generally not admissible if the defendant's sexual orientation is not at issue and no defense is raised based on a victim's gay advance,[215] when such evidence is admitted, ap-

---

[209] 42 U.S.C. § 1983 (1982) enables individuals deprived of federal rights by officials acting under the color of state law to bring a cause of action against such officials for proper redress.

[210] 42 U.S.C. § 1985(3) (1982) provides for a cause of action for damages resulting from the deprivation of individual rights or privileges.

[211] 439 F. Supp. 697 (N.D. Tex. 1977).

[212] *See id.* at 702.

[213] *See supra* p. 11.

[214] Convicted defendants who are gay or lesbian may also experience prejudicial treatment based on their sexual orientation. For a discussion of issues affecting gay prisoners, see Howarth, *The Rights of Gay Prisoners: A Challenge to Protective Custody*, 53 S. CAL. L. REV. 1225 (1980).

[215] *See* People v. Mitchell, 402 Mich. 506, 265 N.W.2d 163 (1978). However, evidence of a defendant's homosexual affair with a witness is uniformly admitted to impeach the witness' credibility. *See* State v. Hise, 738 P.2d 13 (Colo. Ct. App. 1986); Sias v. State, 416 So. 2d 1213 (Fla. Dist. Ct. App. 1982).

pellate courts often find the error nonprejudicial.[216] In addition, prosecutors may impute to defendants a homosexual preference in their opening or closing statements, even if no admitted evidence establishes the defendant's sexual orientation. Although courts generally prohibit such remarks due to their propensity to disparage the defendant in the eyes of the jury,[217] such remarks are generally held nonprejudicial when the court instructs the jury to disregard them.[218] When references to a defendant's homosexuality in a closing argument appear to comment on the evidence presented, courts have also declined to find the commentary to be prejudicial error.[219] However, where a prosecutor focuses on a defendant's imputed homosexuality in closing argument, despite the absence of proof of his or her sexual orientation, and makes other improper arguments, courts have reversed convictions.[220] Courts reviewing the admission of prejudicial evidence of a defendant's homosexuality, or prosecutorial comments imputing a gay or lesbian orientation to the defendant, should weigh heavily the prevalence of anti-gay biases among judges and juries[221] in determining whether to declare a mistrial or reverse a conviction.

   2. *Voir Dire and Homophobic Attitudes.* — Because of the homophobia and anti-gay prejudice permeating popular culture,[222] an unbiased jury is essential to a gay or lesbian defendant's prospects for a fair trial. This is especially important where courts expect jury instructions to cure any prejudice resulting from the erroneous admission of evidence of a defendant's homosexuality or a prosecutor's erroneous reference to a defendant's sexual orientation.[223] Voir dire is the primary means through which the criminal justice system assures an accused of a fair and impartial jury. In general, a court's failure to conduct voir dire regarding juror biases toward homosex-

---

[216] *See, e.g., Sias,* 416 So. 2d at 1213; State v. Dace, 333 N.W.2d 812 (S.D. 1983); Blount v. State, 630 S.W.2d 856 (Tex. Ct. App. 1982). *But see* Gabrielson v. State, 510 P.2d 534 (Wyo. 1973) (reversing the defendant's conviction based, in part, on the admission of testimony as to gay advances made by the defendant).

[217] *See* United States v. Birrell, 421 F.2d 665 (9th Cir. 1970); Killie v. State, 14 Md. App. 645, 287 A.2d 310 (1972).

[218] *See, e.g.,* People v. Hamilton, 27 Ill. App. 3d 249, 327 N.E.2d 35 (1975); Logan v. State, 698 S.W.2d 680 (Tex. Crim. App. 1985).

[219] *See, e.g.,* Commonwealth v. Healy, 393 Mass. 367, 471 N.E.2d 359 (1984); *Logan,* 698 S.W.2d 680.

[220] *See* Commonwealth v. Clary, 388 Mass. 583, 447 N.E.2d 1217 (1983); Bennett v. State, 677 S.W.2d 121, 124–26 (Tex. Ct. App. 1984).

[221] *See supra* note 175.

[222] *See supra* Part I.

[223] Although screening biased jurors probably best ensures gay or lesbian defendants a fair trial, the presence of gay men and lesbians on the jury may also enhance the jury's fairness and representativeness. Although a juror cannot be disqualified for cause because of homosexuality, *see* State v. Viggiani, 105 Misc. 2d 210, 431 N.Y.S.2d 979 (N.Y. Crim. Ct. 1980), no cases have challenged peremptory strikes of jurors based on their sexual orientation.

uality will be reversed only if held to be an abuse of discretion.[224] Judges may refuse to inquire into anti-gay biases when they believe that such questioning would unduly emphasize the issue of homosexuality.[225] Judges also have the discretion not to allow follow-up questions concerning potential bias, and to refuse to conduct individual voir dire, in spite of possible reluctance by jurors to admit anti-gay biases in open court.[226]

Unlike cases involving racial bias, which are generally accorded broader voir dire, courts have held that the mere presence of issues related to homosexuality does not automatically warrant an investigation into potential anti-gay prejudice.[227] Certainly sexual orientation is not as readily discernable as race, nor does it receive heightened scrutiny under the equal protection clause. Nevertheless, jurors with anti-gay prejudices will be more likely to treat gay defendants unfairly. Given the reluctance of courts to reverse convictions or declare mistrials for erroneously admitted evidence or improper prosecutorial remarks concerning a defendant's homosexuality, defense attorneys who anticipate references to a defendant's homosexuality or the presence of gay-related issues at trial should be entitled to conduct voir dire to discover anti-gay biases. Such an opportunity would enable defendants to identify homophobic and anti-gay jurors and eliminate them from the jury through peremptory challenges.

D. Conclusion

In many jurisdictions, the criminal law continues to stigmatize gay men and lesbians through the criminalization of same-sex sodomy and prohibitions on the solicitation of same-sex sexual partners. However, in spite of the Court's decision in *Bowers v. Hardwick* not to recognize a fundamental right of privacy to engage in same-sex sodomy, equal protection and state constitutional privacy challenges remain potential grounds for invalidating such statutes. Whether courts find such challenges persuasive may depend on their disposition toward same-sex sexual conduct and homosexuality in general.

Gay men and lesbians also face obstacles in the criminal justice system, both as victims and as defendants. The increase in hate violence towards minority groups in recent years has taken its toll on gay and lesbian victims, who may be more vulnerable to victimization due to their reluctance to report crimes out of the fear of exposure of their sexual orientation. A long and continuing history of police abuse and insensitivity, in addition to anti-gay biases within the criminal

---

[224] *See* United States v. Click, 807 F.2d 847 (9th Cir. 1987).

[225] *See* Commonwealth v. Boyer, 400 Mass. 52, 507 N.E.2d 1024 (1987).

[226] *See, e.g.*, State v. Lambert, 528 A.2d 890 (Me. 1987).

[227] *See, e.g.*, *Boyer*, 400 Mass. at 52, 507 N.E.2d at 1024.

justice system, has reinforced this reluctance and further impeded the ability of the criminal justice system to control such crimes. The activation of biases and prejudices towards gay and lesbian criminal defendants is another aspect of the victimization of gay men and lesbians based on their sexual orientation, and contributes to the general impression on the part of gay men and lesbians that the criminal law does not always treat them fairly.

III. EMPLOYMENT LAW ISSUES AFFECTING GAY MEN AND LESBIANS

A. Public Employment

Gay men and lesbians face discrimination in three major areas of public employment: military employment, employment in jobs that require a security clearance,[1] and employment in the civil service. Sexual orientation discrimination is most pervasive in military employment.[2] From 1975 to 1985, the military discharged 15,000 persons because of allegations of homosexuality.[3] According to Department of Defense guidelines,[4] the military must discharge individuals who engage or have engaged in homosexual acts,[5] who state that they are

---

[1] Security clearances are required for both public and private sector positions that implicate national security. At the end of 1983, approximately 2,725,000 government civilian and military personnel had security clearances, as did 1,500,000 employees of private contracting firms. *See* SENATE COMM. ON GOVERNMENTAL AFFAIRS, FEDERAL GOVERNMENT'S SECURITY CLEARANCE PROGRAMS, S. REP. NO. 230, 99th Cong., 2d Sess. 2 (1986).

[2] *See generally* K. BOURDONNAY, R. JOHNSON, J. SCHUMAN & B. WILSON, FIGHTING BACK: LESBIAN AND GAY DRAFT, MILITARY AND VETERANS ISSUES (1985) [hereinafter FIGHTING BACK] (examining the military's policies against gay and lesbian servicepersons).

[3] *See* Note, *Homosexuals in the Military: They Would Rather Fight than Switch*, 18 J. MARSHALL L. REV. 937, 937 (1985). From September 1984 to September 1987, the military discharged more than 4600 people from active duty on the grounds of homosexuality. *See* Atkins, *Forced March in the Military*, NATION, Jan. 2, 1989, at 16. The military's anti-gay policies have had a particularly harsh impact on lesbians. Since 1983, "lesbians have been discharged for homosexual conduct at a rate almost 10 times that of homosexual military men." Lewin, *Gay Groups Suggest Marines Selectively Prosecute Women*, N.Y. Times, Dec. 4, 1988, at 34, col. 1; *see also* Berube & D'Emilio, *The Military and Lesbians During the McCarthy Years*, 9 SIGNS 759 (1984) (recounting the military's harsh treatment of lesbians during the 1950's). The military's current campaign against lesbians reflects the generally low level of respect with which women in the military are treated. *See* Moore, *Military Found To Further Limit Women*, Washington Post, Oct. 2, 1988, at A13, col. 1 (reporting General Accounting Office finding that the military services "unnecessarily bar women from thousands of jobs and have established recruiting goals that further limit the number of positions open to women").

[4] 32 C.F.R. pt. 41, app. A, pt. 1.H (1987).

[5] *See id.* pt. 1.H.1.c(1). A "homosexual act" under the regulations is defined in much broader terms than those used in most sodomy statutes, *see supra* p. 1520, the requisite conduct being only "bodily contact, actively undertaken or passively permitted, between members of the same

homosexual or bisexual,[6] or who attempt to marry a member of the same sex.[7] The guidelines permit deviation from these rules only under limited circumstances.[8] Servicepersons discharged on the grounds of homosexuality will receive an honorable or general discharge unless the individual engaged in homosexual acts under certain aggravating circumstances.[9]

---

sex for the purpose of satisfying sexual desires." 32 C.F.R. pt. 41, app. A, pt. 1.H.1.b(3) (1987). Under the regulations, therefore, kissing, holding hands, and even putting an arm around a fellow soldier all might fall within the parameters of homosexual activity. Interestingly, although the discharge regulations are concerned only with same-sex sexual activity, the Uniform Code of Military Justice's proscription on sodomy extends to "unnatural carnal copulation" with a member of either "the same or opposite sex." *See* Uniform Code of Military Justice, 10 U.S.C. § 925 (1983).

[6] *See* 32 C.F.R. pt. 41, app. A, pt. 1.H.1.c(2) (1987).

[7] *See id.* pt. 1.H.1.c(3). The act, statement, or attempted marriage need not occur within the period of military service. *See id.* pt. 1.H.1.c. In addition to discharging gay or lesbian servicepersons under the regulations on homosexuality, the military can discharge gay or lesbian individuals for "fraudulent enlistment," if they did not disclose their sexual orientation at the time they joined the service. *See id.* pt. 1.E.4; *see also* Rich v. Secretary of the Army, 735 F.2d 1220 (10th Cir. 1984) (upholding the discharge of a gay serviceperson for fraudulent enlistment).

[8] Exceptions to discharges based on homosexual acts will be made only when it is determined that the act was uncharacteristic behavior for that individual. *See* 32 C.F.R. pt. 41, app. A, pt. 1.H.1.c(1) (1987). Exceptions to discharges based on declarations of homosexual orientation will be made only if the declaration was false. *See id.* pt. 1.H.1.c(2). Exceptions to discharges based on actual or attempted same-sex marriages will be made only if the individual is found to be heterosexual, and the marriage or attempted marriage is found to be an attempt to avoid or terminate military service. *See id.* pt. 1.H.1.c(3).

[9] The aggravating circumstances include homosexual acts involving force, coercion, or intimidation, acts engaged in with minors or military subordinates, acts performed in public, aboard a military vessel or aircraft or in certain other locations subject to military control, and acts for compensation. *See id.* pt. 1.H.2; *see also* Gay Veterans Ass'n, Inc. v. Secretary of Defense, 850 F.2d 764, 768 (D.C. Cir. 1988) (upholding the less than honorable discharge of a servicewoman for "homosexual conduct open to other members' observation" under the "aggravating circumstances" provision of the regulations). The military may discharge gay and lesbian servicepersons under other than honorable conditions in "fraudulent enlistment" cases, *see supra* note 7, regardless of the existence of aggravating circumstances. *See* 32 C.F.R. pt. 41, app. A, pt. 1.E.4.c(4) (1987).

Despite the regulations' limitation of the circumstances in which other than honorable discharges may be issued, a Navy Board of Officers has recently recommended the other than honorable discharge of Captain Judy Meade for "engaging in public association and [a] long term personal relationship with a known lesbian"; Meade has never been charged with being a lesbian herself. Telephone interview with Martin Kripner, Meade's attorney (Mar. 27, 1989); *see also* Bull, *Lesbian Purge by Marines Continues,* Gay Community News, Mar. 12–18, 1989, at 1, col. 1 (discussing Meade's case). It is not clear whether the Navy Board's recommendation will stand up. *Cf.* Stapp v. Resor, 314 F. Supp. 475, 476, 479 (S.D.N.Y. 1970) (invalidating the undesirable discharge of a servicemember for maintaining a "close, continuing, and sympathetic association with the Communist Party" and with "an active member of the Socialist Workers Party" because the charges failed to allege any military misconduct or matters affecting the plaintiff's military record).

In jobs requiring security clearances, treatment of gay men and lesbians is only slightly better.[10] The Department of Defense has argued that gay and lesbian applicants constitute security risks under a number of criteria used in processing security clearance applications.[11] Although the Defense Department has asserted that openly gay men and women are not barred from receiving security clearances,[12] it nonetheless subjects security clearance applications by all gay men and lesbians to expanded investigations and mandatory adjudications.[13] Moreover, cases involving the security clearance policies of the FBI and the CIA suggest that these agencies have effectively established a per se ban on the employment of any gay or lesbian applicant.[14]

In general, the civil service is much more hospitable to gay and lesbian employees. The civil service's policy toward gay men and lesbians has changed more in the past several decades than has that of any other sector of the federal government. During the McCarthy era, homosexuality was grouped with communism as a grave evil to be rooted out of the federal government.[15] From 1947 through mid-1950, the federal government denied 1700 individuals employment because of alleged homosexuality.[16] In the mid-1960's, however, plaintiffs began to attack successfully the civil service's policy of mandatory exclusion of gay and lesbian employees.[17] At present, the rights of gay men and lesbians in the civil service remain ambiguous: although the civil service will not deny an individual a job solely on the basis of sexual orientation, the job security of gay and lesbian

---

[10] For an early discussion of issues involving security clearances, see Note, *Security Clearances for Homosexuals*, 25 STAN. L. REV. 403 (1973) [hereinafter Note, *Security Clearances*].

[11] *See* High Tech Gays v. Defense Indus. Sec. Clearance Office, 668 F. Supp. 1361, 1365 (N.D. Cal. 1987) (citing "disregard of public law," "criminal or dishonest conduct," "acts indicating poor judgment, unreliability, or untrustworthiness," "mental condition [that] may cause defect in judgment or reliability," "[v]ulnerability to coercion" and "[a]cts of sexual misconduct or perversion") (quoting 32 C.F.R. § 154.7(g)–(k), (q) (1987)).

[12] *See* Williams, *Pentagon Asking Employees About Sex Practices*, N.Y. Times, May 14, 1987, at A18, col. 3.

[13] *See High Tech Gays*, 668 F. Supp. at 1364–65.

[14] *See* Padula v. Webster, 822 F.2d 97, 98–99 (D.C. Cir. 1987) (discussing the FBI's effective ban on hiring gay or lesbian applicants); Dubbs v. Central Intelligence Agency, 866 F.2d 1114, 1118 (9th Cir. 1989) (finding that the evidence supports "a finding that the CIA in fact denies security clearances to all persons known to commit homosexual acts").

[15] *See* J. D'EMILIO, SEXUAL POLITICS, SEXUAL COMMUNITIES: THE MAKING OF A HOMO-SEXUAL MINORITY IN THE UNITED STATES 1940–1970, at 41–44 (1983); SENATE COMM. ON EXPENDITURES, EMPLOYMENT OF HOMOSEXUALS AND OTHER SEX PERVERTS IN GOVERNMENT, INTERIM REPORT, S. DOC. NO. 241, 81st Cong., 2d Sess. (1950), *reprinted in* GOVERNMENT VERSUS HOMOSEXUALS (J. Katz ed. 1975).

[16] *See* J. D'EMILIO, *supra* note 15, at 44.

[17] *See infra* p. 48.

persons who are not discreet about their sexual orientation continues to be uncertain.[18]

This section primarily addresses substantive constitutional[19] protections against sexual orientation discrimination in public employment.[20] First, it considers the issues that arise when courts apply rational relationship review to government employment decisions based on sexual orientation. Second, this section explores how the issues change when courts apply heightened equal protection scrutiny. Finally, this section examines cases in which courts consider whether sexual orientation discrimination violates first amendment guarantees of freedom of speech. After examining these substantive protections, this section briefly addresses the constitutional procedural safeguards available to gay and lesbian employees who have been dismissed from their jobs.

1. Substantive Protections. — (a) Rational Relationship Review. — In reviewing government actions under lower-tier substantive due process or equal protection review,[21] courts must determine whether the action is "rationally related to a legitimate governmental purpose."[22] In the context of sexual orientation discrimination in public

---

[18] *See id.*

[19] This section will address only federal constitutional issues. State constitutional provisions may, however, offer greater protection to public employees. *See infra* note 182.

[20] In addition to challenging sexual orientation discrimination on constitutional grounds, gay and lesbian public employees may bring challenges under title VII of the 1964 Civil Rights Act or other federal statutory schemes. *See infra* pp. 68–72. Furthermore, twelve states and at least 87 cities and counties explicitly prohibit discrimination against gay men and lesbians in public employment. *See American Bar Association Mid-Year Meeting*, 57 U.S.L.W. 2479 (1989).

[21] Due process and equal protection jurisprudence are generally divided into levels, or "tiers," of scrutiny. The lowest tier of both due process and equal protection review requires only that the governmental action at issue be "rationally related" to a legitimate governmental purpose. *See, e.g.*, Kelley v. Johnson, 425 U.S. 238, 247 (1976) (due process); McLaughlin v. Florida, 379 U.S. 184, 191 (1964) (equal protection). In cases that implicate fundamental rights, however, courts employing due process analysis will subject the government's actions to a stricter standard of review. *See, e.g.*, Roe v. Wade, 410 U.S. 113, 155 (1973) (subjecting laws banning abortion to strict scrutiny because of their burden on the constitutional right to privacy). Similarly, courts will apply heightened equal protection scrutiny to governmental actions that implicate fundamental interests, *see, e.g.*, Harper v. Virginia Bd. of Elections, 383 U.S. 663, 670 (1966) (invalidating a state poll tax on the grounds that it burdened the fundamental right to vote), or that employ classifications that are considered "suspect" or "quasi-suspect," *see infra* p. 54. The cases discussed in this section are all based on lower-tier substantive due process, although the courts' reasoning would apply equally to cases involving rational relationship equal protection review.

[22] Kadrmas v. Dickinson Pub. Schools, 108 S. Ct. 2481, 2487 (1988); *see also* Kelley v. Johnson, 425 U.S. 238, 247 (1976) (finding that due process requires the government to show only a "rational connection" between the regulation at issue and the asserted governmental interests). The rational connection standard is the most deferential standard of review of governmental actions, and generally permits any action that can be supported by at least some shred of logical reasoning. *See, e.g.*, United States R.R. Retirement Bd. v. Fritz, 449 U.S.

employment, this standard of review provides almost no protection for military personnel and persons in positions requiring security clearances. Rational basis review does, however, provide some protection for gay and lesbian individuals employed in the civil service. In *Norton v. Macy*,[23] the D.C. Circuit held that the due process clause requires that, before the civil service fires or refuses to hire an individual on the grounds of sexual orientation, it must establish a rational relationship between that person's sexual orientation and the efficiency of governmental operations.[24]

The *Norton* court's framing of the rational relationship test indicates the limits of such review of sexual orientation discrimination in civil service employment. In *Norton*, the court, although holding that there was no rational relationship between the plaintiff's homosexuality and the efficiency of the service, emphasized that the plaintiff's homosexual conduct was off-duty, and that he neither "flaunt[ed] nor carelessly display[ed] his unorthodox sexuality in public."[25] The court's emphasis on these facts leaves open the possibility that gay and lesbian employees whose openness on the job offends co-workers or the public could legally be dismissed.[26]

In *Singer v. United States Civil Service Commission*,[27] the Ninth Circuit adopted the *Norton* court's reasoning to uphold against a due

---

166, 179 (1980) ("Where . . . there are plausible reasons for Congress' action, our inquiry is at an end."). The Supreme Court has, however, occasionally struck down governmental classifications under a stricter standard of rational relationship review. *See, e.g.*, City of Cleburne v. Cleburne Living Center, Inc., 473 U.S. 432 (1985) (invalidating discrimination against the mentally retarded); United States Dep't of Agric. v. Moreno, 413 U.S. 528 (1973) (striking down denial of food stamps to households made up of unrelated individuals); *see also infra* p. 1563.

[23] 417 F.2d 1161 (D.C. Cir. 1969).

[24] *See id.* at 1164–65; *see also* Scott v. Macy, 349 F.2d 182, 184–85 (D.C. Cir. 1965) (holding that the government may not rely on mere allegations of homosexuality to discharge an employee, but must specify the particular conduct it finds immoral, and state why that conduct relates to operational fitness). In *Norton*, the plaintiff was a "veterans preference eligible" employee, and as a result, could only be discharged for "'such cause as will promote the efficiency of the service.'" 417 F.2d at 1162 (quoting 5 C.F.R. § 731.201(b) (1968)). Yet, although the court emphasized the statutory protection accorded the plaintiff, it also relied on the requirements of the due process clause, which, it noted, apply with equal force to employees not protected by "for cause" statutes. *See id.* at 1164. Since *Norton*, courts have held that *Norton*'s rational relationship test is mandated by the due process clause, and applies to both protected and unprotected public employees. *See, e.g.*, Society for Individual Rights, Inc. v. Hampton, 63 F.R.D. 399 (N.D. Cal. 1973), *aff'd*, 528 F.2d 905 (9th Cir. 1975); Morrison v. State Bd. of Educ., 1 Cal. 3d 214, 461 P.2d 375, 82 Cal. Rptr. 175 (1969) (applying the *Norton* test to state public employment).

[25] 417 F.2d at 1167.

[26] The distinction between protected, private homosexual conduct and unprotected, public homosexual activity or advocacy is also determinative in many of the teacher dismissal cases discussed in Part IV below. *See infra* pp. 89–91.

[27] 530 F.2d 247 (9th Cir. 1976), *vacated*, 429 U.S. 1034 (1977).

process challenge the dismissal of a federal civil servant who "flaunted" his homosexuality on the job.[28] The court seized on the distinction between private homosexual activity and public homosexual expression and held that the plaintiff's "openly and publicly flaunting his homosexual way of life and indicating further continuance of such activities while identifying himself as a member of a federal agency" brought discredit upon the government and impeded the efficiency of the service.[29]

Although rational relationship review does not fully protect the rights of gay and lesbian civil servants who are open about their sexuality, it at least provides them with some protection against discrimination based on their sexual orientation. In reviewing discrimination against gay and lesbian security clearance applicants, however, courts employing rational relationship review have generally declined to scrutinize the basis of the government's actions at all,[30] once homosexual conduct has been established.[31]

---

[28] See id. at 249.

[29] Id. at 251, 255. The court summarily dismissed Singer's first amendment claims as well. See id. at 256. Singer was subsequently vacated by the Supreme Court after the adoption of new civil service regulations, see infra, and the plaintiff ultimately prevailed at an administrative hearing. See Rivera, Queer Law: Sexual Orientation Law in the Mid-Eighties (pt. 1), 10 U. DAYTON L. REV. 459, 485 (1985). Nonetheless, the Ninth Circuit's reasoning represents the logical extension of Norton, and continues to be cited. See, e.g., Childers v. Dallas Police Dep't, 513 F. Supp. 134, 141 (N.D. Tex. 1981); Opinion of the Attorney General of the State of West Virginia (Feb. 24, 1983) (concluding that gay and lesbian schoolteachers may be dismissed for immorality), cited in Rivera, supra, at 535 n.511.

After Norton, and while Singer was being litigated, the federal civil service codified Norton's rational relationship requirement. The Federal Personnel Manual now provides that a person is not unsuitable for federal employment merely because such person is gay or lesbian or has engaged in homosexual acts. See Singer, 530 F.2d at 254 n.14. Specific factors, such as "[c]riminal, dishonest, infamous or notoriously disgraceful conduct," however, can provide the requisite link between a person's sexual orientation and job performance. 5 C.F.R. § 731.202(b)(2) (1988). Protection of gay and lesbian federal employees under the guidelines appears to continue to depend on the degree to which the employee's sexual orientation is kept quiet. See United States Customs Serv. v. National Treasury Union, Chapter 142, 77 Lab. Arb. (BNA) 1113, 1117 (1982) (Rocha, Arb.) (reinstating a dismissed Customs officer because his homosexuality "did not manifest itself in any way that resulted in notoriety or public censure which would reflect unfavorably on Customs").

[30] Courts' reluctance to scrutinize closely governmental decisions involving national security stems in part from a concern that judicial scrutiny might lead to exposure of confidential information. See Weinberger v. Catholic Action of Haw., 454 U.S. 139, 146–47 (1981). But see Webster v. Doe, 108 S. Ct. 2047, 2054 (1988) (allowing judicial review of a constitutional attack on the CIA's termination of a gay employee despite the government's claim that such review would entail "extensive 'rummaging around' in the Agency's affairs to the detriment of national security").

[31] See, e.g., McKeand v. Laird, 490 F.2d 1262 (9th Cir. 1973); Adams v. Laird, 420 F.2d 230 (D.C. Cir. 1969), cert. denied, 297 U.S. 1039 (1970); see also Padula v. Webster, 822 F.2d 97, 104 (D.C. Cir. 1987) (upholding the FBI's refusal to hire a lesbian job applicant, noting that "FBI agents perform counterintelligence duties that involve highly classified matters" making gay and lesbian agents open to "blackmail"). But see High Tech Gays v. Defense Indus. Sec.

Courts that have upheld denials of security clearances to gay men and lesbians have accepted arguments that gay and lesbian persons are likely to be subjected to blackmail,[32] that they are untrustworthy,[33] and that they regularly violate the criminal law.[34] The blackmail rationale, the most prevalent of these arguments,[35] is usually based on the assumption that gay men and lesbians fear disclosure of their sexual orientation, and that, as a result, foreign agents who become aware of an employee's homosexuality could threaten to expose that person unless she divulges classified information.[36] Even in cases involving openly gay or lesbian individuals, however, courts have upheld job denials to gay and lesbian persons in fields implicating national security on the grounds that such persons may divulge secret information in an attempt to protect the identities of their intimate partners.[37]

The government's claim that gay and lesbian individuals are greater blackmail risks than the population at large is simply not supported by evidence. None of the approximately forty significant espionage cases presented by the FBI and the Defense Department at a recent Senate hearing involved gay people blackmailed into espionage.[38] Moreover, the government's assertion that, because of a desire to protect the identities of their intimate partners, even openly gay or

---

Clearance Office, 668 F. Supp. 1361, 1368 (N.D. Cal. 1987) (subjecting the government's policy of extended investigations and mandatory adjudications of gay and lesbian security clearance applicants to heightened equal protection scrutiny).

Despite the general acceptance of blanket denials of security clearances to gay and lesbian applicants, the government is prohibited from relying on overly intrusive questioning about sexual practices during the investigative process. *See* Gayer v. Schlesinger, 490 F.2d 740 (D.C. Cir. 1973). *But see* Brief of Amicus Curiae National Gay Rights Advocates at 7 n.2, High Tech Gays v. Defense Indus. Sec. Clearance Office (9th Cir. 1989) (No. 87-2987) (reporting that "[o]ne applicant was asked whether he was on top or on bottom during sexual acts").

[32] *See McKeand,* 490 F.2d at 1263–64; *Adams,* 420 F.2d at 239 n.7; *see also Padula,* 822 F.2d at 104 (upholding the FBI's refusal to hire a lesbian applicant on the grounds that she might be subject to blackmail threats).

[33] *See McKeand,* 490 F.2d at 1266 (Peckham, J., dissenting) (quoting the hearing examiner's finding that the plaintiff's homosexuality indicated a "'lack of reliability and trustworthiness as to suggest that he might disclose classified information'"); *Adams,* 420 F.2d at 240.

[34] *See* Note, *Security Clearances, supra* note 10, at 412 (citing cases).

[35] This is true despite the fact that blackmail is not a significant cause of security breaches. *See* SENATE SELECT COMM. ON INTELLIGENCE, MEETING THE ESPIONAGE CHALLENGE: A REVIEW OF UNITED STATES COUNTERINTELLIGENCE AND SECURITY PROGRAMS, S. REP. NO. 522, 99th Cong., 2d Sess. 26 (1986) (finding that "the most common motivation [for espionage] is financial gain, often combined with conscious or unconscious anger at the employer" and that foreign agents use blackmail only as "a last resort").

[36] *See McKeand,* 490 F.2d at 1263; *Adams,* 420 F.2d at 240.

[37] *See* Padula v. Webster, 822 F.2d 97, 104 (D.C. Cir. 1987) (upholding the FBI's denial of a job to an openly lesbian applicant).

[38] *See* SENATE PERMANENT SUBCOMM. ON INVESTIGATIONS OF THE COMM. ON GOVERN-MENTAL AFFAIRS, FEDERAL GOVERNMENT'S SECURITY CLEARANCE PROGRAMS, S. HRG. NO. 166, 99th Cong., 1st Sess. 171–87, 913–26 (1985) [hereinafter SECURITY CLEARANCE PROGRAMS].

lesbian individuals are security risks is untenable. Certainly, the fact that many non-gay people may enter into clandestine relationships with, for example, married individuals does not justify a wholesale ban on heterosexuals from jobs involving national security.

In rational relationship cases involving the military, courts have required neither the individualized consideration demanded of the civil service nor the evidence of specific homosexual acts mandated by the security clearance guidelines. Because of the deference generally given military judgments,[39] courts using a rational relationship test have found that even a blanket policy of excluding from the military all persons who so much as state that they are gay or lesbian does not offend due process.[40]

Courts have accepted as rational several justifications put forth by the military.[41] First, the military has claimed that the presence of gay men and lesbians in the service would exacerbate anti-gay feelings among other servicepersons, and lead to discipline and morale problems, "tensions and hostilities," and a lack of trust or respect for gay officers. In addition, the military has argued that gay men and lesbians would be unable to perform their duties effectively, because of both their involvement in emotional relationships with other gay and lesbian persons and their fear that their homosexuality might be disclosed. Other factors cited by the military include the danger that gay and lesbian officers would enter into sexual relationships with soldiers under their command, the possibility that parents who know that gay men and lesbians are present in the military would be reluctant to allow their children to enlist, and the risk that people in foreign countries might react negatively to the presence of gay and lesbian servicepersons stationed there. Finally, one court has asserted that "toleration of homosexual conduct, as expressed in a less broad prohibition, might be understood as tacit approval."[42]

The military's justifications for banning gay and lesbian persons from the service contradict even its own research on the relationship between sexual orientation and military performance. A study prepared by the Navy in 1957 found that, rather than being less effective than their heterosexual counterparts, the records of gay servicepersons, on average, actually displayed superior performance to those of Navy

---

[39] See, e.g., Goldman v. Weinberger, 475 U.S. 503, 507 (1986) (upholding discipline of an orthodox Jewish officer for wearing a yarmulke because of the deference owed to military judgments concerning the need to "foster instinctive obedience, unity, commitment, and esprit de corps").

[40] See, e.g., Dronenburg v. Zech, 741 F.2d 1388 (D.C. Cir. 1984); Rich v. Secretary of the Army, 735 F.2d 1220 (10th Cir. 1984); Beller v. Middendorf, 632 F.2d 788 (9th Cir. 1980), cert. denied, 452 U.S. 905 (1981).

[41] The justifications are set forth in Beller, 632 F.2d at 811; and Dronenburg, 741 F.2d at 1398.

[42] Beller, 632 F.2d at 811.

personnel as a whole.[43] Moreover, the military's reasons for excluding gay men and lesbians, if taken to their logical conclusions, would require excluding women and racial minorities from the service, as the presence of both women and men might lead to sexual tensions and officer-subordinate relationships,[44] and the presence of different races might lead to racial tensions.[45]

Nonetheless, in *Beller v. Middendorf*,[46] the Ninth Circuit, accepting all of the military's justifications, upheld the Navy's policy of discharging all persons who have engaged in homosexual conduct.[47] Judge (now Justice) Kennedy wrote that, although the policy is "perhaps broader than necessary to accomplish some of its goals," it "represents a reasonable effort to accommodate the needs of the Government with the interests of the individual."[48] In *Dronenburg v. Zech*,[49] Judge Bork, writing for the D.C. Circuit, went further than Judge Kennedy and argued that "[t]he effects of homosexual conduct within a naval or military unit are almost certain to be harmful to morale and discipline."[50]

Although courts have refused to strike down the military's policy of exclusion of gay men and lesbians under rational relationship review, a number of courts have held that, because the military provides that gay and lesbian servicepersons may be retained under exceptional circumstances,[51] it must articulate why the circumstances of a particular case are not exceptional.[52] Such decisions, however, offer only limited protection to gay and lesbian members of the military. The requirement that the military state why the circumstances of a particular case are not "exceptional" would seem to be quite easy to meet,

---

[43] *See* FIGHTING BACK, *supra* note 2, at 4. Rather than change its anti-gay policy to comport with the study's findings, however, the Navy classified the report and, apparently, destroyed parts of it. *See id.*

[44] *See* Dronenburg v. Zech, 746 F.2d 1579, 1581 (D.C. Cir. 1984) (Robinson, C.J., dissenting from denial of rehearing en banc) ("The dangers hypothesized by the panel provide patently inadequate justification for a ban on homosexuality in a Navy that includes personnel of both sexes and places no parallel ban on all types of heterosexual conduct.").

[45] Exclusion of women or racial minorities would, of course, be prohibited because such groups constitute quasi-suspect or suspect classifications. *See infra* note 65. For an argument that sexual orientation classifications should be considered suspect or quasi-suspect, see pp. 57–60 below.

[46] 632 F.2d 788 (9th Cir. 1980), *cert. denied*, 452 U.S. 905 (1981).

[47] The court, noting the possibility that the Navy's regulations might interfere with constitutionally protected privacy rights, used a vague standard of review somewhere between rational relationship and heightened scrutiny. *See id.* at 808–09.

[48] *Id.* at 812.

[49] 741 F.2d 1388 (D.C. Cir. 1984).

[50] *Id.* at 1398.

[51] *See supra* note 8 and accompanying text.

[52] *See* Berg v. Claytor, 591 F.2d 849 (D.C. Cir. 1978); Matlovich v. Secretary of the Air Force, 591 F.2d 852 (D.C. Cir. 1978); Woodward v. Moore, 25 Fair Empl. Prac. Cas. (BNA) 695 (D.D.C. 1981).

given that the general policy of discharging gay men and lesbians regardless of their individual performance has been upheld.[53]

In the civil service, security clearance, and military cases discussed above, courts have granted broad deference to governmental assertions that an individual's sexual orientation is a relevant basis for hiring and firing decisions.[54] This practice, although consistent with the Supreme Court's treatment of ordinary economic and social policies, ignores the closer scrutiny the Court has required in rational relationship review of classifications that risk embodying prejudice against unpopular groups. In *City of Cleburne v. Cleburne Living Center, Inc.*,[55] for example, the Court struck down under rational relationship review a city's refusal to grant a permit to a home for mentally retarded people.[56] Despite its conclusion that mental retardation is not a quasi-suspect classification,[57] the Court rejected the city's justifications for denying the permit, holding that the desire to avoid negative reactions by neighbors is not an acceptable basis for discriminatory treatment, and that even the legitimate goal of avoiding city congestion cannot be achieved by prohibiting only certain types of group homes while allowing others.[58] The Court's refusal to accept all of the city's goals as legitimate, and its scrutiny of the means by which the city chose to achieve even its legitimate goals, suggest that, even under rational relationship review, distinctions based on gross, atavistic stereotypes about gay men and lesbians should not be accepted.

The difficulty with basing protection for gay men and lesbians on rational relationship review, however, is that the flexibility of the

---

[53] For example, in *Matlovich*, much of the court's analysis indicates that its concern was merely that the Air Force might use its policy of separating gay and lesbian personnel to mask racist or otherwise unlawful discharge policies. *See* 591 F.2d at 856; *see also* Urban Jacksonville, Inc. v. Chalbeck, 765 F.2d 1085, 1086 (11th Cir. 1985) (upholding the discharge of a gay Naval officer despite the fact that all three members of the administrative board that adjudicated his case stated that there were "no conceivable circumstances under which they would retain a [gay or lesbian person] in the Navy").

[54] Although some lower courts have invalidated sexual orientation classifications under rational relationship review, no court of appeals has yet applied their reasoning. *See, e.g.,* benShalom v. Marsh, 703 F. Supp. 1372 (E.D. Wis. 1989); High Tech Gays v. Defense Indus. Sec. Clearance Office, 668 F. Supp. 1361, 1377 (N.D. Cal. 1987); Martinez v. Brown, 449 F. Supp. 207 (N.D. Cal. 1978) (preliminary injunction); Saal v. Middendorf, 427 F. Supp. 192, 201 (N.D. Cal. 1977), *rev'd sub nom.* Beller v. Middendorf, 632 F.2d 788 (9th Cir. 1980), *cert. denied,* 452 U.S. 905 (1981).

[55] 473 U.S. 432 (1985).

[56] *See id.* at 447–50.

[57] *See id.* at 442.

[58] *See id.* at 448–50; *see also* United States Dep't of Agric. v. Moreno, 413 U.S. 528 (1973) (striking down under rational relationship review a provision of the Food Stamp Act that excluded households containing unrelated individuals because of the illegitimacy of Congress' desire to harm hippies).

rationality standard gives courts enormous discretion to uphold sexual orientation discrimination regardless of the soundness of the governmental action in question. Without a clear statement by the Supreme Court that sexual orientation classifications should be given heightened scrutiny, even in cases in which there is absolutely no relationship between sexual orientation and governmental interests, because of incorrect understandings of the nature of homosexuality, gay and lesbian employees will still not be guaranteed protection against governmental discrimination. For example, incorrect assumptions about the ability of gay men and lesbians to be good soldiers,[59] or about the likelihood that gay and lesbian individuals will disclose secrets,[60] may lead judges to uphold as rational discrimination that is based only on their own incorrect stereotypes.

Moreover, unless courts employ the level of scrutiny adopted in cases like *Cleburne*, when the relationship between sexual orientation classifications and the government's asserted interests is plausible, but the interests themselves are illegitimate, rational relationship review is unlikely to provide protection to gay and lesbian employees. For example, because courts employing rationality analysis rarely scrutinize whether the goal of avoiding homophobic reactions is legitimate, discrimination that is based on the likelihood that gay and lesbian individuals might inspire "tensions and hostilities,"[61] or make other employees or the public uncomfortable,[62] is likely to be upheld.[63]

(b) Heightened Equal Protection Scrutiny. — Although courts employing equal protection analysis will uphold most legislative classifications as long as they have some conceivable relationship to a legitimate governmental interest,[64] certain classifications are deemed to be "suspect" or "quasi-suspect," and governmental actions based on such classifications will be subjected to heightened scrutiny.[65] Judicial

---

[59] *See supra* pp. 51–52.

[60] *See supra* note 33 and accompanying text.

[61] *See* Beller v. Middendorf, 632 F.2d 788, 811 n.22 (9th Cir. 1980), *cert. denied*, 452 U.S. 905 (1981).

[62] *See* Singer v. United States Civil Serv. Comm., 530 F.2d 247, 251, 255 (9th Cir. 1976), *vacated*, 429 U.S. 1034 (1977); Norton v. Macy, 417 F.2d 1161, 1167 (D.C. Cir. 1969).

[63] *Cf.* Strauss, *The Myth of Colorblindness*, 1986 SUP. CT. REV. 99, 115 (noting the rationality of the fear that hostilities might arise when members of different races are forced to interact).

[64] *See* McLaughlin v. Florida, 379 U.S. 184, 191 (1964).

[65] The Supreme Court has found that classifications based on race, *see McLaughlin*, 379 U.S. at 192, national origin, *see* Korematsu v. United States, 323 U.S. 214, 216 (1944), and, in some cases, alienage, *compare* Graham v. Richardson, 403 U.S. 365, 372 (1971) (holding that alienage is a suspect classification) *with* Ambach v. Norwick, 441 U.S. 68, 75 (1979) (granting wide latitude to the states to exclude aliens from some functions of government), constitute suspect classifications. In addition, classifications based on gender, *see* Craig v. Boren, 429 U.S. 190 (1976), and illegitimacy, *see* Trimble v. Gordon, 430 U.S. 762 (1977), are considered "quasi-suspect" and trigger a form of "intermediate scrutiny" that is more rigorous than basic rational relationship review. In addition to subjecting suspect or quasi-suspect classifications to strict scrutiny, courts will apply strict scrutiny to classifications that burden fundamental interests. *See supra* note 21.

review of governmental actions that burden members of a suspect or quasi-suspect class requires a standard higher than rational relationship review in two respects. First, these classifications must be supported by more than merely a "legitimate" interest: governmental actions that burden a quasi-suspect classification must be based on an "important" interest,[66] while actions that burden a suspect classification must serve a "compelling" governmental goal.[67] Second, the connection between the discriminatory action and the governmental goal must be more than merely "rational": for quasi-suspect classifications the relationship must be "substantial,"[68] and for suspect classifications the discriminatory action must be "precisely tailored" to the governmental interest at issue.[69]

The Supreme Court has focused on several factors in determining whether a classification is suspect: whether the group has suffered a history of discrimination,[70] whether it has been excluded from the political process,[71] whether the classification is based on incorrect stereotypes,[72] and whether the classification rests on an "immutable" characteristic.[73] Courts have usually declined to find that classifications based on sexual orientation deserve any form of heightened scrutiny.[74] In reaching this conclusion, some courts have simply relied on the absence of Supreme Court precedent holding that homosexuality is a suspect classification.[75] Other courts, erroneously equating homosexual orientation with participation in acts outlawed by state sodomy statutes,[76] have held that if states may constitutionally criminalize sodomy, classifications based on whether or not a person engages in sodomy cannot be invalid.[77]

---

[66] *See* Craig v. Boren, 429 U.S. 190, 197 (1976).

[67] *See* Palmore v. Sidoti, 466 U.S. 429, 432 (1984).

[68] *See Craig*, 429 U.S. at 197.

[69] *See* Plyler v. Doe, 457 U.S. 202, 217 (1981).

[70] *See* Massachusetts Bd. of Retirement v. Murgia, 427 U.S. 307, 313 (1976) (declining to hold that classifications based on age are suspect).

[71] *See Plyler*, 457 U.S. at 217 n.14.

[72] *See* Frontiero v. Richardson, 411 U.S. 677, 685 (1973) (opinion of Brennan, J.).

[73] *See id.* at 686.

[74] *See, e.g.*, Woodward v. United States, No. 86-1283 (Fed. Cir. Mar. 29, 1989) (LEXIS, Genfed library, Courts file); Padula v. Webster, 822 F.2d 97, 103 (D.C. Cir. 1987); Baker v. Wade, 769 F.2d 289, 292 (5th Cir. 1985), *cert. denied*, 478 U.S. 1022 (1986); Dronenberg v. Zech, 741 F.2d 1388, 1391 (D.C. Cir. 1984); Childers v. Dallas Police Dept., 513 F. Supp. 134, 147 n.22 (N.D. Tex. 1981). *But see* Watkins v. United States Army, 847 F.2d 1329, 1349 (9th Cir.), *reh'g granted en banc*, 847 F.2d 1362 (9th Cir. 1988); benShalom v. Marsh, 703 F. Supp. 1372 (E.D. Wis. 1989); High Tech Gays v. Defense Indus. Sec. Clearance Office, 668 F. Supp. 1361, 1368 (N.D. Cal. 1987); *infra* p. 56.

[75] *See, e.g.*, *Childers*, 513 F. Supp. at 147 n.22. The Supreme Court has never held, however, that classifications based on sexual orientation are *not* suspect; it has simply never addressed the issue of suspectness in the context of sexual orientation.

[76] *See infra* pp. 58–59.

[77] *See, e.g.*, *Padula*, 822 F.2d at 103; *see also* Woodward v. United States, No. 86-1283 (Fed. Cir. Mar. 29, 1989) (LEXIS, Genfed library, Courts file) (following *Padula*).

Courts that have rejected assertions that sexual orientation classifications should be accorded heightened equal protection scrutiny have taken far too narrow a view of the values that modern equal protection jurisprudence seeks to protect. As Professor Tribe has argued, the requirement of equal protection of the laws implies that the government may not "perennially reenforce the subordinate status of any group."[78] Governmental discrimination on the basis of sexual orientation violates this prohibition, and contravenes the principle that all people have equal worth as human beings.[79]

Recently, some courts have begun to look more closely at the relationship between sexual orientation and the values of equal protection. In two recent cases, courts have employed heightened equal protection scrutiny to strike down classifications based on sexual orientation. In *Watkins v. United States Army*,[80] the Ninth Circuit found that gay and lesbian people constitute a suspect class, and, consequently, that the Army's policy of discharging gay men and lesbians from the service violates the equal protection clause.[81] In *High Tech Gays v. Defense Industrial Security Clearance Office*,[82] the district court found that gay men and lesbians constitute a quasi-suspect class, and on that basis invalidated the government's policy of subjecting gay and lesbian security clearance applicants to extended investigations and mandatory adjudications.[83]

Watkins and *High Tech Gays* focused on the same criteria used by the Supreme Court in finding that classifications based on race and national origin are suspect. The *Watkins* and *High Tech Gays* courts

---

[78] L. TRIBE, AMERICAN CONSTITUTIONAL LAW § 16–21, at 1516 (2d ed. 1988).

[79] As Professor Dworkin has argued:

We may therefore say that justice as fairness rests on the assumption of a natural right of all men and women to equality of concern and respect, a right they possess not by virtue of birth or characteristic or merit or excellence but simply as human beings with the capacity to make plans and give justice.

R. DWORKIN, TAKING RIGHTS SERIOUSLY 182 (1977). *But cf.* Perry, *Modern Equal Protection: A Conceptualization and Appraisal*, 79 COLUM. L. REV. 1023, 1067 (1979) (arguing that, because sexual activity is something in which a person "chooses to engage," classifications based on homosexual activity are morally relevant and therefore acceptable for equal protection purposes). It is not clear whether Perry would extend his argument to classifications based on sexual orientation, a factor which is arguably not a product of individual choice, *see* R. MOHR, GAYS/JUSTICE 37–42 (1988). Nonetheless, his implication that equal protection protects only those attributes over which an individual has no control grossly oversimplifies the basis of modern equal protection jurisprudence. *See* City of Cleburne v. Cleburne Living Center, Inc., 473 U.S. 432, 472 n.24 (1985) (opinion of Marshall, J.) ("No single talisman can define those groups likely to be the target of classifications offensive to the Fourteenth Amendment and therefore warranting heightened or strict scrutiny; experience, not abstract logic, must be the primary guide.").

[80] 847 F.2d 1329 (9th Cir.), *reh'g granted en banc*, 847 F.2d 1362 (9th Cir. 1988).

[81] *See id.* at 1352; *see also* benShalom v. Marsh, 703 F. Supp 1372, 1379–80 (E.D. Wis. 1989) (following *Watkins*).

[82] 668 F. Supp. 1361 (N.D. Cal. 1987).

[83] *See id.* at 1377.

found that gay men and lesbians have suffered a history of purposeful discrimination, that sexual orientation bears no relation to ability to perform or contribute to society, that prejudices and inaccurate stereotypes have led to discrimination against gay men and lesbians, that sexual orientation is sufficiently immutable, and, finally, that gay men and lesbians lack the political power necessary to obtain redress from the political branches.[84]

The findings in *Watkins* and *High Tech Gays* that gay men and lesbians satisfy the criteria for suspect class status are supported by a wide range of evidence.[85] First, gay men and lesbians have suffered from a history of discrimination. They face dismissal from their jobs if their sexual orientation is discovered, they are prohibited from serving in the military, and, in many cases, they are prevented from raising children.[86] Second, classifications that discriminate against gay men and lesbians are based on inaccurate stereotypes that frequently bear no relation to ability to perform or contribute to society. Many stereotypes about homosexuality assume, for example, that gay men and lesbians are likely to molest children,[87] that they cannot be trusted to keep secrets,[88] and that homosexuality is "contagious."[89] These assumptions have repeatedly been proven false.[90] Third, gay men and lesbians cannot rely on the political process to make themselves heard. Because people who openly declare their homosexuality face harassment, loss of employment, and social ostracism, most gay men and lesbians are not likely to risk publicly calling for changes in policies.[91] Moreover, even if the majority of gay and lesbian people suddenly opened up about their sexuality, because of both moral disapproval of homosexuality and the fact that gay men and lesbians constitute a minority of the population, discriminatory practices would probably continue.[92] Finally, scientific research has suggested that

---

[84] *See Watkins*, 847 F.2d at 1345–49; *High Tech Gays*, 668 F. Supp. at 1369–70.

[85] *See generally* Note, *An Argument for the Application of Equal Protection Heightened Scrutiny to Classifications Based on Homosexuality*, 57 S. CAL. L. REV. 797, 816–27 (1984) (basing an argument for the application of heightened equal protection scrutiny to sexual orientation classifications on standard criteria of suspectness).

[86] *See infra* Part VI (discussing gay and lesbian families).

[87] *See* Part VI, note 68 and accompanying text, *infra* p. 128.

[88] *See supra* note 33 and accompanying text.

[89] *See* Part VI, note 66 and accompanying text, *infra* pp. 127–28.

[90] *See, e.g.*, R. GEISER, HIDDEN VICTIMS: THE SEXUAL ABUSE OF CHILDREN 75 (1979) (finding that almost all child molesters are heterosexual men); SECURITY CLEARANCE PROGRAMS, *supra* note 38, at 171–87, 913–26 (reporting that the majority of governmental security breaches are by non-gay people); Green, Mandel, Hotvedt, Gray & Smith, *Lesbian Mothers and Their Children: A Comparison with Solo Parent Heterosexual Mothers and Their Children*, 15 ARCHIVES SEXUAL BEHAV. 167, 181 (1986) (finding no greater likelihood that children raised by lesbian mothers will become homosexual than will children raised by non-lesbian mothers).

[91] *See* Rowland v. Mad River Local School Dist., 470 U.S. 1009, 1014 (1985) (Brennan, J., dissenting from denial of certiorari); J. ELY, DEMOCRACY AND DISTRUST 163 (1980).

[92] *See* Tribe, *The Puzzling Persistence of Process-Based Constitutional Theories*, 89 YALE

sexual orientation is largely immutable:[93] once an individual's sexual orientation is established early in life, it is difficult, if not impossible, for her to alter it.[94]

Bowers v. Hardwick,[95] in which the Supreme Court held that there is no constitutionally protected privacy right to engage in homoosexual sodomy, does not preclude a finding that sexual orientation classifications should be accorded heightened equal protection scrutiny.[96] *Hardwick* dealt only with the constitutional status of laws that criminalize sodomy, and only considered the validity of those laws in the context of a substantive due process challenge.[97] Sexual orientation classifications and sodomy, however, are two entirely separate phenomena: sexual orientation classifications are based on the direction of an individual's sexual and affectional attractions, while sodomy

---

L.J. 1063, 1075 (1980) (arguing that "[c]oming out of the closet could dispel ignorance, but it may not alter belief").

[93] *See* Coleman, *Changing Approaches to the Treatment of Homosexuality*, in HOMOSEXUALITY: SOCIAL, PSYCHOLOGICAL, AND BIOLOGICAL ISSUES 81–88 (W. Paul, J. Weinrich, J. Gonsiorek & M. Hotvedt eds. 1982) (discussing the limited success of therapists' attempts to replace their patients' homosexual activity with heterosexual activity and concluding that the "illness model of homosexuality is slowly being put to rest"). Even a change in the gender of an individual's sexual partners will not usually produce a shift in sexual orientation. In prisons, for example, non-gay male inmates frequently engage in homosexual sex without adopting a same-sex sexual orientation. *See* W. WOODEN & J. PARKER, MEN BEHIND BARS 250 (1982) (reporting that 55.7% of heterosexual inmates had engaged in homosexual acts while in prison).

[94] Even if change is possible for some people, complete immutability is not a prerequisite to a finding that a classification is suspect. *See* Graham v. Richardson, 403 U.S. 365 (1971) (finding alienage — a mutable characteristic — a suspect classification); Tribe, *supra* note 92, at 1074 n.52 (arguing that "even if race or gender became readily mutable by biomedical means . . . laws burdening those who choose to remain black or female would properly remain constitutionally suspect"). Rather than focusing on whether it is *possible* for an individual to alter a particular characteristic, courts should ask whether it would be *offensive* to condition legal protection on the requirement that one change a highly personal, often self-defining, trait. *See* Watkins v. United States Army, 847 F.2d 1329, 1347–48 (9th Cir.), *reh'g granted en banc*, 847 F.2d 1362 (9th Cir. 1988); *see also* Note, *The Constitutional Status of Sexual Orientation: Homosexuality as a Suspect Classification*, 98 HARV. L. REV. 1285, 1304 (1985) (arguing that, rather than basing the application of heightened scrutiny on the immutability of a characteristic, courts should ask whether a characteristic is an aspect of personality fundamental to individual identity). *But cf.* Rubenfeld, *The Right of Privacy*, 102 HARV. L. REV. 737, 779–82 (1989) (arguing that legal theories asserting that sexual orientation is a fundamental aspect of personal identity only exacerbate society's erroneous assumption that gay men and lesbians are fundamentally different from non-gay people).

[95] 478 U.S. 186 (1986).

[96] Nor does it preclude a finding that forms of homosexual intimacy not proscribed by the sodomy statutes should be accorded constitutional protection. *See* High Tech Gays v. Defense Indus. Sec. Clearance Office, 668 F. Supp. 1361, 1370 (N.D. Cal. 1987) (finding that sexual orientation classifications "must withstand strict scrutiny because they impinge upon the right of lesbians and gay men to engage in any homosexual activity, not merely sodomy, and thus impinge upon their exercise of a fundamental right").

[97] For an analysis of sodomy laws in the context of both due process and equal protection, see pp. 11–24 above.

statutes proscribe particular sexual acts in which persons of any sexual orientation may participate.[98] Many people who consider themselves gay or lesbian rarely or never engage in such acts,[99] others remain entirely celibate,[100] and some, in an attempt to conform to socially accepted behavior, may actually enter heterosexual relationships while still identifying themselves as gay.[101] Sodomy — or even homosexual sex, broadly defined — is simply not the defining characteristic of a homosexual sexual orientation.

Discrimination against gay men and lesbians, moreover, often has little to do with a disapproval of homosexual sodomy. For example, the Defense Department regulations concerning homosexuality provide that if a member of the service has engaged in a homosexual act, but it is determined that the act was atypical and that the person is primarily heterosexual in orientation, the person will be retained.[102] If, however, a serviceperson indicates that her sexual orientation is homosexual, she will be dismissed regardless of whether she has engaged in any sexual acts at all.[103] Because discrimination against gay men and lesbians is based on more than just a desire to regulate conduct governed by sodomy statutes, *Bowers v. Hardwick* is simply irrelevant to the constitutional status of classifications that discriminate against gay men and lesbians as a group.

Even in cases in which discrimination against gay men and lesbians is limited to those who do engage in homosexual sodomy, *Hardwick* does not preclude the application of heightened equal protection scrutiny. *Hardwick* dealt only with due process and never reached the question of equal protection. As Professor Sunstein has argued,

---

[98] The majority of sodomy statutes outlaw both homosexual and heterosexual sodomy. *See* Part II, note 5 and accompanying text, *supra* p. 10 (noting that just seven states prohibit sodomy only between persons of the same gender). Heterosexuals, as well as homosexuals, frequently engage in conduct covered by the statutes. *See, e.g.,* S. HITE, THE HITE REPORT ON MALE SEXUALITY 1121 (1981) (reporting that approximately 96% of all respondents had orally stimulated a female partner); C. TAVRIS & S. SADD, THE REDBOOK REPORT ON FEMALE SEXUALITY 163 (1977) (finding that 85% of women surveyed perform fellatio with their husbands "often" or "occasionally," and 20.3% had engaged in anal intercourse with their husbands more than once).

[99] *See, e.g.,* P. BLUMSTEIN & P. SCHWARTZ, AMERICAN COUPLES 236 (1983) (finding that 23% of lesbians rarely or never engage in oral sex); Martin, *The Impact of AIDS on Gay Male Sexual Behavior Patterns in New York City,* 77 AM. J. PUB. HEALTH 578, 580–81 (1987) (reporting that, in an attempt to reduce their exposure to AIDS, gay men engage in sodomy less frequently than in the past).

[100] *See, e.g.,* Sister Marla, *Gay and Celibate at Sixty-Five,* in LESBIAN NUNS 133 (R. Curb & N. Manahan eds. 1985) ("I know that I'm gay. I love women. I adore women — in and out of the convent. At the same time, I am celibate.").

[101] *See, e.g.,* Wolfe, *Epilogue: Coming Around,* in THE COMING OUT STORIES 243 (S. Wolfe & J. Stanley eds. 1980) (recounting both homosexual and heterosexual experiences of a woman who "was perfectly sure that [she] was a Lesbian at the age of sixteen").

[102] *See* 32 C.F.R. pt. 41, app. A, pt. 1.H.1.c(1) (1987).

[103] *See id.* pt. 1.H.1.c(2).

"it is always immaterial to an equal protection challenge that members of the victimized group are engaging in conduct that could be prohibited on a general basis."[104] Equal protection, Sunstein contends, is intended to provide judicial protection to disadvantaged groups, regardless of whether traditional attitudes condone or condemn the particular conduct in which members of such groups engage.[105] In contrast, the *Hardwick* Court's due process analysis is designed to protect only rights "deeply rooted in this Nation's history and tradition."[106] That the *Hardwick* court found no barrier in substantive due process to laws that criminalize acts in which gay men and lesbians may engage, therefore, says more about the tradition-based nature of due process than about the merits of an equal protection challenge to sexual orientation classifications. Because sexual orientation classifications meet the traditional criteria for heightened equal protection scrutiny, and because discrimination based on sexual orientation implicates precisely the kinds of concerns that the equal protection clause addresses, courts should apply heightened scrutiny to such classifications.

In addition to applying heightened scrutiny to discrimination against gay men and lesbians because sexual orientation is a suspect or quasi-suspect classification, courts should apply heightened scrutiny to anti-gay discrimination because such discrimination is based on a desire to perpetuate traditional sex role stereotypes, and, as such, constitutes a form of gender discrimination. This argument is examined in Part II, above.[107]

Whatever the basis of the application of heightened scrutiny to sexual orientation classifications, once heightened scrutiny is applied, the government's asserted interests in discriminating against gay and lesbian public employees will fail.[108] Under heightened scrutiny, merely "conceivable" possibilities that gay or lesbian employees will succumb to blackmail threats, or will cause discipline problems in the military, will be an insufficient basis for discriminatory action by the government.[109] Because many individuals other than gay men and lesbians may cause the security and discipline problems that the government fears, discrimination based solely on sexual orientation is

---

[104] Sunstein, *Sexual Orientation and the Constitution: A Note on the Relationship Between Due Process and Equal Protection*, 55 U. CHI. L. REV. 1161, 1167 (1988).

[105] *See id.* at 1168.

[106] Moore v. City of E. Cleveland, 431 U.S. 494, 503 (1977) (opinion of Powell, J.).

[107] *See supra* pp. 16–18.

[108] *See supra* pp. 54–55 (discussing the magnitude of the government's interests required under heightened equal protection scrutiny).

[109] The military's integration of soldiers of different races and of both sexes, and other countries' integration of openly gay and non-gay soldiers, *see* R. MOHR, *supra* note 79, at 196, suggest that the discipline and morale problems that the military postulates are simply not "compelling" governmental concerns.

neither "substantially related" nor "precisely tailored" to the governmental interest at issue. More importantly, under heightened scrutiny, the argument at the heart of governmental discrimination against gay men and lesbians — that the presence of gay or lesbian workers will inspire "tensions and hostilities" or other negative attitudes on the part of coworkers or the public — will fail, because the prevention of negative attitudes by prejudiced people is simply not a compelling governmental interest.[110]

(c) First Amendment. — The government's discharge of a gay or lesbian individual may also implicate that person's first amendment right to freedom of speech. If the speech that gave rise to the government's discriminatory treatment dealt with a matter of "public concern," courts must balance the government's interests in discharging the plaintiff against the burden on the plaintiff's right to free speech.[111] Although most free speech issues regarding gay and lesbian public employees arise in teacher dismissal cases,[112] several courts have also applied free speech analysis to cases outside of the schools.

The definition of "public concern" is particularly important in the military: if a person's declaration of homosexual orientation or desire constitutes speech on a matter of public concern, military regulations that provide for discharge of servicepersons who declare that they are gay or lesbian, but who have not engaged in homosexual acts, can survive only if the interests served by the regulations outweigh the servicemember's first amendment right to speak on matters of public concern.[113] Courts that have addressed this issue remain

---

[110] *See* City of Cleburne v. Cleburne Living Center, Inc., 473 U.S. 432, 448 (1985); *see also* Brown v. Board of Educ., 347 U.S. 483 (1954) (integrating public schools despite the likelihood that racial tensions would result); *cf.* Palmore v. Sidoti, 466 U.S. 429, 433 (1984) (reversing denial of custody to a white mother due to her second marriage to a black man, based on a finding that it was unconstitutional to take into account the "pressures and stresses" the child might suffer as a result of racial prejudice).

[111] *See* Pickering v. Board of Educ., 391 U.S. 563, 568 (1968); *see also* Connick v. Myers, 461 U.S. 138, 149–50 (1983) (following *Pickering*).

[112] *See infra* pp. 86–89.

[113] This first amendment argument is premised on the view that the military's ban on statements of homosexual orientation, *see* 32 C.F.R. pt. 41, app. A, pt. 1.H.1.c(2) (1987), regulates just that — *statements* of homosexual orientation — and should not be read as a general prohibition on gay or lesbian servicepersons who neither state that they are homosexual, engage in homosexual acts, *see id.* pt. 1.H.1.c(1), nor attempt to marry a member of their own sex, *see id.* pt. 1.H.1.c(3). Such a reading is more generous to the military than one that contends that the regulations as a whole reflect a desire to exclude from the military all gay and lesbian persons regardless of their conduct and regardless of whether they have made any effort to inform others about their sexual orientation. Moreover, a literal reading of the regulations makes sense from the military's standpoint: it seems reasonable to assume that, in banning acts, statements, and attempted marriages, the military chose to target only those gay and lesbian servicepersons whose sexual orientation would actually become known to other members of the service.

split.[114]   In *benShalom v. Secretary of the Army*,[115] the district court
overturned the Army's dismissal of a servicemember for declaring her
homosexual orientation. The court found that the Army's ban on
expressions of homosexuality violated the plaintiff's first amendment
right to meet with gay men and lesbians, to advocate change, and to
receive information and ideas about homosexuality.[116] Other courts,
however, have upheld discharges based on statements of homosexual
orientation on the grounds that an individual's disclosure of homosexuality is a matter only of private concern,[117] and that an acknowl-
edgement of homosexuality is nothing more than an admission that
one "comes within a classification of people whose presence in the
Army is deemed by the Army to be incompatible with its . . .
goals."[118]

In determining whether declarations of homosexual orientation
constitute speech on a matter of public concern, courts must recognize
the political nature of stating that one is gay or lesbian. First, when
an individual states that she is gay, she indicates her identification
with a group of people that suffers from societal discrimination. By
making such a statement, she implicitly asks that whatever respect
the listener accords to her as an individual be extended to the disfavored group with which she is identifying. A declaration of homosexuality is, therefore, a plea that oppression of gay men and lesbians
cease.[119]

---

[114] *Compare* benShalom v. Marsh, 703 F. Supp. 1372 (E.D. Wis. 1989) [hereinafter *ben-Shalom II*] (finding for a lesbian plaintiff) *and* benShalom v. Secretary of the Army, 489 F. Supp. 964 (E.D. Wis. 1980) [hereinafter *benShalom I*] (same) *with* Johnson v. Orr, 617 F. Supp. 170 (E.D. Cal. 1985) (finding for the military), *aff'd mem.*, 787 F.2d 597 (1986) *and* Pruitt v. Weinberger, 659 F. Supp. 625 (C.D. Cal. 1987) (same).

[115] 489 F. Supp. 964 (E.D. Wis. 1980); *see also benShalom II* (following *benShalom I*).

[116] *See benShalom I*, 489 F. Supp. at 974; *see also benShalom II*, 703 F. Supp. at 1377 (following the first amendment holding in *benShalom I* despite the fact that the regulation at issue in that case, allowing for the discharge of any soldier whose statements evidenced "ho-mosexual tendencies, desire, or interest," had since been narrowed to exclude only those whose statements evidenced homosexual "desire").

[117] *See Johnson*, 617 F. Supp. at 176–77.

[118] *See Pruitt*, 659 F. Supp. at 627. The *Pruitt* court's reasoning rests on the questionable assumption that there is a category of people — beyond individuals who *state* that they are gay or lesbian — that the military regulations seek to exclude. *See supra* note 113.

[119] *See* Gay Law Students v. Pacific Tel. & Tel., 24 Cal. 3d 458, 488, 595 P.2d 592, 610, 156 Cal. Rptr. 14, 32–33 (1979) (finding that "one important aspect of the struggle for equal rights is to induce homosexual individuals to 'come out of the closet,' acknowledge their sexual preferences, and to associate with others in working for equal rights"); *see also infra* pp. 1586–87 (discussing the first amendment protection accorded declarations of homosexual orientation). Indeed, a declaration of homosexuality may be the most effective civil rights statement possible. *See* Herek, *The Social Psychology of Homophobia: Toward a Practical Theory*, 14 N.Y.U. Rev. L. & Soc. Change 923, 933 (1986) (arguing that the most effective way to overcome homophobia is for gay and lesbian people to be open about their sexual orientation).

Second, as discussed above,[120] gay men and lesbians challenge conventional norms about the proper behavior of the sexes. Gay and lesbian people challenge the notion that intimate relationships must incorporate traditional male/female dichotomies; lesbians, in addition, challenge the belief that a woman's life is incomplete without a man.[121] In the context of the military, the mere presence of openly gay men and lesbians calls into question the military's ideology of male dominance and female submissiveness.[122] Regulations that penalize individuals who state that they are gay or lesbian, therefore, burden the right to express dissenting views on sexuality and sex roles, and, as such, contravene the first amendment's goal of preserving a multiplicity of world views and attitudes.[123]

Once a plaintiff has established that the speech which gave rise to her dismissal was protected under the first amendment, the government "bears the burden of justifying the discharge on legitimate grounds."[124] The few courts that have examined the sufficiency of the government's interests in regulating off-duty speech involving gay and lesbian rights often ignore the question whether the speech at issue is actually disruptive, and instead base their decisions on whether they believe that sexual orientation, divorced from the potential effect of particular statements, is a relevant criterion in governmental employment decisions. In the civil service, for example, in which homosexual orientation per se is not a valid basis for discharge,[125] courts have found that the government has no compelling interest in regulating employees' off-duty advocacy of gay rights.[126] In the police force, however, where the mere presence of gay men and lesbians is presumed to affect discipline and provoke disharmony, courts have found that gay employees have no right to "publicly advocate[] homosexuality," even in their off-duty activities.[127]

---

[120] *See supra* pp. 17–18.

[121] *See* Law, *Homosexuality and the Social Meaning of Gender*, 1988 WIS. L. REV. 187, 218 (postulating that opposition to homosexuality derives from gay and lesbian peoples' challenge to traditional male/female roles).

[122] *See* FIGHTING BACK, *supra* note 2, at 108–09 (commenting on the importance of "sexist ideology" in military training).

[123] *Cf.* Police Dep't v. Mosley, 408 U.S. 92, 95 (1972) ("But, above all else, the First Amendment means that government has no power to restrict expression because of its message, its ideas, its subject matter, or its content.").

[124] Rankin v. McPherson, 107 S. Ct. 2891, 2898 (1987).

[125] *See supra* note 29.

[126] *See* Van Ooteghem v. Gray, 628 F.2d 488, 492 (5th Cir. 1980) (refusing to find a compelling interest in preventing a county civil servant from changing his working hours to address a public body on gay rights issues), *aff'd en banc on other grounds*, 654 F.2d 304 (1981), *cert. denied*, 455 U.S. 909 (1982).

[127] *See* Childers v. Dallas Police Dept., 513 F. Supp. 134, 140–42 (N.D. Tex. 1981). *But cf. benShalom II*, 703 F. Supp. 1372, 1377 (E.D. Wis. 1989) (finding no compelling interest behind the Army's desire to regulate servicepersons' declarations of homosexual orientation); *benShalom I*, 489 F. Supp. 964 (E.D. Wis. 1980) (same).

2. Procedural Protections. — The right to procedural due process prevents the government from depriving citizens of interests in life, liberty or property without first providing them with notice and an opportunity to be heard.[128] In the context of public employment, procedural due process requires that the government attach procedural safeguards to dismissals of employees who have a "property interest" in their jobs and to dismissals that implicate a protected "liberty interest."[129]

In determining whether a public employee has a "property" interest in her job, courts focus on whether "rules and understandings" officially promulgated and fostered might create a "legitimate claim of entitlement" to continued employment.[130] The only issue that relates solely to gay and lesbian employees is whether military employees, aware of regulations that bar gay men and lesbians from the service,[131] can have a "legitimate claim of entitlement" to employment. Courts that have addressed this question have held that the military does not deprive a serviceperson of a property interest by discharging her for homosexuality, because there is "no reasonable expectation of continued employment once a person is determined to fall within the categories described in the applicable regulations."[132]

When gay men and lesbians are dismissed from government employment, courts must also decide whether such dismissals impose a stigma sufficient to constitute a deprivation of constitutionally protected liberty interests.[133] In the context of military discharges, courts have argued that no liberty interest is implicated when gay servicepersons are discharged honorably,[134] or when the charges against them

---

[128] *See* L. TRIBE, *supra* note 78, § 10-7, at 664 & n.5.

[129] *See* Perry v. Sinderman, 408 U.S. 593, 599 (1972); Board of Regents v. Roth, 408 U.S. 564, 569–70 (1972).

[130] *See Perry,* 408 U.S. at 602. For the application of this standard to gay and lesbian employee cases, see Rich v. Secretary of the Army, 735 F.2d 1220, 1226 (10th Cir. 1984); Ashton v. Civiletti, 613 F.2d 923, 930 (D.C. Cir. 1979); Swift v. United States, 649 F. Supp. 596, 599–600 (D.D.C. 1986); and Neal v. Secretary of the Navy, 472 F. Supp. 763, 784–85 (E.D. Penn. 1979), *rev'd on other grounds,* 639 F.2d 1029 (3d Cir. 1981).

[131] *See supra* pp. 44–45 (discussing the military's regulations).

[132] Beller v. Middendorf, 632 F.2d 788, 805 (9th Cir. 1980), *cert. denied,* 452 U.S. 905 (1981); *see also* Berg v. Claytor, 436 F. Supp. 76, 81 (D.D.C. 1977) ("Having admitted there was cause for dismissal, plaintiff's expectation of continued employment has been extinguished."), *vacated,* 591 F.2d 849 (D.C. Cir. 1978).

[133] In general, liberty interests are implicated by government employment decisions containing charges that "might seriously damage [an individual's] standing and associations in his community" or impose a "stigma or other disability that foreclose[s] his freedom to take advantage of other employment opportunities." Board of Regents v. Roth, 408 U.S. 564, 573 (1972). Damage to reputation alone, however, without harm to other more "tangible" interests such as employment, is insufficient to implicate a liberty interest. *See* Paul v. Davis, 424 U.S. 693, 701 (1976).

[134] *See Berg,* 436 F. Supp. at 80–81 & n.2.

have been kept secret,[135] because such dismissals do not foreclose future employment opportunities.[136] Moreover, in *Rich v. Secretary of the Army*,[137] even when Army records mentioning the plaintiff's homosexuality were disclosed, the court refused to find an infringement of liberty, arguing that, because the plaintiff consented to the dissemination of the circumstances of his discharge, he was required to suffer the consequences.[138] The court did not consider it relevant that the plaintiff was required to reveal the reasons for his discharge in order to be eligible for unemployment compensation.[139]

Procedural protections alone, therefore, have proven insufficient to attack the problem of sexual orientation discrimination in public employment. Because the government remains generally free to hire or fire gay and lesbian employees at will, even the most elaborate set of procedural protections available will be inadequate to protect the rights of gay men and lesbians in public sector employment.

B. Private Employment

1. Employment-at-Will and the Problem of Discrimination. — Nearly one-third of all gay men surveyed report being discriminated against in some form on the job, and seventeen percent report having lost or having been denied employment because they were gay.[140] Similarly, nearly one-quarter of lesbians surveyed report that they have been discriminated against in the workforce.[141] Despite this widespread discrimination, legal protection for gay men and lesbians in the private sector remains largely nonexistent.

The absence of legal restraints on private discrimination against gay men and lesbians stems from basic differences in the law of public

---

[135] *See* Neal v. Secretary of the Navy, 472 F. Supp. 763, 785–86 (E.D. Penn. 1979), *rev'd on other grounds*, 639 F.2d 1029 (3d Cir. 1981).

[136] *See id.* In one nonmilitary case, the court asserted that even if the plaintiff could establish that future employment opportunities would be foreclosed, he could not prevail unless he could establish the "loss of present or future *government* employment" or the deprivation of some legal right. *See* Swift v. United States, 649 F. Supp. 596, 600 (D.D.C. 1986) (emphasis in original).

[137] 735 F.2d 1220 (10th Cir. 1984).

[138] *See id.* at 1227.

[139] *See id.* at 1227 n.6.

[140] *See* Levine, *Employment Discrimination Against Gay Men*, in HOMOSEXUALITY IN INTERNATIONAL PERSPECTIVE 27 (J. Harry & M. Das eds. 1980).

[141] *See* Levine & Leonard, *Discrimination Against Lesbians in the Work Force*, 9 SIGNS 700, 706 (1984) (reporting both "formal" discrimination, including firing or refusing to hire, limiting promotions, salary increases, or increases in job responsibilities, and "informal" discrimination, including harassment and other unofficial actions taken by supervisors or co-workers). For additional statistics concerning the prevalence of anti-gay discrimination in private employment, see *Report of the American Sociological Association's Task Group on Homosexuality*, 17 AM. SOCIOLOGIST 164, 164 (1982), which reports that 63% of the heads and chairpersons of sociology departments stated that hiring a "known homosexual" would produce "serious problems" or that "it just could not be done."

and private employment. In public employment, the constitutional requirements of due process, equal protection, and the first amendment limit the government's ability to hire and fire at will.[142] Although constitutional safeguards have proven inadequate to protect fully the rights of gay men and lesbians, these protections indicate that, at least in theory, basic principles of fairness and equal treatment control the exercise of governmental discretion.

The starting point in discussions of private employment law is precisely the reverse. Under the American common-law doctrine of "employment-at-will," employers traditionally have had unfettered discretion to fire their workers, regardless of the moral worthiness of their decisions, and regardless of the fact that similar decisions, if made by the government, might be unconstitutional.[143] Under the common-law framework, fairness and equal treatment by private employers are, at best, secondary concerns.

Although employment-at-will continues to provide the basis for the current law of private employment, the doctrine has been modified considerably over the past several decades.[144] Federal, state, and local anti-discrimination statutes limit the ability of employers to consider race, sex, national origin, handicap, and other factors in hiring or firing decisions.[145] Collective bargaining agreements and labor legislation further restrict the employer's exercise of discretion.[146] Finally, common-law tort and contract doctrines sometimes have been used successfully to challenge the employer's ability to fire employees at will.[147] None of these developments, however, has seriously limited the employer's ability to discriminate against gay men and lesbians in the private sector.

This section primarily explores the common-law theories and federal statutes that are most applicable to the question of sexual orien-

---

[142] See supra pp. 47–65.

[143] See M. PLAYER, EMPLOYMENT DISCRIMINATION LAW 1–3 (1988).

[144] Some commentators have argued that, because of the modifications of the employment-at-will regime, the at-will doctrine no longer accurately reflects the expectations of most employees. For these and other reasons, they have suggested that the doctrine be discarded. See, e.g., Leonard, A New Common Law of Employment Termination, 66 N.C.L. REV. 631, 671–83 (1988). But see Epstein, In Defense of the Contract at Will, 51 U. CHI. L. REV. 947, 962–77 (1984).

[145] The federal statutes most relevant to sexual orientation discrimination are title VII of the 1964 Civil Rights Act, 42 U.S.C. §§ 2000e–2000e-17 (1982), see infra pp. 68–71, and the Rehabilitation Act, 29 U.S.C. §§ 701–796i (1982), see infra p. 1581. For a discussion of state and local ordinances, see pp. 72–73 below.

[146] See infra p. 72.

[147] See infra pp. 67–68. The extent to which common-law claims are available to unionized employees remains unclear. In Lingle v. Norge Div. of Magic Chef, Inc., 108 S. Ct. 1877 (1988), the Supreme Court held that § 301 of the Labor Management Relations Act did not preempt an employee's state law tort claim for wrongful discharge, but left open the possibility that state law claims that "require[] the interpretation of a collective-bargaining agreement" might be preempted. See id. at 1885.

tation discrimination, and suggests ways in which existing doctrines could be employed to counter sexual orientation discrimination in private employment. It concludes by addressing state and local ordinances and executive orders that explicitly ban employment discrimination based on sexual orientation.

2. *Common-Law Modifications of Employment-at-Will.* — (a) *Public Policy Exceptions.* — Although private employers generally may discharge employees without cause, several courts have limited employers' discretion by refusing to uphold dismissals that violate a clearly stated public policy.[148] Public policy arguments are most successful when the plaintiff can point to a specific statutory articulation of the policy alleged to have been violated.[149] Some courts, however, have invalidated employment dismissals on public policy grounds despite the absence of a statutory expression of the policy. In one such case, *Payne v. Rozendaal*,[150] the court held that public policy prevents all employment decisions that are "cruel or shocking to the average man's conception of justice."[151]

No court has held that dismissals based on an employee's sexual orientation violate public policy. In the absence of statutory prohibitions against sexual orientation discrimination, gay or lesbian plaintiffs are unlikely to prevail on public policy grounds unless they can convince courts to interpret public policy goals broadly. Faced with evidence of widespread anti-gay sentiments, courts that see the relevant issue as merely whether dismissals of gay or lesbian employees offend the "average man's conception of justice" might be forced to answer in the negative.[152] If, however, courts view dismissals of gay

---

[148] *See, e.g.*, Thompson v. St. Regis Paper Co., 102 Wash. 2d 219, 685 P.2d 1081 (1984); Petermann v. International Bhd. of Teamsters, Local 396, 174 Cal. App. 2d 184, 344 P.2d 25 (Dist. Ct. App. 1959).

[149] The most successful cases are those in which the plaintiff was fired for exercising a personal statutory right or for refusing to commit a crime. *See, e.g.*, *Thompson*, 102 Wash. 2d at 234, 685 P.2d at 1090 (recognizing a possible public policy exception to the discharge of an employee-at-will when the dismissal was in retaliation for the employee's implementing an accounting practice required by the Foreign Corrupt Practices Act); *Petermann*, 174 Cal. App. 2d at 189, 344 P.2d at 27 (finding that the dismissal of an employee who refused to commit perjury violated public policy).

[150] 147 Vt. 488, 520 A.2d 586 (1986) (holding that the discharge of an employee based solely on age violated public policy despite the absence of statutory protection against age discrimination).

[151] *Id.* at 493, 520 A.2d at 588–89 (quoting Pittsburgh, C.C. & St. L. Ry. v. Kinney, 95 Ohio St. 64, 68, 115 N.E. 505, 507 (1916)). In a similar manner, some courts have inferred an obligation of good faith and fair dealing in all employment contracts. *See, e.g.*, Fortune v. National Cash Register Co., 373 Mass. 96, 104, 364 N.E.2d 1251, 1257 (1977); Monge v. Beebe Rubber Co., 114 N.H. 130, 133, 316 A.2d 549, 551 (1974).

[152] *Cf.* Bowers v. Hardwick, 478 U.S. 186, 196–97 (1986) (Burger, C.J., concurring) (basing the decision to uphold Georgia's sodomy statute on the historical moral and legal proscription of homosexuality).

and lesbian employees as punishment for an individual's private choices concerning her personal life, they might find such actions offensive to public policy goals favoring privacy.[153]

(b) Implied Contractual Limitations. — Absent explicit agreement to the contrary, courts will presume that an employment contract is intended to be at-will. Some courts, however, have held that employers who state, either orally or, more commonly, in an official handbook or manual, that they have a "for cause" or an anti-discrimination policy create limitations to the at-will regime, and thereby limit their discretion to fire employees.[154]

Statements by employers condemning sexual orientation discrimination are not uncommon, although it is unclear how many of these statements are included in official handbooks or manuals. In a survey conducted in the early 1980's, each of the top ten "Fortune 500" companies reported that sexual orientation was not a factor in hiring or firing decisions, and roughly half of the top 100 Fortune 500 companies responded similarly.[155] In the only reported case dealing with gay or lesbian employees, however, the Fifth Circuit held that statements in an employee handbook that the company would not discriminate on the basis of sexual orientation did not alter the status of the employee as an employee-at-will.[156]

3. Federal Statutory Protection. — *(a) Title VII.* — Title VII of the 1964 Civil Rights Act prohibits employment discrimination by private employers and federal and state governments on the basis of race, color, religion, sex, and national origin.[157] Efforts to amend title VII to include sexual orientation as a protected characteristic

---

[153] *Cf.* Cordle v. General Hugh Mercer Corp., 325 S.E.2d 111, 117 (W. Va. 1984) (holding that, despite the absence of a statutory right not to submit to a polygraph examination, public policy favoring the individual right to privacy prevents the discharge of an employee for refusing to take a lie detector test). Several states have constitutional provisions guaranteeing a right to privacy, *see* Part II, note 108, *supra* p. 24, which constitute clear statements that privacy is an important state interest.

[154] *See, e.g.*, Toussaint v. Blue Cross & Blue Shield, 408 Mich. 579, 614–15, 292 N.W.2d 880, 892 (1980) (oral statement); Pine River State Bank v. Mettille, 333 N.W.2d 622, 625–27 (Minn. 1983) (handbook statement); Weiner v. McGraw-Hill, Inc., 57 N.Y.2d 458, 465, 443 N.E.2d 441, 445, 457 N.Y.S.2d 193, 197 (1982) (handbook statement).

[155] *See* Rivera, *supra* note 29, at 479 n.125 (citing National Gay Task Force Corporate Survey).

[156] *See* Joachim v. AT&T Information Sys., 793 F.2d 113 (5th Cir. 1986). The court based its decision on Texas precedent that required an "express reciprocal agreement" for a modification of the employment-at-will doctrine. *See id.* at 114. One year later, however, the Fifth Circuit found that statements in employee manuals can constitute express written contracts under Texas law. *See* Aiello v. United Air Lines, Inc., 818 F.2d 1196, 1198–99 (5th Cir. 1987). It is not clear, then, whether the Fifth Circuit would now uphold a claim similar to that made by the plaintiff in *Joachim*.

[157] *See* 42 U.S.C. §§ 2000e–2000e-17 (1982). Title VII does not cover employers with fewer than 15 regular employees. *See id.* § 2000e.

have consistently failed.[158] Gay and lesbian employees have, however, attempted to invoke the protections of title VII on the theory that sexual orientation discrimination is essentially a form of gender discrimination.[159] To date, no plaintiff has recovered under this theory.[160] Indeed, no title VII cases involving lesbian or gay employees have been reported since the early 1980's.

In bringing sex discrimination claims, gay and lesbian plaintiffs have advanced both disparate treatment[161] and disparate impact[162] arguments. The disparate treatment theory contends that sexual orientation discrimination is, in fact, intentional gender discrimination. Employers, plaintiffs argue, will fire men who are intimately involved with other men but will not fire women who are similarly involved with men (the converse being true with respect to relationships with women). This argument was rejected in *DeSantis v. Pacific Telephone & Telegraph Co.*,[163] in which the court observed that "whether dealing

---

[158] *See, e.g., Civil Rights Act Amendments of 1981: Hearings on H.R. 1454 Before the Subcomm. on Employment Opportunities of the House Comm. on Education and Labor*, 97th Cong., 2d Sess. 1–2 (1982); *Civil Rights Amendments Act of 1979: Hearings on H.R. 2074 Before the Subcomm. on Employment Opportunities of the House Comm. on Education and Labor*, 96th Cong., 2d Sess. 6–7 (1980).

[159] *See, e.g.*, DeSantis v. Pacific Tel. & Tel. Co., 608 F.2d 327, 329 (9th Cir. 1979); Smith v. Liberty Mutual Ins. Co., 569 F.2d 325, 326–27 (5th Cir. 1978); *cf.* Ulane v. Eastern Airlines, Inc., 742 F.2d 1081, 1085–86 (7th Cir. 1984) (rejecting a claim that discrimination against transsexuals constitutes sex discrimination), *cert. denied*, 471 U.S. 1017 (1985); Holloway v. Arthur Andersen & Co., 566 F.2d 659, 661–62 (9th Cir. 1977) (same).

[160] The Equal Employment Opportunity Commission ruled early on that title VII does not prohibit sexual orientation discrimination. *See* EEOC Decision 76–75, 19 Fair Empl. Prac. Cas. (BNA) 1823, 1824 (1975).

Although gay and lesbian employees have been unsuccessful in challenging hiring or firing decisions on title VII grounds, at least one court has held that title VII may prohibit same-sex sexual harassment. In Wright v. Methodist Youth Servs., 511 F. Supp. 307 (N.D. Ill. 1981), the court held that a man fired for rejecting homosexual advances made by his male supervisor could bring a title VII action against his employer. The plaintiff, wrote the court, was treated differently because he was a man, as he would not have been harassed had he been female. *See id.* at 310. The *Wright* court's holding suggests that title VII would not cover sexual harassment by bisexual employers, because both male and female employees would be equally susceptible to attacks. This peculiar conclusion is also supported by dicta in Barnes v. Costle, 561 F.2d 983, 990 n.55 (D.C. Cir. 1977); *see also* Vinson v. Taylor, 760 F.2d 1330, 1333 n.7 (D.C. Cir. 1985) (Bork, J., dissenting from denial of rehearing en banc) (criticizing the "bizarre result" that "only the differentiating libido runs afoul of Title VII"), *aff'd sub nom.* Meritor Sav. Bank v. Vinson, 477 U.S. 57 (1986).

[161] Disparate treatment claims are based on allegations that an employer "treats some people less favorably than others because of their race, color, religion, sex, or national origin." International Bhd. of Teamsters v. United States, 431 U.S. 324, 335 n.15 (1977). In a disparate treatment case, proof of discriminatory motive is required for the plaintiff to prevail. *See id.*

[162] Disparate impact claims are based on the theory that a facially neutral selection standard disproportionately affects members of protected groups. Selection criteria that have a disproportionate impact on protected groups will survive only if justified by a "business necessity." *See* Griggs v. Duke Power Co., 401 U.S. 424, 431 (1971).

[163] 608 F.2d 327 (9th Cir. 1979). In addition to rejecting the plaintiffs' title VII claims, the

with men or women the employer is using the same criterion: it will not hire or promote a person who prefers sexual partners of the same sex."[164]

In contrast to disparate treatment claims, which have been brought by both gay men and lesbians, disparate impact arguments are available only to gay men. The disparate impact argument is based on the theory that sexual orientation discrimination disproportionately affects men, because of the supposed greater incidence of homosexuality in the male population and because an employer is allegedly more likely to discover a man's homosexuality than a woman's.[165] In rejecting this argument, the *DeSantis* court claimed that it was an attempt to "bootstrap" title VII protection for gay men "under the guise of protecting men generally."[166]

Rather than focusing on the gender of their intimate partners, or debating whether gay men or lesbians are more oppressed in the workplace, gay and lesbian employees bringing sexual orientation discrimination claims under title VII should emphasize the sexually stereotypical attitudes that lead employers to ban gay and lesbian workers.[167] As discussed above,[168] lesbians and gay men challenge conventional notions about the sexes.[169] Because they reject traditional assumptions about the proper relationship between men and

---

DeSantis court rejected the contention that 42 U.S.C. § 1985(3), which proscribes private conspiracies to deny individuals their civil rights, outlaws employment discrimination against gay men and lesbians. *See id.* at 332–33; *see also* Gay Veterans Ass'n v. American Legion, 621 F. Supp. 1510, 1515–16 (S.D.N.Y. 1985) (following the *DeSantis* court's interpretation of § 1985).

[164] 608 F.2d at 331. *But cf.* Faraca v. Clements, 506 F.2d 956 (5th Cir. 1975) (finding that refusal to hire a white man married to a black woman constituted race disrimination under 42 U.S.C. § 1981 when the employer had previously hired black men married to black women). Under the *DeSantis* court's reasoning, a ban on mixed-race couples would not constitute race discrimination because the ban would apply evenhandedly to both white and nonwhite workers. The Supreme Court has explicitly rejected this conclusion. *See* Loving v. Virginia, 388 U.S. 1, 10 (1967).

[165] *See* Siniscalco, *Homosexual Discrimination in Employment*, 16 SANTA CLARA L. REV. 495, 508–10 (1976).

[166] 608 F.2d at 330.

[167] For arguments that title VII was designed to eliminate sexually stereotypical job criteria, see Phillips v. Martin Marietta Corp., 400 U.S. 542, 545 (1971) (Marshall, J., concurring), which cites the EEOC Guidelines on Discrimination Because of Sex, 29 C.F.R. § 1604.1(a)(1)(ii); and Sprogis v. United Air Lines, Inc., 444 F.2d 1194, 1198 (7th Cir.), *cert. denied*, 404 U.S. 991 (1971).

[168] *See supra* pp. 17–18.

[169] Although many gay men and lesbians do not self-consciously challenge traditional gender roles, sexual orientation discrimination may still stem from the perception of gay and lesbian people as sex role deviants. *See* Taylor, *Conceptions of Masculinity and Femininity as a Basis for Stereotypes of Male and Female Homosexuals*, 9 J. HOMOSEXUALITY 37, 50 (1983) (finding that "those who value traditional sex roles devalue homosexuals because they perceive them to be role deviants, and those who do not value the roles so highly do not care [about homosexuality]").

women, gay men and lesbians cast doubt on the validity of accepted male and female roles.[170] Discrimination against gay men and lesbians, therefore, constitutes gender discrimination because it penalizes individuals who do not conform to stereotypical ideas about the way men and women should behave. Moreover, because gay men are penalized for behavior and attitudes that would be acceptable for female workers, and lesbians are penalized for behavior and attitudes that would be acceptable for male workers,[171] sexual orientation discrimination burdens men and women for different reasons, and is therefore precisely the sort of gender-specific discrimination that title VII was designed to eradicate.

(b) *Other Federal Statutory Protections.* — Section 504 of the Rehabilitation Act prohibits discrimination against persons with handicaps in programs that receive federal financial assistance or in activities conducted by any executive agency or the United States Postal Service.[172] Under the Act, "handicapped" is defined as "any person who (i) has a physical or mental impairment which substantially limits one or more of such person's major life activities, (ii) has a record of such an impairment, or (iii) is regarded as having such an impairment."[173]

Because sexual orientation discrimination often stems from a perception that gay men and lesbians are "sick,"[174] gay and lesbian employees might attempt to challenge discriminatory practices under section (iii) of the Rehabilitation Act's definition of handicap.[175] Moreover, discrimination against gay men that stems from the belief that all gay men have AIDS might also present a cognizable claim under the same provision.[176]

---

[170] *See* Rubenfeld, *supra* note 94, at 800 ("Homosexual couples by necessity throw into question the allocation of specific functions — whether professional, personal, or emotional — between the sexes.").

[171] *Cf.* Hopkins v. Price Waterhouse, 825 F.2d 458, 463 (D.C. Cir. 1987) (finding a title VII violation in the denial of partnership to a female accountant who did not "walk more femininely, talk more femininely, dress more femininely, wear make-up, have her hair styled, and wear jewelry"), *cert. granted*, 108 S. Ct. 1106 (1988).

[172] *See* 29 U.S.C. § 794 (1982). In addition, the federal government and firms contracting with the federal government in excess of $2500 must take "affirmative action" in employing qualified people with handicaps. *See id.* §§ 791, 793.

[173] 29 U.S.C. § 706(8)(B) (Supp. 1987). State laws banning discrimination against people with handicaps often provide greater protection than the federal statutory scheme. *See, e.g.,* State Div. of Human Rights v. Xerox, 65 N.Y.2d 213, 480 N.E.2d 695, 491 N.Y.S.2d 106 (1985) (holding that a state handicap discrimination statute bars discrimination on the basis of obesity).

[174] *See supra* p. 4.

[175] *But see* Blackwell v. United States Dep't of Treasury, 830 F.2d 1183, 1183 (D.C. Cir. 1987) (holding that the Rehabilitation Act's prohibition of discrimination does not encompass discrimination on the basis of sexual orientation). A drawback to the handicap discrimination argument is that it might reinforce society's assumption that homosexuality is abnormal.

[176] Approximately half of all state anti-discrimination agencies believe that laws protecting

Lesbian and gay employees might also seek protection under the National Labor Relations Act (NLRA),[177] which imposes a duty on unions of fair representation of union members.[178] Some unions have actively supported gay or lesbian employees discharged on the basis of sexual orientation.[179] Several unions have, moreover, issued statements in support of gay and lesbian employment and civil rights.[180] In addition, union contracts that require just cause to be shown for dismissal of a union member may provide the basis for successful claims by dismissed gay and lesbian employees.[181]

4. *State and Local Regulations.* — Given the lack of federal statutory protection for gay men and lesbians, and the limited usefulness of common-law theories attacking discrimination in employment decisions, a number of localities, as well as a few states,[182] have adopted executive orders or ordinances explicitly prohibiting sexual orientation discrimination in private and/or public employment.[183] Few cases interpreting the regulations are available, and the extent to which

---

people with handicaps prohibit discrimination against anyone perceived to have AIDS, whether or not he actually has the disease or has tested HIV-positive. Telephone interview with Benjamin Schatz, Director, AIDS Civil Rights Project, National Gay Rights Advocates (Jan. 9, 1989); *cf.* School Bd. v. Arline, 480 U.S. 273, 284 (1987) (finding that the Rehabilitation Act proscribes denial of employment benefits that are based on "the prejudiced attitudes or the ignorance of others").

[177] 29 U.S.C. §§ 151–168 (1982).

[178] *See* Vaca v. Sipes, 386 U.S. 171, 177 (1967).

[179] *See* Hughes Air Corp. v. Association of Flight Attendants, 73 Lab. Arb. (BNA) 148, 157–58 (1979) (Barsamian, Arb.) (invalidating the discharge of an airline employee who engaged in off-duty homosexual activity because "[i]nsufficient record evidence exists that the Company's reputation, product or legitimate interests has or have been harmed in any way by Grievant's off duty conduct").

[180] *See* Rivera, *supra* note 29, at 477–78 (reporting pro-gay and lesbian policies of the AFL-CIO, the International Ladies Garment Workers Union, the American Federation of State, County, and Municipal Employees, the Service Employees International Union, the Communication Workers of America, and the Newspaper Guild).

[181] *See* Note, *Challenging Sexual Preference Discrimination in Private Employment*, 41 OHIO ST. L.J. 501, 520–22 (1980).

[182] Wisconsin is the only state that statutorily proscribes employment discrimination based on sexual orientation. *See* WIS. STAT. ANN. §§ 111.31–.395 (West 1988). Other states have executive orders banning some forms of sexual orientation discrimination. *See, e.g.*, N.Y. COMP. CODES R. & REGS. tit. 4, § 28 (1983) (banning sexual orientation discrimination in state employment). In addition, some state constitutional provisions have been interpreted to provide protection to gay and lesbian employees. *See, e.g.*, Gay Law Students Ass'n v. Pacific Tel. & Tel., 24 Cal. 3d 458, 595 P.2d 592, 156 Cal. Rptr. 14 (1979) (holding that the California Constitution and the California Public Utilities Code bar California public utilities from arbitrary employment discrimination, including dismissals based on sexual orientation absent a showing that the employee's sexual orientation renders her unfit for the job at issue). In *Gay Law Students*, the court noted that the California Constitution does not contain an explicit state action requirement, rendering it applicable to privately owned utilities, which are "more akin to a governmental entity than to a purely private employer." *Id.* at 469, 595 P.2d at 598–99, 156 Cal. Rptr. at 20–21.

[183] For a list of cities and counties that have enacted some type of regulation proscribing sexual orientation discrimination, see Part VII, note 51, below at p. 158.

these regulations have affected discrimination against gay men and lesbians therefore remains unclear. In at least one case, however, the existence of a local anti-discrimination ordinance caused an employer to implement a uniform nondiscrimination policy throughout its offices nationwide, thus extending the ordinance's impact beyond the locality in which it was enacted.[184]

Because they explicitly ban employment discrimination based on sexual orientation, state and local executive orders and ordinances represent the greatest potential source of legal protection for gay men and lesbians. Local regulation of employment discrimination against gay and lesbian people is, however, limited in several important respects. First, executive orders are subject to rescission by referendum or judicial invalidation.[185] Second, local anti-discrimination ordinances may be unenforceable when they conflict with federal interests or constitutional rights.[186] Finally, local regulations necessarily offer only spotty legal protection; in contrast to a uniform federal ban on employment discrimination based on sexual orientation, local regulations can cover only a limited number of employees and reach only selected regions of the country.

C. Conclusion

Employment decisions based on sexual orientation result in second-class status for gay and lesbian people in society,[187] solely because their personal lives or affectional preferences do not conform to those of the majority. In the area of public employment, the constitutional requirements of due process, equal protection, and the first amendment have provided some protection to gay and lesbian employees, but have left unprotected numerous others, particularly those in the military and those in jobs requiring security clearances. In the context of private employment, common-law doctrines and federal statutes

---

[184] See Lambert, MCI, Settling Gay Rights Suit, Issues Bias Ban, N.Y. Times, Dec. 18, 1988, at 61, col. 1 (reporting that MCI Communications Corporation issued a written policy statement proscribing discrimination on the basis of sexual orientation throughout its offices, as part of a settlement of a claim filed by a gay employee who charged that he was fired in violation of the New York City anti-discrimination ordinance).

[185] See sources cited in Part VII, at note 53, below.

[186] See, e.g., Madsen v. Erwin, 395 Mass. 715, 481 N.E.2d 1160 (1985) (dismissing on free exercise grounds a lesbian employee's claims against the Christian Science Monitor for wrongful discharge, breach of contract, deprivation of constitutional rights, and deprivation of civil rights guaranteed by Massachusetts statutes); see also infra pp. 158–60 (discussing free exercise challenges to state and local anti-discrimination ordinances).

[187] See Levine, supra note 140, at 28 (suggesting that fear of discrimination leads some gay men to enter professions that are known to "tolerate homosexuality," despite the fact that they may be over-qualified for such jobs, and that anticipated discrimination causes many gay men to distance themselves in the workplace in an attempt to "pass" as heterosexual, thus hurting their chances for upward mobility).

offer only minimal protection for gay and lesbian people. Although public policy, contractual, and title VII theories offer substantial legal grounds for challenging sexual orientation discrimination, no plaintiff has successfully used these arguments. Similarly, litigation under the Rehabilitation Act and the NLRA does not appear to have made much of an impact. State and local anti-discrimination ordinances and executive orders are a promising source of legal protection, but such regulations are few in number and limited in scope.

Because the existing legal framework does not adequately protect the rights of gay and lesbian employees, Congress should adopt legislation explicitly forbidding public and private employers from basing hiring or firing decisions on an individual's sexual orientation. As with race, gender, or national origin, sexual orientation has no relationship to an individual's ability to perform effectively on the job. The only conceivable bases for sexual orientation discrimination are employers' or co-workers' aversions to working with gay men and lesbians; by using these concerns to justify discriminatory treatment, the law merely reinforces and perpetuates those prejudices that led to the stigmatization of gay and lesbian individuals in the first place. Title VII, the Rehabilitation Act, and other anti-discrimination laws reflect Congress' belief that employers should consider only work-related attributes in choosing their employees. Congress should recognize that sexual orientation discrimination is as offensive to the principles of fairness and equal treatment as discrimination based on any other non-work-related attribute, and amend existing anti-discrimination laws to specify that sexual orientation discrimination will not be tolerated.

IV. Sexual Orientation and the Public Schools

The right of students and faculty members to raise the topic of homosexuality in the public schools has provoked considerable controversy in what has long been a particularly problematic area in first amendment jurisprudence. The Supreme Court has recognized that public schools perform a dual function: they serve both as a forum for free speech by teachers and students,[1] and as a tool for the inculcation of the norms and duties imposed by society.[2] Public schools must thus weigh two values of speech: the inherent value of speech to the speaker and the value of speech as a means of educating

---

[1] Cf. Tinker v. Des Moines Indep. Community School Dist., 393 U.S. 503, 506 (1969) ("It can hardly be argued that either students or teachers shed their constitutional rights to freedom of speech or expression at the schoolhouse gate."). Maintaining the public schools as a forum for student speech in turn teaches students that their opinions have inherent value.

[2] See Ambach v. Norwick, 441 U.S. 68, 75–80 (1979); Brown v. Board of Educ., 347 U.S. 483, 493 (1954).

and preparing young people for life in society. The need to balance these two often conflicting interests creates a unique setting in which greater restrictions on first amendment rights are permissible than in other public institutions.[3]

Legal disputes involving homosexuality in the public schools can be divided into two categories: discrimination claims by gay and lesbian students regarding restrictions on their freedoms of speech and association, and conflicts between school administrators and faculty members regarding the views or sexual orientation of faculty members. Whereas courts have generally supported a student's right to express his or her views regarding sexual orientation,[4] they have largely determined that the unique concerns of the teaching profession give faculty members little discretion to discuss homosexuality or reveal their homosexual orientation.[5]

A. Students' Rights

First amendment issues concerning students' sexual orientation arise in a variety of circumstances,[6] including issues such as the rights of gay and lesbian students to publish statements regarding homosexuality[7] and the right to interact socially with other homosexual students.[8] The courts have generally protected the rights of gay and lesbian students to express political viewpoints regarding sexual orientation and to organize into political groups. However, courts have only rarely extended first amendment protection beyond strictly political speech to non-verbal expression concerning sexual orientation. The courts have thus given insufficient weight to the inherent personal

---

[3] See Hazelwood School Dist. v. Kuhlmeier, 108 S. Ct. 562 (1988) (holding that a high school principal's decision to excise two pages from a student newspaper did not violate students' free speech rights); Bethel School Dist. No. 403 v. Fraser, 478 U.S. 675, 682 (1986) (noting that the rights of public school students "are not automatically coextensive with the rights of adults in other settings").

[4] See cases cited infra note 35.

[5] See infra p. 85.

[6] In order to invoke constitutional protection, a claimant must demonstrate some level of "state" action. See L. TRIBE, AMERICAN CONSTITUTIONAL LAW § 18-1, at 1688 (2d ed. 1988). Alleged discriminatory actions by other students in the course of activities not controlled by the university or school do not constitute state action. See Sinn v. The Daily Nebraskan, 829 F.2d 662 (8th Cir. 1987) (finding no state action in college newspaper's refusal to print advertisements for roommates that mentioned the advertisers' homosexuality because the university authorities exercised only "attenuated" control over the newspaper). But see Gay & Lesbian Students Ass'n v. Gohn, 850 F.2d 361 (8th Cir. 1988) (finding state action in student senate's decision to deny funding for gay and lesbian student association despite the university's lack of direct involvement).

[7] See, e.g., Sinn, 829 F.2d 662; Mississippi Gay Alliance v. Goudelock, 536 F.2d 1073 (5th Cir. 1976), cert. denied, 430 U.S. 982 (1977).

[8] See, e.g., Gay Students Org. v. Bonner, 509 F.2d 652 (1st Cir. 1974); Fricke v. Lynch, 491 F. Supp. 381 (D.R.I. 1980).

value to the speaker of public expression of sexual orientation. In the context of the public schools, first amendment protection of speech is essential not only as a means of fostering self-fulfillment,[9] but also because restricting the freedom of the young teaches them to discount the academic instruction they receive about the freedoms of a democratic society. This section first explores the types of protected speech, and then analyzes the various justifications offered by school officials for restricting that speech.

1. The Scope of Protected Speech. — Although the first amendment by its literal terms protects only "speech,"[10] the Constitution also protects non-verbal forms of communication. For example, the Supreme Court has ruled that wearing an armband to protest the Vietnam war,[11] labor picketing,[12] pamphlet distribution,[13] fundraising,[14] and civil rights demonstrations[15] are actions aimed at expressing some viewpoint or message to an audience, and therefore constitute protected speech for the purposes of the first amendment.[16]

Similarly, protected speech concerning sexual orientation includes more than purely verbal expression. In one of the most expansive decisions regarding this issue, a district court held in *Fricke v. Lynch*[17] that a male student's desire to bring a male date to the high school prom had "significant expressive content" and therefore was protected by the first amendment.[18] Although attendance at a prom does not, in and of itself, constitute speech, the *Fricke* court found that the student's attendance was protected because his expression of his right to participate was "uniquely consonant" with the setting.[19] *Fricke*

---

[9] *See* Cohen v. California, 403 U.S. 15, 24 (1971) (maintaining that protection of freedom of expression is designed to protect the "premise of individual dignity and choice upon which our political system rests"); T. EMERSON, THE SYSTEM OF FREEDOM OF EXPRESSION 6–9 (1970) (noting that freedom of expression is essential not only for maintaining the political process and promoting truth-seeking, but also for "assuring individual self-fulfillment"); Scanlon, *A Theory of Freedom of Expression,* 1 PHIL. & PUB. AFF. 204, 215–18 (1972) (arguing that restrictions on advocacy of conduct contrary to public policy would deprive citizens of their autonomy).

[10] The first amendment states that "Congress shall make no law . . . abridging the freedom of speech." U.S. CONST. amend. I.

[11] *See* Tinker v. Des Moines Indep. Community School Dist., 393 U.S. 503 (1969).

[12] *See* Thornhill v. Alabama, 310 U.S. 88 (1940).

[13] *See* United States v. Grace, 461 U.S. 171 (1983).

[14] *See* Cornelius v. NAACP Legal Defense & Educ. Fund, 473 U.S. 788 (1985).

[15] *See* Shuttlesworth v. City of Birmingham, 394 U.S. 147 (1969).

[16] *See* L. TRIBE, *supra* note 6, § 12-7, at 827–28 (noting that all communication is a combination of expression and action and that the speech/conduct distinction is less determinative of the impermissibility of a regulation than is the motive behind the regulation).

[17] 491 F. Supp. 381 (D.R.I. 1980).

[18] *See id.* at 384. The court described Fricke's attendance as a political statement. *See id.* at 385.

[19] *See id.* at 385 n.4; *see also* A. FRICKE, REFLECTIONS OF A ROCK LOBSTER 69–71 (1981) (noting that the student/author's political message hinged on his being allowed to participate in the prom); *cf.* Clark v. Community for Creative Non-Violence, 468 U.S. 288 (1984) (noting that

thus represents a particularly broad view of the first amendment's protection of political speech, extending it to include social conduct that expresses homosexual orientation.[20]

Although the *Fricke* case upholds and expands the freedom of political expression regarding sexual orientation, it neglects the inherent value of free speech to the individual. It thus leaves unprotected speech by gay or lesbian students who do not wish to make political statements or thrust themselves into political controversy.[21] The first amendment protects not only political messages but also the right to develop one's own opinions regarding sexual orientation.[22] In the context of sexual orientation, social activity can both contribute to political debate[23] and provide independent value and self-fulfillment to the speaker. Such speech is particularly deserving of first amendment protection.

2. The Right of Association. — In a series of cases involving gay student organizations, gay and lesbian students have advanced first amendment arguments in support of their claims for the right to organize into groups, to be officially recognized by the school, to gain access to school facilities, and to secure school funding. Relying primarily on the right of association, courts have generally held in favor of the gay and lesbian student groups.[24] The right of association is

---

camping in public parks to protest treatment of the homeless is expressive, even though camping *in general* is devoid of expressive value); Jarman v. Williams, 753 F.2d 76 (8th Cir. 1985) (holding that parents cannot demand that a school rent out its gym for high school dances because the dancing did not convey a particular message and therefore was not "speech").

[20] *Cf.* Gomez, *The Public Expression of Lesbian/Gay Personhood as Protected Speech*, 1 LAW & INEQUALITY 121 (1983) (arguing that the expression of lesbian/gay "personhood," whether public or private, is entitled to constitutional protection and that societal pressure on gay people to deny or hide their sexual orientation is tantamount to impermissible forced expression under the first amendment).

[21] Regardless of the speaker's intent, a court could deny protection to statements regarding sexual orientation by finding that sexual orientation is an inherently private concern, devoid of any political import. *Cf. infra* p. 87.

[22] *Cf.* L. TRIBE, *supra* note 6, § 12-1, at 788–89 (arguing that no single rationale for the first amendment adequately describes the scope or purpose of freedom of expression, and that various rationales must be considered simultaneously in determining what constitutes protected speech).

[23] A useful analogy might be drawn to the civil rights demonstrations of the 1960's, in which the political movement for equal rights frequently took the form of demands for equal treatment of individual citizens in social settings. *See, e.g.*, Brown v. Louisiana, 383 U.S. 131, 142 (1965) (holding that the first amendment protects "the right in a peaceable and orderly manner to protest by silent and reproachful presence . . . [the] segregation of public facilities").

[24] However, no damages are awarded in these cases. Because the schools are public, and the cases largely decided on the basis of first amendment claims, courts have held that the eleventh amendment prevents assessing damages against school districts or universities. *See, e.g.*, Gay Student Serv. v. Texas A & M Univ., 737 F.2d 1317 (5th Cir. 1984) (holding that university officials acting in their official capacities are immune from damages under the eleventh amendment), *cert. denied*, 471 U.S. 1001 (1985); Student Serv. for Lesbians/Gays & Friends v. Texas Tech Univ., 635 F. Supp. 776 (N.D. Tex. 1986) (same).

implicit in the right to free speech because of its central importance to the ability to develop and express viewpoints; it is therefore protected under the first and fourteenth amendments.[25]

In *Healy v. James*,[26] the Supreme Court for the first time extended the right of association to university student organizations.[27] Having found an associational right for student groups, the Court focused on the practical effects rather than the form of the restrictions in evaluating the school's interference with the exercise of that right.[28] Whether a denial of official recognition infringes upon students' rights of association therefore depends on whether failure to recognize the group makes it ineligible for funding it might otherwise receive, denies it access to school facilities, or inflicts some other similar burden.[29] The school must demonstrate a compelling interest to justify such a restriction.[30]

The First Circuit, in *Gay Students Organization v. Bonner*,[31] employed the *Healy* standard to protect the on-campus activities of a gay student group. Although university officials had only curtailed the Gay Students Organization's (GSO's) "social" activities, the court found that such restrictions were impermissible for two reasons. First, these limits violated the students' freedom of association by hindering the GSO's efforts to express viewpoints and attract members among the student body, thus restricting their political agenda.[32] Second, the court recognized that the restrictions violated the GSO's freedom of speech because in the context of sexual orientation, even a social event could have fundamental expressive value.[33] Like the *Fricke* decision, this case broadened the definition of political "speech" to include social behavior by gay and lesbian students.[34]

---

[25] *See* NAACP v. Button, 371 U.S. 415 (1963); NAACP v. Alabama, 357 U.S. 449 (1958).

[26] 408 U.S. 169 (1972).

[27] *See id.* at 181; *see also* Widmar v. Vincent, 454 U.S. 263 (1981) (holding that a university could not prohibit a student religious group from meeting on campus).

[28] *See Healy*, 408 U.S. at 183. In Gay Students Org. v. Bonner, 509 F.2d 652 (1st Cir. 1974), the First Circuit interpreted *Healy* to focus "not on the technical point of recognition or nonrecognition, but on the practicalities of human interaction." *Id.* at 658.

[29] *See, e.g.*, Gay Alliance of Students v. Matthews, 544 F.2d 162 (4th Cir. 1976); Wood v. Davison, 351 F. Supp. 543, 546–47 (N.D. Ga. 1972).

[30] For examples of arguments given by school authorities to support such restrictions, see pp. 80–81 below. School authorities in private schools need not meet the compelling interest standard. *See infra* section VII.D.

[31] 509 F.2d 652 (1st Cir. 1974).

[32] The court distinguished the GSO from "purely social" groups, saying that as a "cause-oriented group," it stood on a "different footing" from organizations such as fraternities or sororities. *See id.* at 659.

[33] *See id.* at 660–61.

[34] According to the court, the GSO's "message" was "that homosexuals exist, that they feel repressed by existing laws and attitudes, that they wish to emerge from their isolation, and that public understanding of their attitudes and problems is desirable for society." *Id.* at 661.

In addition, *Bonner*, like *Fricke*, fails to acknowledge that non-political, private speech and association must be protected under the first amendment. Protecting gay and lesbian student groups only for their political importance essentially requires these groups to adopt a public political stance or educational goal. The courts should instead recognize that the formation of such groups is also protected by first amendment protection of free speech intended solely to benefit the individual speaker. Subsequent cases involving gay and lesbian student groups have uniformly followed the political focus in *Bonner*.[35] Under current law, whether gay and lesbian organizations receive first amendment protection depends largely on the context of their actions; only those individuals or groups that encounter resistance are protected. Failure to acknowledge the inherent value of such organizations may, in subsequent cases, mandate that a purely social gay organization be denied status and access to facilities on university campuses if a court finds that an insufficient "message" is conveyed, or that the surrounding community would not benefit from the organization's message.

3. *Justifications for First Amendment Infringements.* — (a) *Applicable Standards of Review.* — In the unique context of the public schools, the state's interest in inculcating values in students vests considerable discretion in school administrators. The standard of review used to assess restrictions on student speech varies according to the context in which the speech occurs. School administrators may regulate student speech made within the context of official school curricula because of the nonpublic nature of the academic courses,[36] provided that the regulation does not violate other federal interests[37] and is not solely an attempt to discriminate against particular viewpoints.[38]

---

[35] *See, e.g.*, Gay & Lesbian Students Ass'n v. Gohn, 850 F.2d 361 (8th Cir. 1988); Gay Student Serv. v. Texas A & M Univ., 737 F.2d 1317 (5th Cir. 1984), *cert. denied*, 471 U.S. 1001 (1985); Gay Lib v. University of Mo., 558 F.2d 848 (8th Cir. 1977); Gay Alliance of Students v. Matthews, 544 F.2d 162 (4th Cir. 1976); Student Coalition for Gay Rights v. Austin Peay State Univ., 477 F. Supp. 1267 (M.D. Tenn. 1979).

[36] In Perry Educ. Ass'n v. Perry Local Educators' Ass'n, 460 U.S. 37 (1983), the Supreme Court described three types of forums subject to differing levels of permissible restriction on speech: (1) the "quintessential public forums" such as streets and public parks; (2) a "limited public forum," consisting of public property opened by the State for first amendment purposes; and (3) unopened, nonpublic property. *See id.* at 47. Academic curricula fall into this third category.

[37] *See, e.g.*, Edwards v. Aguillard, 107 S. Ct. 2573, 2577 (1987) (invalidating a Louisiana law mandating equal treatment of creation-science theory and evolutionary theory in the Louisiana public schools as violative of the establishment clause).

[38] *See Perry*, 460 U.S. at 46 (establishing that use of non-public forums may be restricted "as long as the regulation on speech is reasonable and not an effort to suppress expression merely because public officials oppose the speaker's view"); *see also* Board of Educ. v. Pico, 457 U.S. 853, 879 (1982) (Blackmun, J., concurring) (stating that the "State may not act to deny

Furthermore, the Supreme Court's recent decision in *Hazelwood School District v. Kuhlmeier*[39] extended school officials' control by broadening the Court's holding in *Board of Education v. Pico*,[40] which established that restriction of extracurricular speech requires a higher level of scrutiny than does restriction within the confines of an academic curriculum.[41] Holding that restrictions are permissible when schools are required to "sponsor" the speech, the Court in *Hazelwood* allowed school officials to censor a school newspaper written by a high school journalism class. Defining curricular activity in terms of "sponsorship" gives virtually unbridled discretion to school administrators. Students who use classrooms to meet, illustrate their points with school chalk on school blackboards, or post notices on school bulletin boards may be subject to censorship. By expanding the definition of curricula, and by allowing public schools to restrict speech contrary to majority values, *Hazelwood* may severely curtail protected expression regarding sexual orientation in the nation's schools.

Students do, however, have considerably more freedom in extracurricular contexts.[42] When a school allows students to use school facilities or property to express their opinions, it establishes a limited public forum, and can regulate the use of that forum only to the extent that it can establish that some intended student expression will substantially disrupt the educational process.[43] For example, in *Gay Student Services v. Texas A & M University*,[44] the Fifth Circuit held that because Texas A & M had allowed other campus groups and employees to take a negative stance on homosexuality, it had established a limited forum and could not deny a gay organization official recognition.[45] If a public school wishes to deny the use of its facilities, it must be able to articulate rational and objective criteria for the denial independent of the viewpoints expressed.[46]

(b) Justifications Offered by Schools for Restrictions on Speech. — Schools have advanced three major interests in support of restrictions on extracurricular student speech and associations: first, the need to

---

access to an idea simply because state officials disapprove of that idea for partisan or political reasons").

[39] 108 S. Ct. 562 (1988).

[40] 457 U.S. 853 (1982).

[41] *See id.* at 861–63.

[42] *See id.* (distinguishing between regulation of curricula and regulation of library books, which are necessarily extracurricular).

[43] *See* Gay & Lesbian Students Ass'n v. Gohn, 850 F.2d 361, 362 (8th Cir. 1988); Gay Student Serv. v. Texas A & M Univ., 737 F.2d 1317, 1332–33 (5th Cir. 1984).

[44] 737 F.2d 1317 (5th Cir. 1984).

[45] *See id.* at 1332–33.

[46] If the Court were to find sexual orientation a suspect class, any alleged discrimination on the basis of sexual orientation would be subject to strict scrutiny under the equal protection clause. *See supra* p. 1564.

prevent disruption of the learning process; second, the need to avoid potential increases in unlawful behavior (in jurisdictions in which sodomy and other criminal statutes apply to gay men and lesbians); and third, the school's "right" to decline to endorse homosexuality as contrary to public policy. This section explores each of these arguments in turn.

Perhaps the most common argument advanced by schools attempting to regulate gay and lesbian student groups is that the groups' presence and activities disrupt the learning process. Under *Tinker v. Des Moines Independent Community School District*,[47] restriction of student expression is constitutional only when the restriction is "necessary to avoid material and substantial interference with schoolwork or discipline."[48] *Tinker* requires a demonstration that administration fears arise from a reasonable probability of interference rather than a "mere desire to avoid the discomfort and unpleasantness that always accompany an unpopular viewpoint."[49]

Defining disruption is therefore the crucial element in finding a sufficient state interest to justify any restriction of free speech in the public schools. The standards for disruption depend largely on the age of the students involved.[50] At the university level, school authorities have not been successful in arguing that the presence of gay and lesbian student groups will materially and substantially disrupt campus order.[51] In contrast, at the elementary and secondary school levels, disruption is not limited to physical interference with school order. The Supreme Court has recently defined disruption to include interference with the inculcative process. In *Bethel School District No. 403 v. Fraser*,[52] the Court determined that a high school student

---

[47] 393 U.S. 503 (1969).

[48] *Id.* at 511.

[49] *Id.* at 508–09.

[50] The age of students has been given weight in assessing the effect of speech on their learning process. *See, e.g.*, Edwards v. Aguillard, 107 S. Ct. 2573, 2577 n.5 (1987) (noting that "[t]he potential for undue influence is far less significant with regard to college students who voluntarily enroll in courses"); Bethel School Dist. No. 403 v. Fraser, 478 U.S. 675, 683–84 (1986). The Supreme Court has recognized the effect of age on susceptibility to undue influence and has, for example, drawn a distinction between the presence of religious activities in public secondary schools and in universities. *Compare* Grand Rapids School Dist. v. Ball, 473 U.S. 373, 385 (1985) (finding that government support of secular programs in a religious school might well appear to young students to be government endorsement of particular religious beliefs) *with* Widmar v. Vincent, 454 U.S. 263, 274 n.14 (1981) (noting that university students should be able to realize that such government support does not constitute state endorsement of religion).

[51] *See* Gay Lib v. University of Mo., 558 F.2d 848 (8th Cir. 1977) (holding that mere fear of disruption or increased unlawful behavior does not justify denial of gay organization's request for access to university facilities and financial support); Gay Alliance of Students v. Matthews, 544 F.2d 162 (4th Cir. 1976) (holding that mere fear that exposure to gay organization will harm other students is not grounds for restriction of first amendment rights); Gay Activists Alliance v. Board of Regents, 638 P.2d 1116 (Okla. 1981).

[52] 478 U.S. 675 (1986).

could be sanctioned for a sexually suggestive speech, because allowing lewd speech would "undermine the school's basic educational mission"[53] and transgress the "boundaries of socially appropriate behavior."[54] The *Fraser* test dangerously alters the *Tinker* test by allowing censorship of disapproved viewpoints or subject matter.[55] Under *Fraser*, "inappropriateness" replaces disruption as the threshold justification for restriction of student speech, leaving school authorities with broad discretion to bar any references to sexual orientation as inappropriate.[56]

Fraser represents an unfortunate shift away from the educational philosophy that "educating the young for citizenship is reason for scrupulous protection of Constitutional freedoms of the individual, if we are not to strangle the free mind at its source."[57] Public schools must consider how their restrictions on individual thought and expression concerning a subject as fundamental as sexual orientation affect students' perceptions of the meaning of freedom of speech and association.

Second, in jurisdictions with sodomy statutes, school officials have argued that recognition or support of gay and lesbian student organizations will encourage or facilitate violations of those statutes.[58] These arguments assume that the presence of gay and lesbian student groups leads to a greater incidence of sodomy.[59] Courts have been reluctant to accept these arguments.[60] Even in jurisdictions that still

---

[53] *Id.* at 685.

[54] *Id.* at 681.

[55] *See* Hazelwood School Dist. v. Kuhlmeier, 108 S. Ct. 562, 570 n.4 (1988) (noting that *Fraser* did not rest on any disruptive potential of the speech in question). *But see id.* at 575 (Brennan, J., dissenting).

[56] *Cf.* Board of Educ. v. Pico, 457 U.S. 853, 873 (1982) (noting that appropriateness to the educational environment and to the age and grade levels of the students is a permissible consideration in selecting school library books).

[57] West Virginia Bd. of Educ. v. Barnette, 319 U.S. 624, 637 (1943).

[58] *See, e.g.*, Gay Student Serv. v. Texas A & M Univ., 737 F.2d 1317, 1323 (5th Cir. 1984) (including testimony by a witness for school authorities that "'it would be a shock really, if there were not homosexual acts engaged in at or immediately after' a meeting of a homosexual student organization"); Gay Lib v. University of Mo., 558 F.2d 848 (8th Cir. 1977); Student Coalition for Gay Rights v. Austin Peay State Univ., 477 F. Supp. 1267, 1269 (M.D. Tenn. 1979). The state's interest in discouraging criminal behavior may in very limited circumstances be a compelling justification for restricting speech. *See* Brandenburg v. Ohio, 395 U.S. 444, 447 (1969).

[59] It is, however, important in these cases to note that homosexuality is not an "unlawful activity" under the nation's sodomy laws. No state outlaws *being* homosexual; the mere fact that one is homosexual does not justify restricting student speech under the theory that it tends to encourage or lead to violations of the sodomy statutes. *See* Gay & Lesbian Students Ass'n v. Gohn, 850 F.2d 361, 368 (8th Cir. 1988); *Gay Student Serv.*, 737 F.2d at 1328; *Student Coalition for Gay Rights*, 477 F. Supp. at 1269; *supra* pp. 9–10; *cf.* Robinson v. California, 370 U.S. 660 (1962) (holding that the "status" of narcotic addiction cannot be criminally punishable).

[60] *See Student Coalition for Gay Rights*, 477 F. Supp. at 1273–74 (relying on psychiatric

have sodomy statutes,[61] student groups cannot be sanctioned or prevented from merely advocating revision of sodomy laws or other relevant statutes governing homosexuality issues, so long as such advocacy is not "directed to inciting . . . imminent lawless action" as defined under the rule of Brandenburg v. Ohio.[62] Cases involving restrictions on gay and lesbian student groups do not meet this test. First, defining homosexuality as merely the state of wanting to commit an illegal act, or being predisposed to do so, ignores the fact that homosexuality is an affectional preference that connotes far more than sexuality. Second, even sexually active gay men and lesbians do not necessarily violate the sodomy laws.[63] Third, the "imminent lawless action" test has been extremely narrowly defined; the danger must be truly "imminent."[64] Thus, even if speech did lead to violations of the sodomy statutes, this does not constitute a compelling justification for the purposes of the first amendment. Consensual sodomy does not pose the threat of anarchy and violence contemplated in Brandenburg.

Furthermore, the right to lobby for change has been fundamental to social progress; without protection of advocacy of all types, there could be no advancement over the course of time in accordance with society's changing beliefs and mores.[65] Denial of facilities and forums for gay and lesbian students unconstitutionally infringes on students' rights to advocate change of laws with which they disagree.[66]

Third, school officials have attempted to justify restrictions of speech by arguing that endorsing gay and lesbian groups is inimical

---

testimony that the presence on a university campus of an organization advocating homosexuality would not lead to a greater incidence of homosexual conduct); Gay Lib v. University of Mo., 558 F.2d at 854 (dismissing unsupported psychiatric testimony that gatherings of gay students would necessarily lead to an increased incidence of homosexual activities and sodomy). But see Ratchford v. Gay Lib, 434 U.S. 1080 (1978) (Rehnquist, J., dissenting from denial of certiorari).

[61] See Part II, note 2, supra p. 9.

[62] 395 U.S. 444 (1969). See, e.g., Gohn, 850 F.2d at 368 (holding that advocacy of sodomy would be protected by the first amendment even in a state that outlaws sodomy); Student Coalition for Gay Rights v. Austin Peay State Univ., 477 F. Supp. 1267 (M.D. Tenn. 1979) (holding that a state university cannot restrict speech that merely advocates revision of laws outlawing sodomy in Tennessee); Wood v. Davison, 351 F. Supp. 543 (N.D. Ga. 1972).

[63] See Part II, note 11 and accompanying text, supra p. 11.

[64] See Brandenburg, 395 U.S. at 447. This exception to first amendment protection evolved in circumstances involving mob violence, and is inapplicable to the state's interest in preventing violations of sodomy statutes. Cf. Whitney v. California, 274 U.S. 357, 377 (1927) (Brandeis, J., concurring) (noting that "even imminent danger cannot justify resort to prohibition of [first amendment rights], unless the evil apprehended is relatively serious").

[65] Advocacy of change in the law has resulted in numerous landmark cases of social advancement. See, e.g., Roe v. Wade, 410 U.S. 113 (1973) (mandating that women be given the freedom to choose abortion despite abortion's criminal status in most states); Loving v. Virginia, 388 U.S. 1 (1967) (approving interracial marriage at a time when inter-marriage was criminal in Virginia).

[66] See Brandenburg, 395 U.S. at 448 (noting that the abstract advocacy of violence or unlawful behavior is protected speech under the first amendment).

to public policy.[67] This argument is grounded in the theory that students should be protected from material deemed inappropriate for their age or grade level. As was the case in determining the standard for disruption, restriction of the "inappropriate" is constitutional only for primary and secondary school students, and then only as concerns school curricula or the maintenance of order;[68] university students are far less susceptible to undue influence by teachers or from perceived school actions.[69] Public policy arguments therefore do not justify restrictions of speech and association beyond the secondary school level.

Even at the primary and secondary school levels, standards of appropriateness at given ages should be viewpoint neutral. A school district cannot legitimately argue that it is attempting to shield students from shocking subjects if it permits a negative portrayal of the subject and excludes only the opposite viewpoint. Any public policy argument directed at limiting students' exposure to sexual orientation cannot restrict speech based on the viewpoint, as distinguished from the subject matter, of that speech.

4. Conclusion. — Gay and lesbian students have been granted first amendment protections based on courts' interpretations of the political and educational nature of public expression regarding sexual orientation. Courts have not, however, recognized the inherent value of such expression to the speaker. This narrow definition of protected speech fails to protect gay men and lesbians who do not wish to enter the political arena. Only by recognizing the private, individual value of speech and association can the courts remove the burden on gay and lesbian students to assert political, public motives for their actions.

The recent *Fraser* and *Hazelwood* decisions suggest that freedom to address gay and lesbian issues and to express one's homosexual orientation within the secondary schools may be restricted. The Supreme Court's endorsement of an inculcative, locally governed public school system threatens to permit censorship of discussion and expression regarding sexual orientation in primary and secondary schools, and to negate the precedents established to date. Courts should recognize the limits of the *Fraser* and *Hazelwood* standards, and should thus restrict their application to students below university age and to expression that takes place within the confines of the curriculum. Furthermore, determinations of "inappropriateness" must

---

[67] *See, e.g.,* Gay & Lesbian Students Ass'n v. Gohn, 850 F.2d 361, 363 (8th Cir. 1988) (noting the student council's comparison of a gay and lesbian group to a group of arsonists); Student Coalition for Gay Rights v. Austin Peay State Univ., 477 F. Supp. 1267, 1269 (M.D. Tenn. 1979).

[68] *See supra* pp. 81–82.

[69] *See supra* note 50.

be based on the subject matter at issue, rather than the viewpoint expressed.

B. Faculty Members' Rights

Legal disputes regarding sexual orientation also arise in the public schools when faculty members are dismissed or sanctioned because of their sexual orientation or expression of their views regarding homosexuality. Teachers have been dismissed or sanctioned for a range of behavior connected to sexual orientation, including convictions under sodomy or solicitation statutes,[70] public homosexual displays,[71] unauthorized comments made in the classroom regarding homosexuality,[72] and private declarations of homosexual orientation.[73]

Teachers, as public employees, may be dismissed without cause.[74] Furthermore, teachers have a duty to provide role models for their students[75] and to shield their students from "inappropriate" subjects or behavior.[76] Dismissals may not, however, be based on the teacher's exercise of constitutional privileges.[77] More specifically, teachers and

---

[70] See, e.g., Board of Educ. v. Calderon, 35 Cal. App. 3d 490, 110 Cal. Rptr. 916 (affirming the dismissal of a teacher who had been acquitted of a criminal charge of oral copulation, but who in a subsequent civil proceeding was found to have engaged in the act), cert. denied, 419 U.S. 807 (1973); Moser v. State Bd. of Educ., 22 Cal. App. 3d 988, 101 Cal. Rptr. 86 (1972) (upholding a teacher's dismissal and revocation of his teaching certificate based on a criminal conviction for public masturbation and touching another man's genitals); Sarac v. State Bd. of Educ., 249 Cal. App. 2d 58, 57 Cal. Rptr. 69 (1967) (affirming the dismissal of a teacher convicted of disorderly conduct for fondling another man at a public beach), overruled by Morrison v. State Bd. of Educ., 1 Cal. 3d 214, 461 P.2d 375, 82 Cal. Rptr. 175 (1969).

[71] See, e.g., Ross v. Springfield School Dist. No. 19, 56 Or. App. 197, 641 P.2d 600 (1982) (upholding a dismissal based on the "resultant notoriety" of an elementary school librarian's homosexual activity in an adult bookstore); Singer v. United States Civil Serv. Comm'n, 530 F.2d 247 (9th Cir. 1976) (holding that a civil servant may be fired for "flaunting" his homosexuality), vacated, 429 U.S. 1034 (1977).

[72] See, e.g., United States v. Coffeeville Consol. School Dist., 513 F.2d 244 (5th Cir. 1975) (examining a teacher's dismissal for an unauthorized discussion about homosexuality and holding that the discussion was not a just cause for dismissal).

[73] See, e.g., Rowland v. Mad River Local School Dist., 730 F.2d 444 (6th Cir.) (upholding the firing of a public high school guidance counselor solely based on her expression of her sexual preference), cert. denied, 470 U.S. 1009 (1984).

[74] See, e.g., Board of Regents v. Roth, 408 U.S. 564 (1972) (holding that public employees may be discharged without cause and without a prior hearing). For a more detailed discussion of discriminatory terminations in public employment, see section III.A above.

[75] See Edwards v. Aguillard, 107 S. Ct. 2573, 2577 (1987).

[76] See, e.g., Bethel School Dist. No. 403 v. Fraser, 478 U.S. 675 (1986).

[77] See Pickering v. Board of Educ., 391 U.S. 563 (1968) (forbidding the discharge of public employees for exercising first amendment rights of free speech absent overriding concerns with discipline or harmony in the workplace); cf. Mt. Healthy City School Dist. Bd. of Educ. v. Doyle, 429 U.S. 274, 283–84 (1977) (holding that a teacher's exercise of constitutional freedoms may contribute to his or her dismissal so long as it was not the motivating factor in the decision to terminate the employment). See generally Developments in the Law — Public Employment,

other public employees retain their rights of free speech. The Supreme Court has, however, declined to establish a general standard for the scope of permissible speech in this context; instead, it has held that the conflict between a teacher's right of expression and the state's interest in maintaining an efficient workplace must be weighed against each other on a case by case basis.[78] This breadth of discretion has resulted in varying levels of restriction on gay and lesbian faculty members' right to free speech.[79]

In circumstances in which a teacher's exercise of a constitutional right is not at issue, the state's right to dismiss faculty members is limited by the due process and equal protection clauses. Dismissals may not, under these tests, be arbitrary and capricious.[80] In part because of the unique concerns of public schools, gay and lesbian teachers have been largely unsuccessful in their attempts to challenge their dismissals on these grounds.

1. First Amendment Protections. — The public school environment places special constraints on the first amendment rights of primary and secondary school instructors.[81] Because the Supreme Court has vested considerable discretion in local school boards to establish school curricula, courts are unlikely to interfere with school board decisions to sanction a teacher for permitting or introducing "inappropriate" conversation in the classroom.[82] The courts, however, have been hesitant to allow school boards to sanction teachers for advocating gay rights or discussing their homosexual orientation outside of the classroom in their capacity as private citizens.[83] Courts have had

---

97 HARV. L. REV. 1614, 1738–49 (1984) (reviewing the historical treatment of the constitutional rights of public employees).

[78] *See Pickering,* 391 U.S. at 569 ("[W]e do not deem it either appropriate or feasible to attempt to lay down a general standard against which all such statements may be judged.").

[79] *Compare* Aumiller v. University of Delaware, 434 F. Supp. 1273 (D. Del. 1977) (awarding damages to a university lecturer dismissed for granting public interviews in which he discussed his homosexuality) *with* Rowland v. Mad River Local School Dist., 730 F.2d 444 (6th Cir. 1984) (holding that a faculty member's discussion of her homosexual orientation was permissible grounds for transferring her to a position not involving student contact), *cert. denied,* 470 U.S. 1009 (1985).

[80] *See, e.g., Pickering,* 391 U.S. at 563. Furthermore, dismissals that discriminate against a protected class are subject to strict scrutiny. *See supra* p. 54.

[81] *Cf. supra* p. 80.

[82] *Cf.* Peterson, *Taking Risks at Mead High,* THE ADVOCATE, Jan. 17, 1989, at 12–13 (noting that a high school teacher was officially reprimanded for inviting a gay student to speak to his class regarding homosexuality). *But see* United States v. Coffeeville Consol. School Dist., 513 F.2d 244 (5th Cir. 1975) (reinstating a teacher in spite of school board's determination that her discussion of homosexuality with eighth grade students justified dismissal).

[83] *See, e.g.,* National Gay Task Force v. Board of Educ., 729 F.2d 1270 (10th Cir. 1984) (holding that the portion of an Oklahoma statute that barred mere advocacy of gay rights without demanding an overriding state interest violated the first amendment and was therefore facially overbroad and unconstitutional), *aff'd by an equally divided Court,* 470 U.S. 903 (1985); *see also Aumiller,* 434 F. Supp. at 1273 (awarding compensatory and punitive damages to a

more difficulty determining which standard is applicable to faculty speech made in the workplace but outside the ambit of curricular activity. They have tended to defer to local board decisions in these cases, even though such extracurricular speech has a limited impact on the efficiency of the workplace.

In *Rowland v. Mad River Local School District*,[84] for example, the Sixth Circuit defined the realm of school board discretion extremely expansively in situations involving the sexual orientation of faculty members. In that case, the court held that a school district could transfer a guidance counselor to a position that did not involve student contact merely because she had revealed her bisexuality to a colleague.[85] In doing so, the court relied on *Connick v. Myers*,[86] in which the Supreme Court held that first amendment protection for speech by public employees made in the workplace extends only to speech regarding matters of "public concern."

The "public concern" criterion addresses the danger of unregulated disruption of the workplace.[87] The *Rowland* decision misapplied this doctrine by ignoring that the speech was neither given in the workplace nor disruptive. First, the court in *Rowland* ignored the fact that the speech had taken place beyond the workplace, outside of the classroom walls. Second, *Connick* involved the dismissal of an employee who had circulated an employee questionnaire soliciting grievances against her employer.[88] The conversation involved in *Rowland* was confidential and was not disruptive of the workplace. Thus, *Rowland* places a burden of silence on gay and lesbian teachers that does nothing to maintain or enhance governmental efficiency.

Furthermore, under the *Connick* standard, even if Rowland's speech has been made in the workplace, or caused some level of disruption, legal and societal treatment of gay men and lesbians is a matter of current public concern and worthy of first amendment protection.[89] A teacher's public revelation of her sexual orientation involves her in the ongoing public debate about sexual orientation as well as in any ensuing debate concerning her employment.[90] In the

---

university lecturer dismissed after granting three interviews with the press in which he discussed his homosexuality).

[84] 730 F.2d 444 (6th Cir. 1984), *cert. denied*, 470 U.S. 1009 (1985).

[85] *See id.* at 449.

[86] 461 U.S. 138 (1983).

[87] *See id.* at 141. This doctrine complements that of Pickering v. Board of Educ., 391 U.S. 563 (1968), which mandates that a teacher's first amendment rights be restricted only when the state's interest in efficiency outweighs the employee's interest in exercising his or her right to free speech. *See id.* at 569; *supra* pp. 85–86.

[88] *See Connick*, 461 U.S. at 141.

[89] *See supra* pp. 76–77.

[90] *See* Rowland v. Mad River Local School Dist., 470 U.S. 1009, 1012 (1985) (Brennan, J., dissenting from denial of certiorari) (noting that "[s]peech that 'touches upon' this explosive issue

instant case, the school's immediate and extreme reaction to Rowland's confidences indicates that her sexuality was not considered a strictly private matter.

Moreover, the *Connick* rule, even when properly applied, imposes undue burdens on gay men and lesbians who wish to discuss their sexual orientation privately, without the fear that such speech will be sanctioned in their workplaces. Private speech, particularly confidential speech, is no less deserving of first amendment protection than is public speech.[91] Such private speech is crucial to self-development and self-esteem. Furthermore, a teacher's right to speak privately cannot be restricted in the interests of governmental efficiency, because confidential speech does not hinder the efficient operation of the schools.[92]

The first amendment also protects teachers' freedom of association and limits school authorities' regulation of a teacher's associations outside of the classroom. In *Shelton v. Tucker*,[93] the Supreme Court held that a state may not require teachers to reveal all of their organizational affiliations as a condition of employment.[94] Schools may only require that applicants reveal those associational ties that are relevant to a teacher's effectiveness.[95] Courts have, however, interpreted this requirement to include associations with gay and lesbian organizations, even though those associations were strictly extracurricular.[96]

Permitting school authorities to require disclosure of faculty members' personal activities may force gay and lesbian applicants for teaching positions to reveal their sexual orientation, and thus risk unemployment. In *Acanfora v. Board of Education of Montgomery County*,[97] the Fourth Circuit held that a teacher's failure to include his former membership in a college gay organization on his employment application constituted misrepresentation and was therefore adequate grounds for dismissal.[98] However, school officials admitted

---

[of gay rights] is no less deserving of constitutional attention than speech relating to more widely condemned forms of discrimination").

[91] *See supra* p. 77.

[92] *See* May v. Evansville-Vanderburgh School Corp., 787 F.2d 1105 (7th Cir. 1986) (holding that private conversations are entitled to *greater* first amendment protection because they do not inject the school system into public controversy).

[93] 364 U.S. 479 (1960).

[94] *See id.* at 490; *cf.* NAACP v. Alabama, 357 U.S. 449, 462–63 (1958) (holding that a state may not require organizations to divulge their membership lists because to do so would substantially affect individuals' exercise of their right to freedom of association).

[95] *See Shelton*, 364 U.S. at 490.

[96] *See* Acanfora v. Board of Educ., 491 F.2d 498 (4th Cir. 1974); McConnell v. Anderson, 451 F.2d 193 (8th Cir. 1971), *cert. denied*, 405 U.S. 1046 (1972).

[97] 491 F.2d 498 (4th Cir. 1974).

[98] The court also found that because Acanfora's public speeches were of public interest and

that if Acanfora had informed the school district of his association with a gay organization, they would not have employed him.[99]

The court's failure to address whether a teacher's right to associate with gay organizations outweighs the government's interest in hiring qualified applicants forces gay and lesbian teachers associated with such groups to choose between honest disclosure resulting in unemployment and possible dismissal for fraud. Moreover, it may discourage gay men and lesbians seeking careers in education from joining any organizations concerned with sexual orientation.[100] This holding undermines the rights of association guaranteed to gay and lesbian students;[101] their membership in such organizations may seriously harm their chances for future employment in the public sector.

2. *Due Process Requirements.* — In circumstances in which the first amendment and the *Pickering* balance are not implicated, faculty members challenging their dismissals must rely on due process requirements, which provide that dismissals must be rationally related to a legitimate governmental goal.[102] Under this standard, dismissals and sanctions must have a rational nexus to the maintenance of government efficiency. In the few reported cases involving the sexual orientation of faculty members, courts have held that various types of homosexual behavior bear a rational nexus to teaching ability.[103] Courts have focused on factors such as whether specific homosexual acts are involved, whether the acts in question occurred in public, whether any criminal charges or convictions were involved, and how much publicity surrounded the revelation of a faculty member's sexual orientation.

Several courts have interpreted the "rational nexus" requirement as a public/private distinction, holding that although private homosexual conduct cannot be grounds for punishing an employee,[104] public

---

had not impaired his ability to function professionally, they were protected by the first amendment. *See id.* at 500–01.

[99] *See id.* at 501.

[100] *Cf.* NAACP v. Alabama, 357 U.S. 449 (1958) (noting the potential chilling effect on NAACP membership if membership lists were discoverable).

[101] *See supra* p. 77.

[102] *See* Kelley v. Johnson, 425 U.S. 238, 247 (1976); *supra* pp. 47–54.

[103] *See, e.g.,* Thompson v. Southwest School Dist., 483 F. Supp. 1170 (W.D. Mo. 1980); Kilpatrick v. Wright, 437 F. Supp. 397 (M.D. Ala. 1977); Morrison v. State Bd. of Educ., 1 Cal. 3d 214, 461 P.2d 375, 82 Cal. Rptr. 175 (1969); Weissman v. Board of Educ., 190 Colo. 414, 547 P.2d 1267 (1976); Shipley v. Salem School Dist., 64 Or. App. 777, 669 P.2d 1172 (1983).

[104] *See Morrison,* 1 Cal. 3d at 229, 461 P.2d at 386–87, 82 Cal. Rptr. at 186; Moser v. State Bd. of Educ., 22 Cal. App. 3d 988, 990, 101 Cal. Rptr. 86, 87 (1972). The *Morrison* court listed several factors that a school board might use to determine the effect of homosexual conduct on a teacher's fitness, including the effect on student attitudes, adverse community reactions, adverse effects on students or fellow teachers, the remoteness in time of the conduct, and the type of teaching certificate involved.

conduct is by definition "rationally connected" to an employee's effectiveness.[105] Public homosexual conduct is particularly likely to be held rationally related in cases involving a faculty member's conviction under criminal statutes.[106] In cases involving public homosexual conduct, school boards have little or no duty to establish that the teacher's ability to perform has been affected.[107]

This absolute prohibition of public homosexual conduct places an unconstitutional burden on gay and lesbian teachers' right to free speech. The public/private standard employed in the teacher cases constitutes content-based censorship. Restrictions on homosexual conduct alone, without specifying that the contact is obscene or inappropriate in the schools, discriminates against gay and lesbian teachers on the basis of their sexual orientation.

Furthermore, under heightened scrutiny analysis, this distinction violates the equal protection clause by enforcing conceptions of "immorality" unevenly between gay and non-gay faculty members. School regulations regarding faculty members' private lives generally permit dismissals for "immorality," either through local policy or under state statutes authorizing dismissals for "immorality."[108] By defining immorality as public homosexual conduct, rather than indecent or inappropriate homosexual conduct, courts have differentiated between same-sex and opposite-sex displays. The ambiguous definition of what constitutes a "public display" does not provide notice to gay and lesbian teachers about what behavior is impermissible. A public display of homosexual conduct might be construed as same-sex cohabitation, kissing, or touching, while identical heterosexual conduct would be condoned.[109] Only by adopting a uniform standard of

---

[105] *Cf.* McConnell v. Anderson, 451 F.2d 193 (8th Cir. 1971) (allowing a university to withdraw an unexecuted job offer to a librarian after he applied for a marriage license with another man), *cert. denied*, 405 U.S. 1046 (1972). *But see* Board of Educ. v. M., 19 Cal. 3d 691, 566 P.2d 602, 139 Cal. Rptr. 700 (1977) (holding that a tenured teacher, in spite of his arrest for public homosexual conduct, was not unfit per se to teach elementary school children).

[106] *See, e.g.*, McLaughlin v. Board of Medical Examiners, 35 Cal. App. 3d 1010, 1015–16, 111 Cal. Rptr. 353, 357 (1973) (upholding a five year sentence of probation for a physician for public solicitation of another male, noting that "[t]he distinction between a private, noncriminal act and a criminal act committed in a public place is obvious"); Moser v. State Bd. of Educ., 22 Cal. App. 3d 988, 101 Cal. Rptr. 86 (1972); Sarac v. State Bd. of Educ., 249 Cal. App. 2d 58, 57 Cal. Rptr. 69 (1967).

[107] *See* Governing Bd. v. Metcalf, 36 Cal. App. 3d 546, 111 Cal. Rptr. 724 (1974); Board of Educ. v. Calderon, 35 Cal. App. 3d 490, 110 Cal. Rptr. 916 (1974) (upholding a teacher's dismissal in spite of the fact that he had been acquitted of the criminal charges upon which the firing was based).

[108] *See, e.g.*, CAL. EDUC. CODE §§ 13202, 13556.5 (West 1978) (providing that California faculty members may be dismissed for "immoral" conduct).

[109] *Cf.* Andrews v. Drew Mun. Separate School Dist., 507 F.2d 611 (5th Cir. 1975) (overruling school district rule barring employment of unwed parents as faculty members); Drake v. Covington County Bd. of Educ., 371 F. Supp. 974 (M.D. Ala. 1974) (ruling the dismissal of an unwed pregnant teacher unconstitutional).

morality can the schools eliminate the broad discretion the public/ private distinction gives to local school boards to discriminate against gay and lesbian teachers.

Other courts have grappled with the issue of the relationship between sexual orientation and teaching ability by stressing a teacher's function as a role model. Because the state has an interest in educating students in the "boundaries of socially appropriate behavior,"[110] gay and lesbian teachers face dismissal or transfer to non-teaching jobs if their sexual orientation, publicly expressed or not, is deemed an "inappropriate" role model for students.

For example, in *Gaylord v. Tacoma School District*,[111] the Washington Supreme Court applied this role model theory to uphold the dismissal of a teacher for immorality based on his status as a "publicly known homosexual."[112] Although Washington had repealed its sodomy statute by the time of the trial,[113] the court found that Gaylord's homosexual conduct was evidence of his immorality and a valid basis for dismissal.[114] In so holding, the court emphasized the need for teachers to instruct students in morality,[115] and the danger that the presence of gay and lesbian teachers might be interpreted as expressing approval and encouraging imitation.[116] *Gaylord* thus strongly affirms the argument that the rational nexus requirement is satisfied by viewing teachers as moral exemplars and justifies a blanket policy of excluding gay people from teaching positions, or at least those involving young children.[117]

The *Gaylord* decision, and the role model theory it prescribes, present problems on several levels. First, the court mistakes sexual orientation for specific sexual acts. Even though there was no evidence that Gaylord had actually committed any sexual acts,[118] the court argued that "sexual gratification with a member of one's own sex is implicit in the term 'homosexual.'"[119] The court interpreted Gaylord's acknowledgment of his homosexual orientation as tantamount to an admission that he had committed such acts.[120] By

---

110 Bethel School Dist. No. 403 v. Fraser, 478 U.S. 675, 681 (1986).

111 88 Wash. 2d 286, 559 P.2d 1340, *cert. denied*, 434 U.S. 879 (1977).

112 *See id.* at 289, 559 P.2d at 1342.

113 *See id.* at 297, 559 P.2d at 1346.

114 *See id.* at 296, 559 P.2d at 1345.

115 The requirement that teachers instruct students in prevailing conceptions of morality was in fact statutorily mandated. *See id.* at 290, 559 P.2d at 1342.

116 *See id.* at 298–99, 559 P.2d at 1347.

117 *Cf.* Safransky v. State Personnel Bd., 62 Wis. 2d 464, 475, 215 N.W.2d 379, 384 (1974) (upholding the dismissal of a tenured houseparent of a state home for retarded boys on the grounds of a violation of his duty to project the "orthodoxy of male heterosexuality").

118 *See Gaylord*, 88 Wash. 2d at 293, 559 P.2d at 1344.

119 *Id.* at 289, 559 P.2d at 1342.

120 *See id.* at 291–96, 559 P.2d at 1343–45.

defining homosexuality solely on the basis of sexual activity, the court ignored the fact that homosexuality is an affectional preference that cannot be limited to sexual acts. Even in those jurisdictions in which sodomy is illegal, a teacher's homosexuality does not indicate that he or she is violating those laws.[121]

The conception of teachers as exemplars of heterosexual morality also ignores benefits that accrue from employing openly gay and lesbian teachers. First, the presence of openly gay men and lesbians in the public schools would both educate public school children about the diversity of the general population and provide opportunities to instruct them in fairness and tolerance.[122] Public schools, long recognized as a "marketplace of ideas," benefit from having student bodies and faculties diverse enough to promote an exchange of viewpoints.[123] No evidence indicates that such an exchange of ideas with young people affects the sexual orientation of those children.[124] Second, gay and lesbian faculty members would serve as role models for gay and lesbian students, reducing the alienation of gay students.[125]

3. Equal Protection Issues. — Because the Supreme Court has declined to define sexual orientation as a suspect classification, discrimination against gay and lesbian teachers remains permissible under the fourteenth amendment.[126] Gay and lesbian faculty members have been removed from student contact under ethical or contractual requirements that are ostensibly neutral regarding sexual orientation.[127] These facially neutral standards have been enforced more

---

[121] *See* Part II, note 11 and accompanying text, *supra* p. 11; *cf.* High Tech Gays v. Defense Indus. Sec. Clearance Office, 668 F. Supp. 1361, 1371 (N.D. Cal. 1987) (finding a fundamental freedom to engage in nonsodomous homosexual activity).

[122] *Cf.* Wygant v. Jackson Bd. of Educ., 106 S. Ct. 1842, 1868 (1986) (Stevens, J., dissenting) (arguing that a racially integrated faculty benefits not only minority students, but the entire student body). *But see id.* at 1848 (majority opinion) (rejecting a role model justification for upholding a collective bargaining agreement to maintain the percentage of minority faculty members).

[123] In the analogous context of racial diversity, courts have noted that integration leads to greater racial tolerance and understanding. *See* Sweatt v. Painter, 339 U.S. 629, 634 (1950) (mandating integration of a public university law school on the ground that law students benefit from exposure to a variety of viewpoints and from an exchange of ideas); Kromnick v. School Dist., 739 F.2d 894, 905 (3d Cir. 1984), *cert. denied*, 469 U.S. 1107 (1985).

[124] Indeed, studies of the children of gay and lesbian parents indicate that their sexual orientations correspond to the relative proportions of the general population. *See* Part VI, note 76 and accompanying text, *infra* p. 129.

[125] *See* A. BELL, M. WEINBERG & S. HAMMERSMITH, SEXUAL PREFERENCE 95, 163 (1981) (finding that both gay and lesbian adolescents feel alienated from their peers).

[126] *See supra* p. 54.

[127] Such contractual requirements may include provisions barring sexual conduct between students and faculty members, or requirements that a teacher inform the school district of all extracurricular activities. *See* Naragon v. Wharton, 737 F.2d 1403, 1405 (5th Cir. 1984) (upholding a faculty member's dismissal for a same-sex relationship based on the school's ethical code barring faculty/student involvement); Rowland v. Mad River Local School Dist., 730 F.2d 444 (6th Cir. 1984), *cert. denied*, 470 U.S. 1009 (1985); Korf v. Ball State Univ., 726 F.2d

rigorously against gay and lesbian faculty members than against non-gay employees. As a policy matter, gay and lesbian teachers should not be removed from their positions under circumstances in which a non-gay teacher would be permitted to continue teaching. School authorities must consider more than their conceptions of "appropriateness" in employing faculty members; their policies and attitudes toward any minority group or minority viewpoint instructs students in the vitality of first amendment protections and of the constitutional principles being taught. If gay and lesbian teachers are summarily excluded or stigmatized in the school systems, such disregard for the fundamental principles of fairness and equal protection mandated by the Constitution would teach students to "discount important principles of our government as mere platitudes."[128]

4. *Conclusion.* — Sanctions on public school teachers for expressions of sexual orientation or for discussion of gay rights often rely on mistaken conceptions of homosexuality and the potential effects gay and lesbian teachers may have on their students. Courts addressing this issue must consider the needs of students, both gay and non-gay, for diverse role models and for examples of diversity and tolerance in the public school systems. At a minimum, they must, under established due process requirements, assess the effect of sexual orientation on a teacher's effectiveness in the classroom.

Teachers and students face very different standards regarding public expression of sexual orientation in the public schools as a consequence of the differences between public employment and mandatory school attendance. The harsh standards applied to faculty members are not, however, wholly separable from students' rights. Although students consistently have won litigation regarding their rights to take part in student activism or participate in gay or lesbian student groups, the specter of future sanctions may chill such expression even at the student level. Until employment discrimination based on sexual orientation is eliminated, students may only be courting future unemployment when they exercise their hard-won rights to associate with other gay and lesbian students. Only a full examination of the needs of students during and beyond their school years can properly balance students' needs, teachers' rights, and the government interest in maintaining efficient and effective public schools.

V. SAME-SEX COUPLES AND THE LAW

The evolution of social norms and practices has influenced the colloquial and legal definitions of family. Whereas a family was once

---

1222, 1224–25 (7th Cir. 1984) (same as *Naragon*); Acanfora v. Board of Educ., 491 F.2d 498, 503–04 (4th Cir. 1974) (upholding a dismissal of a gay teacher based on an omission from his job application of his membership in a gay student organization).

[128] West Virginia State Bd. of Educ. v. Barnette, 319 U.S. 624, 637 (1943).

seen strictly as a patriarchy, consisting of an income-earning male and a housewife, today's definition is much broader.[1] Society has recognized that many modern families are headed either by two adults who work outside of the home or by a single parent.[2] Similarly the legal definition of family has broadened. In *Moore v. City of East Cleveland*,[3] for example, the Supreme Court granted constitutional protection beyond nuclear families to extended families.[4] Despite this social and legal evolution, courts and legislatures continually have refused to grant gay and lesbian couples family status.[5]

The consequences of the denial of legal status to gay and lesbian couples are severe. Regardless of the quality or length of the relationship, gay and lesbian partners often cannot receive important economic benefits, such as workers' compensation upon the death of their life partners. Nor can gay men and lesbians assume the housing leases of their partners or ensure that wills or trusts assigning property to their partners will be protected from court challenges.[6]

Although the law denies all unmarried couples many legal and economic privileges regardless of sexual orientation, the effect on same-sex relationships is particularly troublesome. The law's seemingly evenhanded treatment of unmarried couples in fact penalizes same-sex couples more severely, because gay men and lesbians do not have the option of marriage. Basic tenets of fairness should compel courts and legislatures to eliminate laws and policies governing private law entitlements that discriminate against same-sex couples, either by affording gay men and lesbians the right to marry or at least by offering them those personal and economic benefits that are vital to their welfare.

This Part addresses two sets of legal issues concerning same-sex couples. Section A examines the right of gay and lesbian couples to marry and argues that state laws prohibiting same-sex marriage are

---

[1] Many Americans continue to regard the nuclear family as the basic unit of social organization and regret what they consider the disintegration of the family. *See* Note, *The Necessity for State Recognition of Same-Sex Marriage: Constitutional Requirements and Evolving Notions of Family*, 3 BERKELEY WOMEN'S L.J. 134, 134 & n.1 (1987–1988).

[2] *See* Bartlett, *Rethinking Parenthood as an Exclusive Status: The Need for Legal Alternatives When the Premise of the Nuclear Family Has Failed*, 70 VA. L. REV. 879, 880–81, nn.5 & 9 (1984) (citing U.S. census figures that report increasing numbers of children who do not live with both natural parents, increasing divorce rates, and increasing numbers of single-parent, never-married households).

[3] 431 U.S. 494 (1977).

[4] *See id.* at 500–06.

[5] The various substitutes for legal marriage — putative spouse marriage, common-law marriage, and marriage by contract or declaration — are available to heterosexual couples in a few jurisdictions, but remain altogether unavailable to gay and lesbian couples. *See* Lovas, *When Is a Family Not a Family? Inheritance and the Taxation of Inheritance Within the Non-Traditional Family*, 24 IDAHO L. REV. 353, 355–63 (1987).

[6] *See* pp. 102–13.

constitutionally invalid. Section B analyzes laws governing private law entitlements that effectively discriminate against same-sex couples. Section C analyzes the legal mechanisms that same-sex couples have used to overcome barriers imposed by those laws. The conclusion argues that courts and legislatures should afford gay and lesbian couples the same legal protections as those afforded married heterosexual couples.

A. The Right of Gay and Lesbian Couples To Marry

Marriage has always been regarded as a central institution in American society. Alongside its strong symbolic meaning to the partners, marriage bestows concrete legal advantages on the couple: tax benefits, standing to recover damages for certain torts committed against spouses, rights to succession, and insurance benefits, to name a few.[7] Thus, states have recognized the special importance of marriage to society. The Supreme Court also has affirmed the special status of marriage. In *Griswold v. Connecticut*,[8] the Court declared that marriage "is an association that promotes a way of life, not causes; a harmony in living, not political faiths; a bilateral loyalty, not commercial or social projects. Yet it is an association for as noble a purpose as any involved in our prior decisions."[9] Moreover, in *Loving v. Virginia*[10] and *Zablocki v. Redhail*,[11] the Court firmly established marriage as a "'basic civil right[] of man,' fundamental to our very existence and survival."[12]

Judicial recognition of a fundamental right to marry represented two major constitutional moves. The first was toward protecting intimate adult unions from societal prejudice. Thus, in *Loving*, the Supreme Court held that a state miscegenation law was unconstitutional.[13] The second move was toward removing unreasonable burdens on an individual's decision to marry. Thus, in *Zablocki*, the Court invalidated a statute that implicitly tied the ability to marry to

---

[7] *See* Turner v. Safley, 107 S. Ct. 2254, 2265 (1987); *see also* Note, *Marital Status Classifications: Protecting Homosexual and Heterosexual Cohabitors*, 14 HASTINGS CONST. L.Q., 111, 115–16 (1986) (listing benefits associated with marriage). Marriage also brings with it liabilities. If the partners divorce, for example, many states require courts to consider "fault" in determining property distribution and/or alimony. *See* Golden & Taylor, *Consideration of Misconduct in Setting Alimony*, in SECTION OF FAMILY LAW, AM. BAR ASS'N, ALIMONY: NEW STRATEGIES FOR PURSUIT AND DEFENSE 2 (1988).

[8] 381 U.S. 479 (1965).

[9] *Id.* at 486; *see also* Maynard v. Hill, 125 U.S. 190, 211 (1888) (declaring that marriage is "the foundation of the family and of society").

[10] 388 U.S. 1 (1967).

[11] 434 U.S. 374 (1978).

[12] *Loving*, 388 U.S. at 12 (quoting Skinner v. Oklahoma, 316 U.S. 535, 541 (1942)); *see also* *Zablocki*, 434 U.S. at 383 (stating that "the right to marry is of fundamental importance").

[13] *See Loving*, 388 U.S. at 12.

a person's wealth.[14]   Yet, despite these two moves, which together connote a respect for the importance to the individual of the right to marry, states — the traditional regulators of marriage[15] — universally have denied this right to persons of the same sex.[16] Marriage statutes either expressly prohibit same-sex marriage,[17] or courts interpret them to contain such a prohibition.[18]

1. Principles Informing the Right To Marry. — At least three constitutional principles inform the right to marry, and each compels extending the right to same-sex couples. First, the right to marry derives in large part from the right to privacy. In *Cleveland Board of Education v. LaFleur,*[19] the Court declared that it "has long recognized that freedom of personal choice in matters of marriage and family life is one of the liberties protected by the Due Process Clause of the Fourteenth Amendment."[20] Autonomy in this area nurtures personhood[21] and individuality.[22] Choice in intimate relationships is no less critical for homosexuals than for heterosexuals. Thus, insofar as the right to marry derives from the right to privacy, it should extend to heterosexuals and homosexuals alike.[23]

---

[14] *See Zablocki,* 434 U.S. at 389–91 (striking down a statute that proscribed the marriage of a person with outstanding child-support obligations).

[15] *See* Pennoyer v. Neff, 95 U.S. 714, 734–35 (1877) ("The State . . . has absolute right to prescribe the conditions upon which the marriage relation between its own citizens shall be created, and the causes for which it may be dissolved.").

[16] *See* Rivera, *Homosexuality and the Law,* in HOMOSEXUALITY: SOCIAL, PSYCHOLOGICAL, AND BIOLOGICAL ISSUES 323, 330 (W. Paul, J. Weinrich, J. Gonsiorek & M. Hotvedt eds. 1982).

[17] *See, e.g.,* CAL. CIV. CODE § 4100 (West 1983) (defining marriage as "a personal relation arising out of a civil contract between a man and a woman"); TEX. FAM. CODE ANN. § 1.01 (Vernon 1975) (stating that "[a] license may not be issued for the marriage of persons of the same sex").

[18] *See, e.g.,* Adams v. Howerton, 486 F. Supp. 1119, 1122–23 (C.D. Cal. 1980) (finding no reason to permit same-sex marriages in the legislature's lack of express prohibition of them), *aff'd,* 673 F.2d 1036 (9th Cir.), *cert. denied,* 458 U.S. 1111 (1982); Baker v. Nelson, 291 Minn. 310, 311–12, 191 N.W.2d 185, 185–86 (1971) (same), *appeal dismissed,* 409 U.S. 810 (1972). The cases involving same-sex marriages fall into two categories: dissolution of same-sex "marriages," *see, e.g.,* Anonymous v. Anonymous, 67 Misc. 2d 982, 325 N.Y.S.2d 499 (N.Y. Sup. Ct. 1971) (dissolving a same-sex marriage in which the plaintiff married the defendant believing the defendant was male), and denial of marriage licenses to gay couples, *see, e.g., Baker,* 291 Minn. at 310, 191 N.W.2d at 185.

[19] 414 U.S. 632 (1974).

[20] *Id.* at 639–40.

[21] *See* L. TRIBE, AMERICAN CONSTITUTIONAL LAW § 15-2, at 1304 (2d ed. 1988) (explaining that "[w]ords like 'personhood' . . . have been thrust into a social and political vacuum to define some reliable limits upon the state's power to shape the behavior of individuals and groups").

[22] *See* Bowers v. Hardwick, 478 U.S. 186, 205 (1986) (Blackmun, J., dissenting) ("[W]e protect the family because it contributes so powerfully to the happiness of individuals, not because of a preference for stereotypical households.").

[23] The Supreme Court's recent decision in *Hardwick* does not foreclose application of the privacy doctrine to same-sex marriage. Although *Hardwick* held that the right to privacy does

A complementary perspective on the right to privacy also supports the protection of same-sex marriages. Freedom of intimate association, a fundamental element of personal liberty, can be understood more as limiting state authority than protecting spheres of personal autonomy. As the Court explained in *Roberts v. United States Jaycees*,[24] freedom of association extends to "certain kinds of highly personal relationships" that "act as critical buffers between the individual and the power of the State."[25] Under this theory, the state simply has no authority to pressure individuals into heterosexual relationships, by giving only those relationships the benefits and protections of the law.[26]

Marriage is also constitutionally protected because it promotes familial and societal stability.[27] This functional view of marriage suggests that any stable and significant relationship between two consenting adults should be accorded constitutional protection. Indeed, the Court's functionalism has moved it to expand, rather than limit, its definition of family. Thus, in *Moore v. City of East Cleveland*,[28] the Court invalidated a city ordinance barring extended families from living in a single unit and held that the scope of the privacy right in family matters extends to families comprised of close relatives who coalesce out of choice, necessity, and duty.[29] Protecting "family," in this sense, promotes social stability by protecting the right of the extended family "to come together for mutual sustenance and to main-

---

not protect the right of homosexuals to engage in sodomy, the right of gay men and lesbians to marry is unrelated to their right to engage in sodomy. Just as Mormons did not forfeit the right to free exercise of religion simply because the state proscribed polygamy, a practice that their religion once espoused, so too homosexuals do not forfeit their fundamental right to marry because the state can proscribe sodomy. *See* Note, *Custody Denials to Parents in Same-Sex Relationships: An Equal Protection Analysis*, 102 HARV. L. REV. 617, 625 (1989). Nor would extending the right of privacy to protect the right of gay men and lesbians to marry necessarily entail extending the right of privacy to protect the right of individuals to marry close relatives. Incestuous relationships, unlike homosexual relationships, create a high risk of birth defects in their offspring. The state, therefore, has a compelling interest in regulating them.

[24] 468 U.S. 609 (1984).

[25] *Id.* at 618–19; *see also* Moore v. City of E. Cleveland, 431 U.S. 494, 506 (1977) (stating that the state cannot not "standardiz[e]" its children and adults "by forcing all to live in certain narrowly defined family patterns").

[26] *See* Rubenfeld, *The Right of Privacy*, 102 HARV. L. REV. 737, 800 (1989). Rubenfeld states:

Homosexual couples by necessity throw into question the allocation of specific functions . . . between the sexes. It is this aspect of the ban on homosexuality — its central role in the maintenance of institutionalized sexual identities and normalized reproductive relations — that have made its *affirmative* or *formative* consequences . . . so powerful a force in modern society.

Id. (emphasis in original).

[27] *See Zablocki*, 434 U.S. at 384.

[28] 431 U.S. 494 (1977).

[29] *See id.* at 505.

tain or rebuild a secure home life."[30] Similarly, the Court's functionalism should move it to expand its definition of marriage. To the extent that marriage is a vehicle for stability because of the commitment it embodies, gay men and lesbians in stable, committed relationships should be no less entitled to marry than their heterosexual counterparts.

Just as courts and legislatures addressing this issue should acknowledge the principles that inform the right to marry, they should recognize which principles do *not* animate the right. For one, the Constitution does not protect marriage because of its link to procreation. While not directly addressing this issue, the Court's holdings in *Griswold v. Connecticut*,[31] *Eisenstadt v. Baird*,[32] and *Roe v. Wade*[33] clearly suggest that marriage can be understood independently of procreation. The state cannot force married persons to have children, nor can it forbid infertile persons to marry.[34]

Even if marriage is protected because it often involves procreation, the argument that gay and lesbian couples should therefore be denied the right to marry is without merit. Given current advances in reproductive technology — in particular artificial insemination and surrogacy — gay men and lesbians can easily produce offspring.[35] Thus, allowing gay men and lesbians to marry would not be inconsistent with policies favoring procreation.

In sum, same-sex marriages are wholly consistent with the theoretical and policy justifications behind the right to marry. If the Court is serious about the interests promoted by protecting the right to marry — self-determination, autonomy from the state, and societal and familial stability — then it should value them for heterosexuals and homosexuals alike and recognize that the fundamental right to marry should extend to gay and lesbian couples.

2. *State Justifications for Prohibiting Same-Sex Marriage.* — Once courts and legislatures acknowledge a constitutionally protected right to marry for same-sex couples, the next inquiry is whether a state's interests in prohibiting same-sex marriage justify a substantial burden on that right. Under *Zablocki*, courts must apply strict scrutiny in testing the validity of state restrictions that "significantly interfere with

---

[30] *Id.*

[31] 381 U.S. 479 (1965) (holding that the right to privacy protects the right of a married person to use contraceptives).

[32] 405 U.S. 438 (1972) (holding that the right to use contraceptives attaches to the individual, irrespective of marriage).

[33] 410 U.S. 113 (1972) (holding that the right to privacy protects a woman's right to decide whether or not to have an abortion).

[34] *See* Marks v. Marks, 191 Misc. 448, 449, 77 N.Y.S.2d 269, 270–71 (Kings County Sup. Ct. 1948) (holding that an inability to procreate cannot be grounds for preventing people from getting married).

[35] *See infra* pp. 138–42.

decisions to enter into the marital relationship."[36] Two arguments further support applying strict scrutiny to same-sex marriage prohibitions. First, gay men and lesbians should constitute a suspect class;[37] and second, same-sex marriage prohibitions arguably burden the associational rights of gay men and lesbians under the first amendment.[38] This section argues that the prohibition on same-sex marriage cannot withstand any level of scrutiny, because states cannot articulate legitimate interests that are rationally related to the restrictions they impose.[39]

States have argued that prohibiting same-sex marriage encourages procreation[40] and promotes traditional values.[41] For reasons ex-

---

[36] 434 U.S. at 386.

[37] *See supra* pp. 54–60; *see also* Adolph Coors Co. v. Wallace, 570 F. Supp. 202, 209 n.24 (N.D. Cal. 1983) (protecting membership in organizations promoting gay rights because gays are a "'discrete and insular minority'" deserving special solicitude (quoting United States v. Carolene Products Co., 304 U.S. 144, 153 n.4 (1938))).

[38] *See* Board of Directors of Rotary Int'l v. Rotary Club, 481 U.S. 537, 545 (1987) ("[T]he First Amendment protects those relationships . . . that presuppose 'deep attachments and commitments to the necessarily few other individuals with whom one shares not only a special community of thoughts, experiences, and beliefs but also distinctively personal aspects of one's life.'" (quoting Roberts v. United States Jaycees, 468 U.S. 609, 619–20 (1984))).

[39] Whether applying heightened scrutiny under a substantive due process or a fundamental right equal protection approach, the Court effectively engages in a balancing process. Justice Marshall, dissenting in Dandridge v. Williams, 397 U.S. 471 (1970), articulated the balancing approach:

> In my view, equal protection analysis . . . is not appreciably advanced by the *a priori* definition of a 'right,' fundamental or otherwise. Rather, concentration must be placed upon the character of the classification in question, the relative importance to individuals in the class discriminated against of the governmental benefits that they do not receive, and the asserted state interests in support of the classification.

Id. at 520–21 (Marshall, J., dissenting). Substantive due process methodology typically requires a balancing of governmental and individual interests, with the degree of justification required of the government increasing with the severity of the burden on the protected right. *See* Moore v. City of E. Cleveland, 431 U.S. 494, 499 (1977) ("[W]hen the government intrudes on choices concerning family living relationships, this Court must examine carefully the importance of the governmental interests advanced and the extent to which they are served by the challenged regulation."). Traditional equal protection analysis uses strict, intermediate, or rational basis scrutiny. Under strict scrutiny, courts must determine whether the law at issue is narrowly tailored to serve a compelling state interest. *See* Shapiro v. Thompson, 394 U.S. 618, 634 (1969). Intermediate scrutiny requires a substantial relationship to an important state interest. *See* Craig v. Boren, 429 U.S. 190, 197 (1976). Rational basis review requires only that the means used to achieve a legitimate state interest be rationally related to that interest. *See* McDonald v. Board of Election Comm'rs, 394 U.S. 802, 809 (1969).

[40] *See, e.g.,* Adams v. Howerton, 486 F. Supp. 1119, 1123 (C.D. Cal. 1980) (stating that "the legal protection . . . afforded to marriage . . . has historically . . . been rationalized as being for the purpose of encouraging the propagation of the race"), *aff'd*, 673 F.2d 1036 (9th Cir.), *cert. denied*, 458 U.S. 1111 (1982); Singer v. Hara, 11 Wash. App. 247, 259, 522 P.2d 1187, 1195 (1974) ("[M]arriage exists as a protected legal institution primarily because of societal values associated with the propagation of the human race.").

[41] *See, e.g., Adams,* 486 F. Supp. at 1123 (noting that Judaism and Christianity vehemently condemn all homosexual relationships); Baker v. Nelson, 291 Minn. 310, 312, 191 N.W.2d 185,

plained above, the procreation argument is flawed.[42] Furthermore, same-sex marriage prohibitions, as instruments through which the procreation interest is served, are overinclusive because gay and lesbian couples can have children. In addition, they are underinclusive because many married heterosexual couples cannot, or elect not to, have children. The prohibition on same-sex marriage may in fact discourage procreation; some same-sex couples may elect not to have children precisely because their relationship is not sanctioned by the state.

The second proffered state interest — the invocation of traditional values — is nothing more than an appeal to eliminate diversity, an interest explicitly rejected by the Supreme Court.[43] As Justice Blackmun has noted, "[t]he legitimacy of secular legislation depends . . . on whether the State can advance some justification for its law beyond its conformity to religious doctrine."[44] Neither "the length of time a majority has held its convictions [n]or the passions with which it defends them can withdraw legislation from [the] Court's scrutiny."[45]

Moreover, anti-homosexual biases are nurtured by ill-founded assumptions about gay and lesbian relationships. Gay men and lesbians can and do have stable and long-lasting relationships.[46] Furthermore, they can and do create favorable environments in which to raise and

---

186 (1971) (noting that the traditional definition of marriage is "as old as the book of Genesis"); *Singer*, 11 Wash. App. at 264, 522 P.2d at 1197 (upholding a statute prohibiting same-sex marriage in part because of the state's "interest in affording a favorable environment for the growth of children").

[42] *See supra* p. 98.

[43] *See Moore*, 431 U.S. at 505–06 (plurality opinion) (striking down a housing ordinance that limited occupancy of a unit to a narrowly defined "family").

[44] Bowers v. Hardwick, 478 U.S. 186, 211 (1986) (Blackmun, J., dissenting); *see also* Stone v. Graham, 449 U.S. 39 (1980) (striking down a statute requiring the posting of a copy of the Ten Commandments on classroom walls because it had no secular legislative purpose).

[45] *Hardwick*, 478 U.S. at 210 (Blackmun, J., dissenting). The irony of the Court's justification of its holding in terms of societal animus towards homosexuality is readily apparent:

> [W]hen the Court uses the history of violent disapproval of the behavior that forms part of the very definition of homosexuality as the basis for denying homosexuals' claim to protection, it effectively inverts the equal protection axiom of heightened judicial solicitude for despised groups . . . and uses that inverted principle to bootstrap antipathy toward homosexuality into a tautological rationale for continuing to criminalize homosexuality.

L. TRIBE, *supra* note 21, § 15-21, at 1428.

[46] *See* P. BLUMSTEIN & P. SCHWARTZ, AMERICAN COUPLES 45 (1983) ("'Couplehood,' either as a reality or an aspiration, is as strong among gay people as it is among heterosexuals."). The level of commitment in same-sex relationships may in fact be higher than that in heterosexual relationships, given the psychological, social, and legal obstacles that gay couples must overcome in order to stay together. For example, gay men and lesbians who decide to share a residence may face more obstacles than their non-gay counterparts. Landlords may be reluctant to rent to them, families may express disapproval for their decision, neighbors may act with hostility towards them, and employers may show their disapproval in many subtle, and some not so subtle, ways.

educate children.[47] Because the state interest in promoting majoritarian morality is based on "irrational prejudice and fear of unconventional activities and lifestyles,"[48] it is illegitimate.[49]

Same-sex marriage prohibitions significantly interfere with the exercise of fundamental constitutional rights and do not withstand even a relatively low level of scrutiny. Courts should, therefore, strike them down. At the very least, courts should recognize that the legal rights of gay and lesbian partners should not depend on marital status classifications. As the following Section indicates, such classifications work an invidious and unjustifiable discrimination against same-sex couples.

B. Same-Sex Couples and Private Law Benefits

Traditionally, the law has denounced cohabitation as a direct threat to the strength and integrity of marriage.[50] Although modern society has been more accepting of heterosexual cohabitation[51] — and, to a lesser degree, gay and lesbian relationships[52] — courts and legislatures have been slow to recognize these contemporary family structures and lifestyles. As a result, unmarried homosexuals and heterosexuals often are denied legal privileges that married couples enjoy.

Generally, courts that have protected the rights of a gay or lesbian couple have required proof that the relationship is sufficiently stable

---

[47] See Part VI, note 57, infra p. 126.

[48] Ingram, A Constitutional Critique of Restrictions on the Right To Marry — Why Can't Fred Marry George — or Mary and Alice at the Same Time?, 10 J. CONTEMP. L. 33, 55 (1984).

[49] See Palmore v. Sidoti, 466 U.S. 429 (1984) (holding that a custody denial based on potential stigmatization of the child due to the mother's interracial remarriage amounted to endorsing public prejudices and, therefore, violated the equal protection clause); see also Sunstein, Public Values, Private Interests, and the Equal Protection Clause, 1982 SUP. CT. REV. 127, 136–37 (proposing that choices "based on a perception that one person is in some sense 'better' than another" or based solely on a person's identity should be considered impermissible justifications under the equal protection clause).

[50] See, e.g., E. FARNSWORTH, CONTRACTS § 5.4, at 345–46 (1982).

[51] See, e.g., Note, Marital Status Classifications: Protecting Homosexual and Heterosexual Cohabitors, 14 HASTINGS CONST. L.Q. 111, 114 & n.26 (1986) [hereinafter Note, Marital Status Classifications] (noting that over fifteen years ago, California legislation dealing with cohabitors started to treat married and unmarried couples more equally).

[52] See, e.g., Leonard, Madison, WI Council Passes Two Domestic Partnership Bills, 1988 LESBIAN/GAY L. NOTES 49 (reporting that Madison, Wisconsin recently approved bills allowing nontraditional families to live in areas previously zoned for single families and mandating that city employees be allowed bereavement and sick leave for "family partners"); see also Housing Rights of Gay Survivors Subject of New York Litigation, 1986 LESBIAN/GAY L. NOTES 66 (reporting that for the first time, the ACLU has adopted a formal policy of endorsing gay and lesbian marriage as well as a provision for spousal benefits for gay and lesbian couples); Los Angeles Times, Feb. 22, 1989, § 2, at 3, col. 5 (reporting that West Hollywood, where 35% of residents are homosexual, will insure partners of unmarried city employees, regardless of their sexual orientation). But cf. Bowers v. Hardwick, 478 U.S. 186 (1986) (holding that consensual homosexual sodomy is not a protected privacy right under the Constitution).

and close to constitute a family. In making such a determination, these courts have considered intangible factors such as interdependence[53] and the quality of the relationship.[54] Although preferable to an outright rejection of their claims, this requirement places an unjust burden on gay men and lesbians in long-term relationships because, unlike their unmarried heterosexual counterparts, they do not have the option of automatic protection through marriage.

This section examines the current legal status of same-sex couples. Subsections 1, 2, and 3 respectively demonstrate how the legal system discriminates against gay and lesbian couples in the areas of housing, workers' compensation, and tort law.[55]

1. Housing Law. — Unmarried homosexual and heterosexual couples are subject to substantial discrimination — both overt and covert[56] — in their efforts to acquire housing. This discrimination is

---

[53] *See infra* pp. 108–109.

[54] *See* Two Assocs. v. Brown, 131 Misc. 2d 986, 989, 502 N.Y.S.2d 604, 607 (N.Y. Sup. Ct. 1986), *rev'd on other grounds*, 127 A.D.2d 173, 513 N.Y.S.2d 966 (N.Y. App. Div. 1987).

[55] Cohabitors — homosexual and heterosexual — have been discriminated against in other ways, from the denial of tax, social security, employment, and insurance benefits to the rejection of claims brought under wrongful death statutes. In addition, common-law states do not permit cohabitors to hold property by the entireties, nor do community property states permit them to hold community property. *See* Note, *Marital Status Classifications, supra* note 51, at 115–16.

In the area of liability insurance, cohabitors have difficulty obtaining policies that cover both partners. Policies often state that only a "resident" or "member" of the same "household" or "family" can recover under the insured's policy. *See* Annotation, *Who Is "Resident" or "Member" of Same "Household" or "Family" as Named Insured, Within Liability Insurance Provision Defining Additional Insureds*, 93 A.L.R.3D 420, 424 (1979). Generally, courts have interpreted these contracts narrowly to include only persons related by marriage or blood. *See, e.g.*, Park v. Government Employees Ins. Co., 396 N.W.2d 900 (Minn. Ct. App. 1986) (holding that an adult foster child is not covered by an insurance policy limiting insureds to those related by blood, marriage, or adoption); Eisner v. Aetna Casualty & Sur. Co., 534 N.Y.S.2d 339 (N.Y. Sup. Ct. 1988) (holding that the insured's lifelong companion and roommate of 20 years did not qualify as a "relative" under the terms of a casualty insurance policy); Continental Casualty Co. v. Weaver, 48 Wash. App. 607, 739 P.2d 1192 (Ct. App. 1987) (holding that rental car insurance which covers "immediate family" does not apply to a driver who had established a household with the lessee and held herself out as the spouse of the lessee). When parties are legally married, however, courts are quite willing to accept legal fictions. For example, courts have recognized spouses as residents, even though they might not be living in the same residence. *See, e.g.*, Reserve Ins. Co. v. Apps, 85 Cal. App. 3d 228, 149 Cal. Rptr. 223 (Dist. Ct. App. 1978); Belling v. Harn, 65 Wis. 2d 108, 221 N.W.2d 888 (1974). In the area of no-fault auto insurance, the courts have taken a pragmatic approach, showing a general willingness to examine such factors as dependency and actual residency. *See, e.g.*, Hartman v. Insurance Co. of N. Am., 106 Mich. App. 731, 308 N.W.2d 625 (1981); James v. Allstate Ins. Co., 201 N.J. Super. 299, 493 A.2d 28 (1985).

Similar legal obstacles exist in tort. Wrongful death statutes have been construed narrowly. Although in Moragne v. States Marine Lines Inc., 398 U.S. 375 (1970), the Supreme Court created a common-law wrongful death action, courts nevertheless have been reluctant to expand the tort of wrongful death beyond its statutory terms and have denied unmarried cohabitants the right to bring wrongful death claims. *See, e.g.*, Aspinall v. McDonnell Douglas Corp., 625 F.2d 325, 327 (1980).

[56] It is difficult to judge the extent of housing discrimination. Landlords seeking to exclude

the product of a variety of factors, including exclusionary zoning laws, restrictive statutory provisions, discriminatory landlord practices, and narrow judicial constructions of the meaning of "family."[57]

Many jurisdictions have enacted exclusionary zoning ordinances that restrict the sale and rental of housing to single families. A typical ordinance defines "family" as biologically or legally related persons who are organized under a single head and/or function as a single household.[58] In general, courts upholding such ordinances have been unwilling to extend family status to unmarried heterosexual couples.[59] One court has argued that the ordinances do not violate federally protected rights, because zoning ordinances may exclude "uses that may impair the stability of [the traditional family] environment and erode the values associated with traditional family life," as long as they do not involve invidious discrimination.[60] Similar reasoning could be used to justify denial of family status to same-sex couples under these ordinances.

Rent control and stabilization laws provide another vehicle for statute-based discrimination against unmarried couples.[61] Some stat-

---

same-sex couples may simply claim that they have better offers or that the dwelling already has been sold or rented to another person. *See* Stauffer, *Tenant Blacklisting: Tenant Screening Services and the Right to Privacy*, 24 HARV. J. ON LEGIS. 239, 264 (1987) (noting that discrimination is difficult, if not impossible, to detect unless "the landlord operates a significant number of rental units and consistently discriminates against a group large enough to make the exclusion readily apparent").

[57] The consequences for homosexual couples are particularly dire in cities like New York where the AIDS epidemic has prompted many property owners to wait until the named tenant dies from the disease and then evict the surviving life partner. *See, e.g.*, Aiello v. Hoffer, N.Y.L.J., Apr. 4, 1988, at 13, col. 2 (N.Y. App. Div. June 12, 1987); Yorkshire Towers v. Harpster, 134 Misc. 2d 384, 510 N.Y.S.2d 976 (N.Y. Civ. Ct. 1987), *rev'd*, No. 92706/87 slip op. (N.Y. App. Div. 1988); Washington Village v. Ahearn, No. L&T 69362/87 slip op. (N.Y. Civ. Ct. 1987).

[58] *See* Annotation, *What Constitutes a "Family" Within Meaning of Zoning Regulation or Restrictive Convenant*, 71 A.L.R.3D 693, 699 (1976).

[59] *See, e.g.*, City of Ladue v. Horn, 720 S.W.2d 745 (Mo. Ct. App. 1986) (upholding the constitutionality of a city zoning ordinance that defined "family" as those persons related by blood, marriage, or adoption, and that thereby prevented an unmarried man and woman from occupying their home).

[60] *Id.* at 751 (footnote omitted). *But see* City of White Plains v. Ferraioli, 34 N.Y.2d 300, 313 N.E.2d 756, 357 N.Y.S.2d 449 (1974) (invalidating a restrictive zoning ordinance that went beyond the function of maintaining particular neighborhoods as residential areas and attempted to control "the genetic or intimate internal family relations of human beings").

[61] More than one-third of the housing in the United States is renter-occupied. *See* Stone, *Community, Home, and the Residential Tenant*, 134 U. PA. L. REV. 627, 699 & n.129 (1985) (citing 1980 U.S. Census). In New York City, the unofficial vacancy rate is minus one percent. *See*, Note, *All in the Family: Succession Rights and Rent Stabilized Apartments*, 53 BROOKLYN L. REV. 213, 213 (1987). Because the competition for housing is so great, rental prices have soared, and the supply of affordable housing has shrunk dramatically. As a result, landlords, particularly those owning affordable and rent-controlled units, have sought to evict unnamed tenants upon the death of the named tenant and return their apartments to the open market. *See id.* at 216–17.

utes limit the right of successorship to "tenants."[62] Landlords have attempted to define this term narrowly to protect their right to select the future occupants of their apartment buildings. Renters and tenant groups, on the other hand, have struggled to broaden the right of successorship to include not only immediate family members, but also nonimmediate family members living in the apartments.[63]

In determining successorship rights, courts generally have construed the relevant statutes narrowly. For example, New York City's rent and eviction regulations — promulgated to enforce the city's rent control law[64] — provide that "[n]o occupant of housing accommodations shall be evicted . . . where the occupant is either the surviving spouse of the deceased tenant or some other member of the deceased tenant's family who has been living with the tenant."[65] Some courts have held that this provision does not extend to gay and lesbian life partners.[66] A New York appellate court prohibited a gay life partner from remaining in an apartment pending the outcome of litigation as to whether he qualified as a member of his deceased partner's family. The court explained that "the right of succession to the leasehold property rights of a rent control tenant . . . is governed purely by statute," and concluded that the statute does not protect gay and lesbian life partners because the state legislature has not granted them legal status as families.[67]

The same rigidity is evident in *Two Associates v. Brown*.[68] In that case, a New York appellate court reversed a trial court decision that held that a gay partner qualified as a "nonimmediate" family member under an emergency bulletin issued by the state and was therefore as entitled to a new lease as other "nonimmediate" family members.[69] The trial court had emphasized the seven-year duration

---

[62] *See* Note, *supra* note 61, at 222.

[63] *See id.* at 223–34.

[64] New York City Rent Control Law § 26-401-415, N.Y. UNCONSOL. LAWS § 8617 (McKinney 1987).

[65] New York City Rent and Eviction Regulations § 2204.6(d), N.Y. UNCONSOL. LAWS § 8597 (McKinney 1987).

[66] *See, e.g.*, Braschi v. Stahl Assocs., 531 N.Y.S.2d 562, 562–63 (1988); Koppelman v. O'Keeffe, N.Y.L.J., Sept. 28, 1988, at 17, col. 1 (N.Y. App. Term. July 8, 1987) (sustaining the eviction of a gay life partner, arguing that equal protection is not offended because unmarried heterosexual couples enjoy no tenant succession rights either), *aff'd*, 533 N.Y.S.2d 412 (1988). Several lower courts, however, have implied that the provision protects unmarried homosexual and heterosexual couples. *See, e.g.*, Gelman v. Castaneda, N.Y.L.J., Oct. 22, 1986, at 13, col. 1 (N.Y. Civ. Ct.); Zimmerman v. Burton, 107 Misc. 2d 401, 403, 434 N.Y.S.2d 127, 128–29 (N.Y. Civ. Ct. 1980).

[67] *Braschi*, 531 N.Y.S.2d at 563.

[68] 131 Misc. 2d 986, 502 N.Y.S.2d 604 (N.Y. Sup. Ct. 1986), *rev'd on other grounds*, 127 A.D.2d 173, 513 N.Y.S.2d 966 (N.Y. App. Div. 1987) (granting summary judgment).

[69] *See Brown*, 131 Misc. 2d at 989–90, 502 N.Y.S.2d at 606–07. The emergency bulletin, issued by the State Division of Housing and Community Renewal, defined nonimmediate as including brothers, sisters, nephews and other relatives. *See id.* at 988, 502 N.Y.S.2d at 605.

of the gay relationship and the financial and emotional interdependence of the partners.[70] Given this closeness, the trial court concluded, it would have been arbitrary to grant family-member status to a distant relative but not a gay partner.[71] The appellate court reversed on other grounds.[72]

In addition to statute-based discrimination, gay and lesbian couples face various forms of private discrimination in housing. Landlords are able to impose their personal preferences and biases on the selection of tenants.[73] Increasingly, landlords have hired private tenant-screening services to identify unacceptable applicants.[74] Condominium and homeowner associations also have excluded "unsavory" buyers from their buildings and have exerted extraordinary control over the conduct, lifestyle, and property rights of association members.[75] Finally, lease clauses may provide that only "immediate family members" can share apartments.[76]

There are few constitutional limitations on the ability of landlords and housing associations to exclude tenants. Although in *Shelley v. Kraemer*[77] the Supreme Court held that judicial enforcement of a racially restrictive covenant violated the fourteenth amendment, lower courts have been reluctant to overturn private agreements, particularly those that do not discriminate against an explicitly protected group.[78] In general, tenants or buyers cannot prove sufficient state involvement

---

[70] *See id.* at 988, 502 N.Y.S.2d at 606.

[71] *See id.* at 990, 502 N.Y.S.2d at 607.

[72] *See* Two Assocs. v. Brown, 127 A.D.2d 173, 513 N.Y.S.2d 966 (N.Y. App. Div. 1987) (finding that the emergency rent regulations were not authorized and that the rent statute referred only to "tenants," not to family members).

[73] *See* Stone, *supra* note 61, at 627; Note, *The Rule of Law in Residential Associations*, 99 HARV. L. REV. 472, 473 (1985) [hereinafter Note, *Residential Associations*]; Note, *Why Johnny Can't Rent — An Examination of Laws Prohibiting Discrimination Against Families in Rental Housing*, 94 HARV. L. REV. 1829, 1836–37 (1981) (noting that critics of exclusionary landlord practices often claim that refusal to rent or sell to families with children serves as a "smokescreen" for racial and sexual orientation discrimination). Residential communities also have employed restrictive standards. *See, e.g.*, Village of Belle Terre v. Boraas, 416 U.S. 1 (1974) (restricting residence in single households in a village to persons related by blood, adoption, or marriage).

[74] *See generally* Stauffer, *supra* note 56 (exploring the propriety of tenant screening services and analyzing possible responses). Tenant screening services — organized in many states with large metropolitan areas, including California, Colorado, Nebraska, New Jersey, New York, Rhode Island, Texas, and Washington, D.C. — collect information on a prospective tenant's financial background and involvement in legal disputes. They also collect more vague and open-ended information about a tenant's "lifestyle." *See id.* at 240–43.

[75] *See, e.g.*, Note, *Residential Associations*, *supra* note 73, at 473–78.

[76] *See, e.g.*, Evangelista Assocs. v. Bland, 117 Misc. 2d 558, 558, 458 N.Y.S.2d 996, 997 (N.Y. Civ. Ct. 1983).

[77] 334 U.S. 1 (1948).

[78] *See, e.g.*, Ginsberg v. Yeshiva of Far Rockaway, 45 A.D.2d 334, 358 N.Y.S.2d 477 (1974) (upholding the use of a restrictive covenant to prevent the operation of a religious school and restricting *Shelley v. Kraemer* to covenants that on their face discriminate on the basis of race).

in discriminatory housing arrangements to satisfy the "state action" doctrine.

Most anti-discrimination laws do not prohibit discrimination on the basis of sexual orientation and thus provide little direct protection against the efforts of landlords to exclude same-sex couples.[79] In *Evangelista Associates v. Bland*,[80] for example, a New York court held that because the applicable law[81] did not include a prohibition on sexual orientation discrimination, the landlord was free to exclude gay couples from his building on the basis of the "immediate family" restriction in the lease.[82] State disability discrimination laws, however, might indirectly protect some same-sex couples. A New Jersey superior court held that a landlord violated the state's disability discrimination law when he refused to rent to three healthy gay men for fear of contracting AIDS.[83] Citing the Supreme Court's decision in *School Board of Nassau County, Florida v. Arline*,[84] the New Jersey court held that those persons irrationally perceived as presenting an AIDS threat come within the protective scope of handicap discrimination principles.[85] Similarly, courts might find that a landlord who refuses to rent to a gay couple out of fear of contracting AIDS violates such disability discrimination principles.

In addition, statutes barring housing discrimination based on marital status promise only limited protection to gay and lesbian couples. In *Hudson View Properties v. Weiss*,[86] for example, a New York civil court held that a landlord's refusal to sell or rent to an unmarried heterosexual couple constituted unlawful discrimination on the basis of marital status in violation of the state's human rights statute.[87]

---

[79] *See, e.g.*, The Fair Housing Act, Pub. L. No. 90-284, 82 Stat. 83 (1968) (codified as amended at 42 U.S.C. § 3604 (1982)) (prohibiting refusal to rent or sell housing units on the basis of the customer's race, color, religion, sex, or national origin, but *not* on the basis of sexual orientation). Wisconsin, on the other hand, expressly prohibits sexual orientation discrimination. *See* WIS. STAT. ANN. §§ 111.32, .321, .322, .36(1)(d) (West 1987 & Supp. 1988). California courts have held that the state's Unruh Civil Rights Act, CAL. CIV. CODE § 51 (West 1976), protects gay men and lesbians from arbitrary discrimination in rental housing. *See, e.g.*, Hubert v. Williams, 133 Cal. App. 3d Supp. 1, 184 Cal. Rptr. 161 (1982).

[80] 117 Misc. 2d 558, 458 N.Y.S.2d 996 (N.Y. Civ. Ct. 1983).

[81] N.Y. EXEC. LAW § 296(5)(a) (McKinney 1982 & Supp. 1989).

[82] *See* 117 Misc. 2d at 562-63, 458 N.Y.S.2d at 999.

[83] *See* Poff v. Caro, 228 N.J. Super. 370, 549 A.2d 900 (Law Div. 1987).

[84] 480 U.S. 273 (1987). The Court in *Arline* held that the federal prohibition on discrimination against handicapped persons in federally funded programs forbids discrimination motivated by irrational fear of contagion against otherwise qualified persons with tuberculosis. *See id.* at 284-86.

[85] *See* 228 N.J. Super. at 373, 549 A.2d at 903.

[86] 106 Misc. 2d 251, 431 N.Y.S.2d 632 (N.Y. Civ. Ct. 1980), *rev'd*, 109 Misc. 2d 589, 442 N.Y.S.2d 367 (App. Term 1981), *rev'd*, 86 App. Div. 2d 803, 448 N.Y.S.2d 649 (1982), *rev'd*, 59 N.Y.2d 733, 450 N.E.2d 234, 463 N.Y.S.2d 428 (1983).

[87] *See Weiss*, 106 Misc. 2d at 256-57, 431 N.Y.S.2d at 637.

The lower court explained that the very existence of a clause outlawing discrimination on the basis of marital status "is consistent with both evolving notions of morality and the realities of contemporary urban society, where couples openly live in heterosexual *and homosexual* units without sanction of state or clergy."[88] The New York Court of Appeals reversed,[89] however, emphasizing that the tenant had violated the lease by allowing a person not a tenant and not a part of her immediate family to occupy the apartment.[90] Expressly refusing to examine the character of the unmarried couple's relationship, the court in *Weiss* concluded that the couple did not qualify as a "family" under the terms of the lease.[91]

Yet, despite the apparent unwillingness of courts to extend protection to nontraditional families — whether heterosexual or homosexual — on the basis of marital-status discrimination laws, recent decisions interpreting such laws as prohibiting housing denials to roommates of the same sex might nevertheless provide some protection to gay and lesbian couples.[92] Because gays cannot marry, the law arguably treats them as single individuals. Thus, in seeking protection under a marital status provision, same-sex couples might emphasize not their similarity to married heterosexual couples but rather their identity as single roommates. Although there are no reported cases in which same-sex couples have used the marital status provision to argue that as same-sex roommates they deserved protection, such an argument might prove effective in the future.

Similarly, same-sex couples might be able to protect their housing needs by shifting the legal debate away from the nature of their relationships to the exigencies of the housing market. In *420 East*

---

[88] *Id.* (emphasis added).

[89] *See* Hudson View Properties v. Weiss, 59 N.Y.2d 733, 450 N.E.2d 234, 463 N.Y.S.2d 428 (1983).

[90] *See id.* at 734, 450 N.E.2d at 235, 463 N.Y.S.2d at 429.

[91] Courts facing this issue in other jurisdictions also have been reluctant to hold landlords in violation of statutes barring discrimination on the basis of marital status. *See, e.g.*, Maryland Comm'n on Human Relations v. Greenbelt Homes, Inc., 300 Md. 75, 475 A.2d 1192 (1984) (holding that an association rule allowing only "family members" to live together did not violate a state statute prohibiting discrimination on the basis of marital status); Prince George's County v. Greenbelt Homes, Inc., 49 Md. App. 314, 431 A.2d 745 (1981) (holding that a cooperative housing development could lawfully deny housing to an unmarried couple, because common-law marriages were not recognized in Maryland). *But see* Hess v. Fair Employment & Housing Comm'n, 138 Cal. App. 3d 232, 187 Cal. Rptr. 712 (1982) (holding that landlords had unlawfully discriminated against unmarried couples on the basis of marital status); Loveland v. Leslie, 21 Wash. App. 84, 583 P.2d 664 (1978) (holding that a landlord's practice of renting apartments only to married couples was unlawful, because the state's anti-discrimination statute prohibited discrimination based solely on the absence or existence of a marital relationship).

[92] *See, e.g.*, Loveland v. Leslie, 21 Wash. App. 84, 583 P.2d 664 (1978) (holding that an owner's refusal to rent to a single man and his male roommate constituted unlawful discrimination on the basis of marital status).

80th Co. v. Chin,[93] for example, a lower New York court held that a tenant's gay partner could not be evicted under a clause limiting tenancy to family members. The court avoided deciding whether the partner constituted an immediate family member under the lease and, instead, based its decision on the housing crisis in New York, which caused people outside of the nuclear family to share apartments.[94]

2. *Workers' Compensation.* — Workers' compensation schemes provide benefits for "dependents" of covered employees.[95] Program regulations define with particularity the classes of persons entitled to receive compensation as dependents.[96] In addition, many statutes include a more general definition of dependency for persons not included in the enumerated categories. Such statutes define "dependents" to include members of the employee's "family or household,"[97] "next of kin,"[98] and "legal beneficiaries."[99]

Courts have differed in their interpretations of these statutes. Some courts have held that a family member is any person living in the same home under a single head;[100] others have included relatives by descent, without regard to residence.[101] Generally, however, courts have not recognized the right of a cohabitant to receive workers' compensation benefits unless he or she is the employee's legal spouse.[102] As explained above, such nonrecognition works an invidious discrimination against gay and lesbian couples.

---

[93] 115 Misc. 2d 195, 455 N.Y.S.2d 42 (App. Term. 1982), *aff'd*, 97 A.D.2d 390, 468 N.Y.S.2d 9 (1984).

[94] *See id.* at 196, 455 N.Y.S.2d at 43–44.

[95] *See* 81 AM. JUR. 2D *Workmen's Compensation* § 186 (1976).

[96] *See id.* § 198. The California workers' compensation statute, for example, reads as follows:

No person is a dependent of any deceased employee unless in good faith a member of the family or household of the employee, or unless the person bears to the employee the relation of husband or wife, child, posthumous child, adopted child or stepchild, *grandchild*, father or mother, father-in-law or mother-in-law, grandfather or grandmother, brother or sister, uncle or aunt, brother-in-law or sister-in-law, nephew or niece.

CAL. LAB. CODE § 3503 (West Supp. 1989) (emphasis in original).

[97] *See, e.g.*, CAL. LAB. CODE § 3503 (West Supp. 1989).

[98] *See, e.g.*, CONN. GEN. STAT. § 31-275 (1987).

[99] *See, e.g.*, TEX. CODE ANN. art. 8306, § 8 (Vernon 1967 & Supp. 1989).

[100] *See, e.g.*, Peterson's Case, 270 Mass. 309, 312, 169 N.E. 779, 780 (1930) (holding that a claimant who lived in the same household but was unrelated to a deceased employee was nevertheless a member of the deceased's family).

[101] *See, e.g.*, Passini v. Aberthaw Constr. Co., 97 Conn. 110, 112–13, 115 A. 689, 690 (1921) (finding that the sister of a deceased employee was a member of the decedent's family, even though she resided in New York City and the decedent resided in Connecticut).

[102] These courts have emphasized that unmarried cohabitation is illegal. *See, e.g.*, Moore v. Capitol Glass & Supply Co., 25 So. 2d 248 (La. Ct. App. 1946), Crenshaw v. Industrial Comm'n, 712 P.2d 247 (Utah 1985). Recent decisions, however, suggest a trend toward allowing recovery for heterosexual couples, particularly for those that hold themselves out to the community as legally married. *See, e.g.*, Department of Indus. Relations v. Workers' Compensation Appeals Bd., 94 Cal. App. 3d 72, 156 Cal. Rptr. 183 (1979); West v. Barton-Malow Co., 394 Mich. 334, 230 N.W.2d 545 (1975).

Only one workers' compensation board has recognized the claim of an insured employee's gay partner. In *Donovan v. County of Los Angeles and State Compensation Insurance Fund*,[103] the California Workers' Compensation Appeals Board (WCAB) held that a deceased county employee's same-sex partner of twenty-seven years was a "good faith member" of the employee's household and was, therefore, entitled to receive workers' compensation benefits.[104] To the WCAB, the absence of a marriage license was not in itself determinative of "good faith membership" in a household.[105] In reaching its conclusion, the WCAB relied on *Marvin v. Marvin*,[106] which held that cohabitation agreements between unmarried couples are enforceable so long as the consideration does not rest on sexual services.[107] The board also cited *Department of Industrial Relations, Division of Industrial Accidents v. Workers' Compensation Appeals Board*,[108] for the proposition that a person's unmarried status does not automatically bar him or her from receiving workers' compensation.[109] The WCAB acknowledged society's interest in encouraging traditional marriage, but concluded that this interest was outweighed by the gay partner's property interests.[110]

Courts in jurisdictions that criminalize cohabitation or homosexual sodomy should not be hindered from applying the *Donovan* standard.[111] Morality-based limitations on recovery shift burdens of workplace injuries from employers to survivors and, therefore, run counter to the twin rationales underlying workers' compensation schemes — compensation and deterrence.[112] In deciding issues of dependency, therefore, courts should recognize the claims of same-sex partners irrespective of state criminal law.

---

[103] 73 LA 385-107 (Cal. Workers' Comp. Appeals Bd., Opinion and Notice of Intention, Nov. 3, 1983).

[104] *See id.* at 9.

[105] *See Donovan*, 73 LA 385-107, 3 (Cal. Workers' Comp. Appeals Bd., Opinion and Order Denying Reconsideration, Jan. 24, 1984).

[106] 18 Cal. 3d 660, 557 P.2d 106, 134 Cal. Rptr. 815 (1976).

[107] *See id.* at 672, 557 P.2d at 114, 134 Cal. Rptr. at 823; *Donovan*, 73 LA 385-107, 3 (Cal. Workers' Comp. Appeals Bd., Opinion and Notice of Intention, Nov. 3, 1983).

[108] 94 Cal. App. 3d 72, 156 Cal. Rptr. 183 (1979).

[109] *See Donovan*, 73 LA 385-107, 3 (Cal. Workers' Comp. Appeals Bd., Opinion and Notice of Intention, Nov. 3, 1983).

[110] *See Donovan*, 73 LA 385-107, 3 (Cal. Workers' Comp. Appeals Bd., Opinion and Order Denying Reconsideration, Jan. 24, 1984).

[111] Although in relying on *Department of Industrial Relations* the *Donovan* board implied that the lack of criminality of cohabitation was an important factor in its decision, that factor was not dispositive. Moreover, in states that criminalize sodomy, courts can apply the *Donovan* precedent because dependent same-sex relationships are possible without sodomy.

[112] *See* Note, Donovan v. County of Los Angeles and State Compensation Insurance Fund: *California's Recognition of Homosexuals' Dependency Status in Actions for Worker's Compensation Death Benefits*, 12 J. CONTEMP. L. 151, 159–60 (1986).

3. Tort Claims. — The legal system generally has been reluctant to recognize and compensate emotional injury.[113] Where the defendant's negligence has caused only mental disturbance, the overwhelming majority of courts deny recovery.[114] Some courts have allowed recovery, however, for certain forms of mental distress.[115] In several instances, in fact, courts have imposed liability where the defendant's conduct, although directed at a third party, has caused emotional injury to the plaintiff.[116] Ordinarily, recovery in such cases has been limited to plaintiffs who were known by the defendant to have been present at the accident so that the mental harm could reasonably have been foreseen.[117] Although nearly all of the cases allowing recovery have involved members of the victim's immediate family, the holdings of the cases could equally apply to persons beyond the immediate family.[118]

In some jurisdictions, a third-party plaintiff who has a "sufficiently close" relationship with the direct victim of negligence may recover damages for negligent infliction of emotional harm[119] or loss of consortium.[120] Although unmarried heterosexual partners have occasionally succeeded in such actions,[121] no court has recognized the cause

---

[113] *See* W. KEETON, D. DOBBS, R. KEETON & D. OWEN, PROSSER AND KEETON ON THE LAW OF TORTS § 54, at 359–60 (5th ed. 1984) [hereinafter PROSSER & KEETON]. A number of objections to allowing recovery have been made: "that mental disturbance cannot be measured in monetary terms . . . ; that its physical consequences are too remote, and so not 'proximately caused'; that there is a lack of precedent, and that a vast increase in litigation would follow." *Id.* at 360.

[114] *See id.* at 361.

[115] *See id.* § 12, at 64. "[T]he law appears to be moving in the direction of liability [for emotional harm] but thus far recovery is clearly limited to the more extreme cases of violent attack, where there is some special likelihood of fright or shock." *Id.* at 66.

[116] *See, e.g.,* Keck v. Jackson, 122 Ariz. 114, 593 P.2d 668 (1979); Dillon v. Legg, 68 Cal.2d 728, 441 P.2d 912, 69 Cal. Rptr. 72 (1968); Stadler v. Cross, 295 N.W.2d 552 (Minn. 1980).

[117] *See, e.g.,* Koontz v. Keller, 52 Ohio App. 265, 3 N.E.2d 694 (1936) (denying recovery where the plaintiff suffered mental and physical distress upon discovering the body of her murdered sister); *see also* PROSSER & KEETON, *supra* note 113, § 12, at 65 & n.5 (citing Magruder, *Mental and Emotional Disturbance in the Law of Torts*, 49 HARV. L. REV. 1033, 1044 (1936)).

[118] *See* PROSSER & KEETON, *supra* note 113, § 12, at 66.

[119] *See, e.g.,* Krouse v. Graham, 19 Cal. 3d 59, 562 P.2d 1022, 137 Cal. Rptr. 863 (1977) (allowing recovery by the victim's husband who was present when she was struck and killed by an automobile); Dillon v. Legg, 68 Cal. 2d 728, 441 P.2d 912, 69 Cal. Rptr. 72 (1968) (allowing recovery by a mother who witnessed the fatal injury of her child); Rickey v. Chicago Transit Auth., 101 Ill. App. 3d 439, 428 N.E.2d 596 (1981) (same); Walker v. Clark Equip. Co., 320 N.W.2d 561 (Iowa 1982) (sibling); Genzer v. City of Mission, 666 S.W.2d 116 (Tex. Ct. App. 1983) (grandparents).

[120] Modern courts have defined loss of consortium to include loss of sexual relations, society, and affection. *See, e.g.,* Wood v. Mobil Chemical Co., 50 Ill. App. 3d 465, 365 N.E.2d 1087 (1977); Whittlesey v. Miller, 572 S.W.2d 665 (Tex. 1978).

[121] *See, e.g.,* Bulloch v. United States, 487 F. Supp. 1078, 1088 (D.N.J. 1980) (holding that

of action of a gay or lesbian partner for either tort.[122] Indeed, even in California, where most of the major case law on these issues has originated, courts have rejected the claims both of heterosexuals and of homosexuals. In *Elden v. Sheldon*,[123] for example, the California Supreme Court held that an unmarried heterosexual partner could not collect damages for negligent infliction of emotional distress or loss of consortium. Although the court in *Elden* recognized that the number of couples who live together without formal marriage has increased dramatically, that some of these couples are bound by emotional ties as strong as those that bind married partners, and that such couples may share financial resources and expenses in the same manner as married couples,[124] the court nevertheless dismissed the plaintiff's cause of action. The court based its decision on three grounds: the inability of courts to determine case-by-case which relationships qualify for the causes of action; the need to establish clear lines for recovery so as not to unreasonably burden human activity; and the state's interest in promoting traditional marriage.[125]

The argument that the judiciary is incompetent to identify which relationships are "sufficiently close" to qualify for these tort actions is unpersuasive. Tort law constantly requires courts to define and interpret standards and to draw lines between those who are entitled to compensation and those who are not. Furthermore, standards already exist in the common law that separate tangential from family-like relations.[126]

Nor would extending the tort actions to unmarried gay or non-gay couples expose defendants to unlimited liability. Not only must the plaintiff make an initial showing that the defendant owed him or her a duty of due care, but also, under *Dillon v. Legg*,[127] the plaintiff

---

proof of legal marriage is not an essential element of a loss of consortium claim); Ledger v. Tippit, 164 Cal. App. 3d 625, 210 Cal. Rptr. 814 (1985) (allowing recovery under the "close relationship" standard for a woman who watched her illegitimate child's father being stabbed to death).

[122] *See, e.g.*, Coon v. Joseph, 192 Cal. App. 3d 1269, 237 Cal. Rptr. 873 (1987) (holding that an intimate homosexual relationship does not fall within the "close relationship" standard for negligent infliction of emotional distress).

[123] 46 Cal. 3d 267, 758 P.2d 582, 250 Cal. Rptr. 254, *modified*, 46 Cal. 3d 1003a (1988).

[124] 758 P.2d at 585–86, 250 Cal. Rptr. at 257–58.

[125] 758 P.2d 586–88, 250 Cal. Rptr. at 258–60.

[126] Where claims of the existence of a common-law marriage have been made, courts have looked closely at the quality of the relationships to determine whether to grant cohabitors legal status. They have considered such factors as the couple's living arrangement, the public perception of the relationship, and the permanence and exclusivity of the relationship. *See, e.g.*, Chivers v. Couch Motor Lines, Inc., 159 So. 2d 544, 549–50 (La. 1964); Daniels v. Mohon, 350 P.2d 932, 935 (Okla. 1960); Marshall v. State, 537 P.2d 423, 429 (Okla. Crim. 1975); Estate of Claveria v. Claveria, 615 S.W.2d 164, 166 (Tex. 1981).

[127] 68 Cal. 2d 728, 441 P.2d 912, 69 Cal. Rptr. 72 (1968).

must prove that his or her relationship was sufficiently close to warrant recovery.[128] A partner who could not demonstrate a reasonably lengthy involvement or financial interdependence with the injured party would be ineligible for damages. Thus, tort law's traditional doctrines would guard against unlimited liability of defendants.

Although the state may have an interest in promoting traditional marriage, denying gay and lesbian partners the right to recover damages for emotional harm and loss of consortium does not further that end. As the dissent in *Elden* recognized, "the state's interest in marriage is not advanced by precluding recovery to couples who could not in any case choose marriage."[129] Thus, courts would not undermine the state's interest in promoting traditional marriage by granting gay and lesbian partners recovery for serious emotional harm caused by tortfeasors.

For several additional reasons, courts should grant unmarried homosexual and heterosexual partners recovery for negligent infliction of emotional harm and loss of consortium. First, courts should not presume that the suffering of an unmarried cohabitant who loses a partner is less real or direct than that of a legal spouse. Second, emotional harms are no longer tied to the loss of spousal services but are recognized as legitimate, compensable harms in and of themselves.[130] Thus, the landmark California cases concerning emotional distress, *Dillon v. Legg* and *Molien v. Kaiser Foundation Hospitals*,[131] construe the cause of action for negligent infliction of emotional distress broadly and grant recovery to persons who are "closely related" to the actual victim.[132]

Moreover, recognition of these causes of action is consistent with the deterrence policy underlying tort law. Given the increase in unmarried cohabitation, a tortfeasor is increasingly likely to injure an unmarried cohabitor — heterosexual or homosexual. By making clear that no tortfeasor will be free from extended liability merely because he or she harmed an unmarried, rather than a married, person, courts would encourage potential tortfeasors to increase their level of care. Assume, for example, that a doctor negligently treats an AIDS patient who has a strong, committed gay relationship. Courts should hold

---

[128] *See Dillon*, 68 Cal. 2d at 741, 441 P.2d at 920, 69 Cal. Rptr. at 80.

[129] *Elden*, 758 P.2d 582, 592 n.2, 250 Cal. Rptr. 254, 264 n.2 (1988) (Broussard, J., dissenting).

[130] *See* Butcher v. Superior Court, 139 Cal. App. 3d 58, 60, 188 Cal. Rptr. 503, 505 (1983).

[131] 27 Cal. 3d 916, 616 P.2d 813, 167 Cal. Rptr. 831 (1980).

[132] *See Molien*, 27 Cal. 3d at 923, 616 P.2d at 816–17, 167 Cal. Rptr. at 835 (finding that the defendant owed the plaintiff a duty of care under *Dillon* and implying that the plaintiff's married status provided prima facie evidence that the plaintiff and victim shared a close relationship); *Dillon*, 68 Cal. 2d at 741, 441 P.2d at 921, 69 Cal. Rptr. at 81 (stating that a defendant would be more likely to foresee that a child's mother, as opposed to a stranger, would be traumatized by witnessing an accident that seriously harms the child).

that doctor liable for any serious emotional harm suffered by the life partner of the patient. In such a case, the emotional harm to the partner is clearly foreseeable.[133]

C. Responses to Current Law

Same-sex couples have employed a number of legal mechanisms to circumvent the barriers posed by state laws.[134] These mechanisms include property ownership, beneficiary designations, powers of attorney,[135] "durable" powers of attorney,[136] reciprocal wills,[137]

---

[133] Of course, this argument only applies in the limited case where the potential tortfeasor knows or has reason to know about the relationship.

[134] Gay and lesbian couples who take the necessary precautions to protect their property arrangements might nevertheless be unable to exercise the same degree of control over their property as similarly situated non-gay couples. There are very few reported cases concerning gay and lesbian couples' rights to property. Thus, gay men and lesbians have few legal precedents on which to rely in court. In addition, at least one commentator has cited evidence suggesting that third parties are more likely to succeed in challenging their wills and trusts than those of similarly situated heterosexual couples. *See* Sherman, *Undue Influence and the Homosexual Testator*, 42 U. PITT. L. REV. 225, 227, 267 (1981). One such challenge might be that the partner unduly influenced the gay or lesbian testator to name him or her as sole beneficiary in a will. For a discussion of the general nature of "undue influence," see 1 PAGE ON THE LAW OF WILLS § 15.1, at 711–12 (W. Bowe & D. Parker rev. ed. 1960).

[135] A "power of attorney" is a written instrument by which one person, as principal, appoints another his or her agent. In effect, a power of attorney confers upon the agent authority to perform specified acts or kinds of acts on the principal's behalf. *See* King v. Bankerd, 303 Md. 98, 105, 492 A.2d 608, 611 (analyzing the concept of "power of attorney").

[136] Only some states have durable power of attorney statutes. *See* SEXUAL ORIENTATION AND THE LAW § 4.07[2], at 4-23 (R. Achtenberg ed. 1987). A durable power of attorney is "a power of attorney designed to become effective upon the incapacity of the principal." *Id.* Typically, a durable power of attorney statute calls for the agent's authority to continue beyond the principal's incapacity for a pre-determined period of time and may begin immediately or upon the principal's incapacitation. *See, e.g.*, CAL. CIV. CODE § 2436.5, tit. 9, art. 3 (West Supp. 1989); MINN. STAT. § 523.08 (West Supp. 1989). For gay and lesbian couples, the crucial question with regard to this method for securing property and personal interests is whether the authority given the agent encompasses the power to make personal decisions, such as medical decisions, on behalf of the incapacitated principal. Only California has expressly addressed this issue by passing the Durable Power of Attorney for Health Care Act. CAL. CIV. CODE § 2430, tit. 9, art. 5 (West Supp. 1989). By virtue of this act, gay and lesbian residents of California might well be able to make personal decisions on behalf of their incapacitated partners.

The importance of the durable power of attorney mechanism for securing personal interests was highlighted by a recent decision by a Minnesota court of appeals. The court granted plenary rights of legal guardianship to the natural father of a mentally and physically incapacitated adult woman over the woman's lesbian partner of four years. *See In re* Guardianship of Kowalski, 382 N.W.2d 861 (Minn. Ct. App. 1986). The court emphasized both the inability of the incapacitated ward to express with consistency her own wishes and the depression suffered by the ward following her partner's hospital visits. *See id.* at 866–67. Had the ward executed a durable power of attorney prior to her accident, the court might well have recognized her partner's right to legal guardianship.

[137] In reciprocal wills, the partners assign their property to each other. Generally, courts have upheld the wills. Often, however, relatives have successfully sought to invalidate these

trusts,[138] life insurance,[139] contracts, and adoption. This section discusses the effectiveness of contract and adoption as mechanisms for securing the shared personal and property interests of gay and lesbian couples.

1. Contract. — Modern courts have shown a willingness to enforce explicit or implied agreements between unmarried heterosexual cohabitants defining the terms of their relationship, so long as the consideration for the contract is severable from the sexual aspect of the relationship.[140] In the seminal case of *Marvin v. Marvin*,[141] the

---

wills on grounds of undue influence. *See generally* Sherman, *supra* note 134 (arguing that wills and trusts executed by gay and lesbian testators bequeathing property to their life partners are more likely than those of heterosexual testators to be challenged successfully by relatives of the testator on grounds of undue influence). Thus, to help ensure protection, same-sex couples should include "no-contest" clauses in their reciprocal wills. A no-contest clause is "a testamentary provision purporting to preclude any legatee or devisee who contests [a] will from receiving any legacy or devise thereunder." *Id.* at 248. Although a no-contest clause might deter relatives from contesting the will, it is not foolproof; heirs might nonetheless bring challenges. As a result, in order to discourage an heir from contesting a will, a gay or lesbian legator might have to bequeath to him or her a substantial piece of property. Even if the heir agrees not to contest the will, however, there is nothing to prevent him or her from doing so in the future, especially if the heir believes that he or she would have little to lose and much to gain. *See id.* at 248–49. Nevertheless, "no-contest" clauses might effectively deter some people from bringing frivolous claims.

[138] "A trust is a fiduciary relationship in which one person is the holder of the title to property subject to an equitable obligation to keep or use the property for the benefit of another." G. BOGERT, TRUSTS 1 (6th ed. 1987).

[139] *See* Sherman, *supra* note 134, at 262.

[140] *See, e.g.*, Mason v. Rostad, 476 A.2d 662 (D.C. 1984) (upholding contracts to share property acquired by unmarried couples during cohabitation); Glasgo v. Glasgo, 410 N.E.2d 1325 (Ind. Ct. App. 1980) (same); Heistand v. Heistand, 384 Mass. 20, 423 N.E.2d 313 (1981) (same); *In re* Eriksen, 337 N.W.2d 671 (Minn. 1983) (same); Brooks v. Kunz, 637 S.W.2d 135 (Mo. Ct. App. 1982) (same); *In re* Estate of Steffes, 95 Wis. 2d 490, 290 N.W.2d 697 (1980) (same); *cf.* Levar v. Elkins, 604 P.2d 602 (Alaska 1980) (recognizing express, but not implied, agreements between unmarried cohabitors); Dominguez v. Cruz, 95 N.M. 1, 617 P.2d 1322 (N. M. Ct. App. 1980) (same); Morone v. Morone, 50 N.Y.2d 481, 413 N.E.2d 1154, 429 N.Y.S.2d 592 (1980) (same). Only three states have refused to enforce express agreements on public policy grounds. *See* Rehak v. Mathis, 239 Ga. 541, 238 S.E.2d 81 (1977); Hewitt v. Hewitt, 77 Ill. 2d 49, 394 N.E.2d 1204 (1979); Roach v. Buttons, 6 Fam. L. Rep. (BNA) 2355 (Tenn. Ch. Ct. Feb. 19, 1980).

The rationale underlying the severability requirement is that agreements in which parties offer sexual services as payment constitute bargains for prostitution. *See* Whorton v. Dillingham, 248 Cal. Rptr. 405, 407 (Ct. App. 1988).

Although most of the cases on point have dealt with property rights in the context of a relationship that has ended, the same principles apply to inheritance rights. *See, e.g., In re* Estate of Eriksen, 337 N.W.2d 671 (Minn. 1983) (granting a portion of a deceased partner's property to the survivor by a constructive trust, even though the couple was not married); *In re* Estate of Thornton, 81 Wash. 2d 72, 499 P.2d 864 (1972) (granting the survivor a portion of the deceased partner's property, under a theory of implied partnership). Some state statutes recognize express written contracts between unmarried heterosexual cohabitants. *See, e.g.*, MINN. STAT. ANN. § 513.075 (West Supp. 1989).

[141] 18 Cal. 3d 660, 557 P.2d 106, 134 Cal. Rptr. 815 (1976).

California Supreme Court upheld one such agreement. The court recognized that unmarried heterosexual cohabitation is common and accepted in modern society.[142] Further, the court in *Marvin* understood that, unlike married partners whose obligations are specified by law, unmarried partners must create and delineate their mutual obligations in accordance with the needs of their relationship.

While courts in numerous jurisdictions have followed *Marvin*, only one court has extended *Marvin* to protect the cohabitation agreement of a same-sex couple. In *Whorton v. Dillingham*,[143] a California appellate court upheld an oral agreement made by a gay couple, finding that the portion of the agreement that called for one of the parties to provide the other with sexual services was severable from the rest of the contract.[144] The *Whorton* court recognized that agreements between unmarried same-sex partners are often indistinguishable from those between unmarried heterosexual partners.

The *Whorton* holding is consistent with other court rulings. First, courts have begun to recognize that gay and lesbian relationships are not per se illicit.[145] Second, as the Louisiana appeals court held in *Succession of Bacot*,[146] the concept of concubinage — "an open, illicit

---

[142] *See id.* at 683, 557 P.2d at 123, 134 Cal. Rptr. at 831; *cf.* Taylor v. Fields, 178 Cal. App. 3d 653, 224 Cal. Rptr. 186 (1986) (holding that a relationship between a married man and his mistress is not governed by *Marvin*'s holding). Prior to *Marvin*, courts universally held that private contracts between unmarried cohabitants — presumably even those in which sexual services placed no part whatsoever — were unenforceable as against public policy. *See* E. FARNSWORTH, CONTRACTS § 5.4, at 345–46 (1982). *See generally* H. KRAUSE, FAMILY LAW 128–33 (2d ed. 1983) (probing issues raised by *Marvin*).

One commentator has stated that "*Marvin*'s importance lies in the court's willingness to use quasi-contractual theories to create an agreement from the context of the relationship." Hunter, *An Essay on Contract and Status: Race, Marriage, and the Meretricious Spouse*, 64 VA. L. REV. 1039, 1085 (1978). *Marvin* allows recovery, when appropriate, under theories of implied contract, quantum meruit, implied partnership, and constructive trust. *See Marvin*, 18 Cal. 3d at 684, 557 P.2d at 122–23, 134 Cal. Rptr. at 831–32. Additional theories courts might use to allow recovery include joint ownership, resulting trust, and partnership. *See* Annotation, *Property Rights Arising from Relationship of Couple Cohabiting Without Marriage*, 3 A.L.R. 4TH 13, §§ 3, 4, 9 (1981).

[143] 248 Cal. Rptr. 405 (Ct. App. 1988).

[144] *See id.* at 410. Prior to *Whorton*, the only decision to address the issue was Jones v. Daly, 122 Cal. App. 3d 500, 176 Cal. Rptr. 130 (1981), which refused to enforce an agreement between a same-sex couple because the language in the complaint stated that the plaintiff had agreed to "render his services . . . as a *lover*" and, thus, strongly indicated that the provision of sexual services "was an inseparable part of the consideration for the 'cohabitors agreement,' and indeed was the predominant consideration." *Id.* at 508, 176 Cal. Rptr. at 133 (emphasis in original).

[145] *See, e.g.*, Bramlett v. Selman, 268 Ark. 457, 465, 597 S.W.2d 80, 85 (1980) (finding a constructive trust in a homosexual relationship and declaring that "a court of equity should not deny relief to a person merely because he is a homosexual"); Weekes v. Gay, 243 Ga. 784, 787, 256 S.E.2d 901, 904 (1979) (rejecting an heir's argument that the decedent's lover should be denied relief because of the "nature" of the relationship, but only because "the evidence was inconclusive as to the exact nature of the relationship").

[146] 502 So. 2d 1118 (La. App. 1987).

sexual relationship approximating marriage"[147] — should apply only to male/female relationships, that is, relationships in which the parties are capable of contracting marriage. "Homosexuals living together, no matter what the duration, can never marry, and therefore such individuals can never be concubines to one another."[148] Thus, it would be consistent for courts following rulings such as that in *Bacot* to extend *Marvin*'s protections to same-sex couples.

2. *Adult Adoption*. — Currently, every state recognizes the inheritance rights of an adopted child of an unmarried intestate decedent over those of the decedent's nonimmediate blood relatives.[149] For this reason, gay men and lesbians have sought to adopt their partners in order to leave property to them. More traditional property assignment devices such as wills or trusts have been challenged successfully in court by blood relatives who claim that the decedent's gay or lesbian partner exercised undue influence over the decedent.[150] Adoption, which becomes final at the moment of execution, provides a more secure mechanism for the assignment of property.[151]

The availability of adult adoption varies from state to state. Some jurisdictions prohibit adult adoption altogether;[152] other jurisdictions

---

[147] *Id.* at 1129.

[148] *Id.* at 1130.

[149] *See* Sherman, *supra* note 134, at 253 (suggesting adoption as an estate planning device for gay and lesbian testators).

[150] *See id.* at 232–48 (discussing four such challenges).

[151] There are, however, several disadvantages to adult adoption. First, unless the adopter can prove undue influence, fraud, or some other special circumstance — such as feeblemindedness, epilepsy, or venereal disease — the adoption is final, as are the attendant property assignments. *See* Pierce v. Pierce, 522 S.W.2d 435, 436 (Ky. 1975); Stevens v. Halstead, 181 A.D. 198, 200, 168 N.Y.S. 142, 143 (1917); *see also In re* Adoption of a Minor, 350 Mass. 302, 214 N.E.2d 281 (1966) (refusing to reverse an adoption despite procedural errors because the errors were due to the parents' own carelessness); *In re* Adoption of L., 56 N.J. Super. 46, 50, 151 A.2d 435, 437 (Essex County Ct. 1959) (noting that the paramount consideration in annulment is the best interests of the child). Consequently, no equivalent to a divorce is available if the parties wish to end their relationship. Secondly, some state statutes prevent an adopted child from inheriting from his or her natural parents. *See, e.g.,* IDAHO CODE § 16-1509 (1979) (stating that an adoptee may not continue to inherit from his or her natural parents, unless the adoption decree so provides or the natural parents provide by will); WASH. REV. CODE ANN. § 11.04.085 (West 1987) (same). Finally, however remote the possibility, adopting one's partner might leave one vulnerable to incest charges. *But see* People v. Baker, 69 Cal. 2d 44, 50, 442 P.2d 675, 678, 69 Cal. Rptr. 595, 598 (1968) (requiring consanguinity for the invocation of the state's incest law); *In re* Adoption of Adult Anonymous I, 106 Misc. 2d 792, 798, 435 N.Y.S.2d 527, 530 (Fam. Ct. 1981) (refusing to apply incest law to relatives by adoption in homosexual context because the relationship lacked consanguinity); State v. Rogers, 260 N.C. 406, 409, 133 S.E.2d 1, 3 (1963) (same in heterosexual context).

[152] *See, e.g.,* Doby v. Carroll, 274 Ala. 273, 276, 147 So. 2d 803, 805 (1962); Appeal of Ritchie, 155 Neb. 824, 828, 53 N.W.2d 753, 755 (1952).

expressly permit it.[153] Still others permit only certain kinds of adult adoptions.[154] In general, courts have been reluctant to allow the adoption of adults who are not wards of the state, because adoption traditionally has been viewed as a mechanism to protect the well-being of a child.[155] Where the statutes are vague, courts have disagreed as to the validity of an adult adoption designed for inheritance purposes only.[156] In cases where the parties to the adoption share a sexual relationship, some courts have allowed the adoption and have argued that the failure of the relevant statute to limit adoption to children shows that the sexual element of the relationship is irrelevant.[157] Courts that have denied such adoptions have argued that courts must uphold the moral values or policy purposes of the adoption statute.[158]

Given the reluctance of many courts to allow adult adoptions, gay men and lesbians openly seeking to adopt their life partners will likely face problems in many jurisdictions.[159] Recent cases in New York — the only jurisdiction with reported cases on point — illustrate the obstacles. Although a lower New York court in *In re Adult Anonymous II*[160] had recognized that the "sober life reality"[161] of a couple's

---

[153] *See, e.g.*, ARK. STAT. ANN. § 9-9-203 (1987) ("Any individual may be adopted."); N.D. CENT. CODE § 14-15-02 (1981) (same).

[154] *See, e.g.*, CAL. CIV. CODE §§ 221, 227p (West Supp. 1988) (stating that an adult adoptee must be younger than the adopter and must not be the adopter's spouse); NEB. REV. STAT. § 43-101 (1988) (stating that adults may be adopted only by a spouse of their natural parent).

[155] *See infra* p. 133.

[156] *Compare* Estate of Fortney, 5 Kan. App. 2d 14, 21, 611 P.2d 599, 604–05 (1980) (validating the adoption of a 65-year-old nephew by his 90-year-old uncle, where the purpose was to allow the nephew to inherit property) *with In re* Estate of Griswold, 140 N.J. Super. 35, 60, 354 A.2d 717, 731 (1976) (invalidating an adult adoption for the purpose of inheritance, because it would "abuse" the adoption process). As early as 1898, Justice Holmes recognized the importance of adult adoption to protect property interests. *See, e.g.*, Collamore v. Learned, 171 Mass. 995, N.E. 518 (1898) (Holmes, J.) (upholding the right of a 70-year-old man to adopt three adults, because adoption for the purposes of protecting a will contract is perfectly proper).

[157] *See, e.g.*, Bedinger v. Graybill's Ex'r & Trustee, 302 S.W.2d 594 (Ky. Ct. App. 1957) (upholding a husband's adoption of his wife because the legislature had not explicitly prohibited such adoptions); Greene v. Fitzpatrick, 220 Ky. 590, 295 S.W. 896 (1927) (holding that the concealment of an unlawful relationship does not constitute fraud practiced on the court and therefore does not provide grounds for invalidating a man's adoption of his mistress), *aff'd on other grounds*, 228 Ky. 850, 16 S.W.2d 477 (1929).

[158] *See, e.g.*, *In re* Adoption of Robert Paul P., 63 N.Y.2d 233, 236, 471 N.E.2d 424, 425, 481 N.Y.S.2d 652, 653 (1984) (denying that adoption may be used as a "quasi-matrimonial vehicle"); Stevens v. Halstead, 181 A.D. 198, 201, 168 N.Y.S. 142, 144 (1917) ("Surely it is against public policy to admit a couple living in adultery to the relation of parent and child.").

[159] The greatest difficulty for gay and lesbian couples may come in states such as Florida that expressly prohibit gays and lesbians from adopting children. *See, e.g.*, FLA. STAT. ANN. § 63.042(2)(3)(d) (West 1985) ("No person eligible to adopt under this statute may adopt if that person is homosexual.").

[160] 88 A.D.2d 30, 452 N.Y.S.2d 198 (1982).

[161] *Id.* at 33, 452 N.Y.S.2d at 200.

economic circumstances should override the public policy concerns about gay adult adoptions,[162] the New York Court of Appeals in *In re Adoption of Robert Paul P.*[163] rejected such reasoning and denied the petition of a man to adopt his lifelong male partner. Viewing the petition as a quasi-marital vehicle for legitimizing a sexual relationship between unmarried partners,[164] the court held that adoption applies only to a parent-child relationship, because the policy underlying the adoption statute is to provide "for the welfare of [a] child."[165] Any departure from such a policy, the court declared, must come from the legislature.[166]

A more recent decision by the New York Court of Appeals suggests that as long as the adoption petition appears on its face to indicate a filial relationship or a wish to secure property rights, the court will not delve deeper to discover the "true" motives propelling the adoption. In *East 53rd Street Associates v. Mann*,[167] the court held that an adoption order motivated by a desire to protect the inheritance rights of the adopted party was not per se fraudulent.[168]

D. Conclusion

Courts and legislatures should legalize same-sex marriage. The state has failed to articulate interests compelling enough to justify burdening the fundamental constitutional rights of gay men and lesbians to due process of law and equal protection under the laws. In the alternative, courts and legislatures should grant gay and lesbian couples personal and economic benefits vital to their welfare. Gay and lesbian relationships are qualitatively similar to heterosexual relationships in many essential aspects and are not inherently harmful either to the partners or to society. Furthermore, stable and secure relationships benefit society, whether heterosexual or homosexual. Society's disapproval of the gay and lesbian lifestyle should not, therefore, entail legal exclusion of gay men and lesbians from private law entitlements.

---

[162] *See id.* at 33–35, 452 N.Y.S.2d at 200–01; *cf. In re* Adoption of Adult Anonymous I, 106 Misc. 2d 792, 435 N.Y.S.2d 527, (Fam. Ct. 1981) (holding that public policy or morality does not bar adoptions between two competent and consenting adults in a homosexual relationship).

[163] 63 N.Y.2d 233, 471 N.E.2d 424, 481 N.Y.S.2d 652 (1984).

[164] *See* 63 N.Y.2d at 235–36, 471 N.E.2d at 425, 481 N.Y.S.2d at 653.

[165] *Id.*

[166] *See id.* at 239, 481 N.Y.S.2d at 655, 471 N.E.2d at 427.

[167] 121 A.D.2d 289, 503 N.Y.S.2d 752 (1986).

[168] *See id.* at 292, 503 N.Y.S.2d at 754–55. As the dissent points out, the court never addressed the issue of whether the adoption — which involved two adult women — was a subterfuge. *See id.* at 292, 503 N.Y.S.2d at 755 (Kupferman, J., dissenting).

Even if society refuses to alter its fundamental opposition to homosexuality, states should nevertheless amend and interpret laws to eliminate their unduly harsh impact on gay and lesbian couples. Such action, in areas ranging from workers' compensation and insurance to housing, adoption, and tort liability claims, would not require a dramatic reversal in current practices.

VI. Family Law Issues Involving Children

Approximately three million gay men and lesbians in the United States are parents, and between eight and ten million children are raised in gay or lesbian households.[1] This Part examines the law concerning parenting by gay men and lesbians in three areas: custody and visitation, adoption and foster parenting, and issues related to becoming natural parents.

A. Custody and Visitation

Custody cases often arise involving gay or lesbian parents and their children.[2] It is useful to distinguish among three types of custody and visitation disputes: those between a child's natural parents, those between a parent and a nonparent, and those that result in termination of the parent's rights with respect to the child. Courts employ different standards in each of these settings. In disputes between parents, courts are required to determine custody and visitation rights based on the "best interests of the child."[3] The law governing disputes between a parent and a nonparent varies by state, but generally some sort of presumption exists in favor of granting custody to the parent.[4] In cases that may lead to termination of a parent's rights with respect to the child, regardless of the parties involved, all states preserve the parent's rights unless the parent is found unfit or continuation of the relationship would be harmful to the child.[5]

---

[1] See ABA Annual Meeting Provides Forum for Family Law Experts, 13 Fam. L. Rep. (BNA) 1512, 1513 (Aug. 25, 1987).

[2] According to one commentator, child custody issues are the most litigated of gay and lesbian issues. See Rivera, Recent Developments in Sexual Preference Law, 30 Drake L. Rev. 311, 327 (1980–1981).

[3] See A. Haralambie, Handling Child Custody Cases § 3.06, at 24, § 7.07, at 82–83 (1983).

[4] See H. Clark, The Law of Domestic Relations in the United States, § 19.6, at 821 (2d ed. 1988); infra p. 124.

[5] See H. Clark, supra note 4, § 19.6, at 823; infra pp. 125–26.

1. Current Law. — (a) Disputes Between Parents. — In custody disputes between parents, statutes[6] and case law[7] generally require courts to award custody based on the "best interests" of the child. Because appellate courts defer to trial court decisions regarding the best interests of the child, usually reversing only upon a showing of a clear abuse of discretion,[8] a trial judge's denial of custody based on a finding that the parent's sexual orientation conflicts with the child's best interests will generally be final.

Courts frequently consider the parent's sexual orientation to be relevant to the child's best interests[9] and several courts have used the

---

[6] *See* ALA. CODE § 30-3-1 (1983) (listing factors to be considered in making the best interests determination); ALASKA STAT. §§ 25.20.060, .24.150(c) (1983) (same); ARIZ. REV. STAT. ANN. § 25-332 (Supp. 1988) (same); ARK. STAT. ANN. § 9-13-101 (1987) (specifying application of best interests standard without listing factors); CAL. CIV. CODE § 4600 (West Supp. 1989) (listing factors); COLO. REV. STAT. § 14-10-124 (1987) (same); CONN. GEN. STAT. § 46b-56 (1987) (without listing factors); DEL. CODE ANN. tit. 13, § 722 (1981) (listing factors); D.C. CODE ANN. § 16-911 (1981) (same); FLA. STAT. §§ 61.13(2)(b)1, 61.13(3)a–j (1988) (same); GA. CODE ANN. § 19-9-3 (Supp. 1988) (without listing factors); HAW. REV. STAT. § 571-46 (1988) (same); IDAHO CODE § 32-717 (1983) (listing factors); ILL. REV. STAT. ch. 40, ¶ 602 (1987) (same); IND. CODE ANN. § 31-1-11.5-21 (Burns 1987) (same); IOWA CODE § 598.41 (1987) (same); KAN. STAT. ANN. § 60-1610 (Supp. 1987) (same); KY. REV. STAT. ANN. § 403.270 (Baldwin 1983) (same); LA. CIV. CODE ANN. art. 146 (West Supp. 1989) (same); ME. REV. STAT. ANN. tit. 19, § 752 (Supp. 1988) (same); MD. FAM. LAW CODE ANN. § 9-202 (1984) (without listing factors); MASS. GEN. L. ch. 208, § 31 (1984 & Supp. 1986) (same); MICH. COMP. LAWS ANN. § 722.25 (West Supp. 1988) (same); MINN. STAT. § 257.025 (1988) (same); MISS. CODE ANN. § 93-5-24 (Supp. 1988) (same); MO. REV. STAT. § 452.375 (Supp. 1988) (listing factors); MONT. CODE ANN. § 40-4-212 (1987) (same); NEB. REV. STAT. § 43-1203 (Supp. 1986) (without listing factors); NEV. REV. STAT. ANN. § 125.480 (Michie 1987) (listing factors); N.H. REV. STAT. ANN. § 458:17 (Supp. 1988) (requiring decisions to be "most conducive to [the child's] benefit"); N.J. STAT. ANN. § 9:2-4 (West 1976) (requiring decisions to be made to promote the "happiness and welfare" of the child); N.M. STAT. ANN. § 40-4-9 (1986) (listing factors); N.Y. DOM. REL. LAW § 240 (McKinney Supp. 1989) (without listing factors); N.C. GEN. STAT. § 50-13.2 (1987) (same); N.D. CENT. CODE § 14-09-06.1 to -06.2 (1981) (same); OHIO REV. CODE ANN. § 3109.04 (Anderson Supp. 1987) (same); OKLA. STAT. ANN. tit. 12, § 1275.4 (1988) (without listing factors); OR. REV. STAT. § 107.137 (1987) (same); PA. STAT. ANN. tit. 23, §§ 5301, 5303 (Purdon Supp. 1988) (same); S.C. CODE ANN. § 20-3-160 (Law. Co-op. 1985) (same); TENN. CODE ANN. § 36-6-101 (Supp. 1988) (same); TEX. FAM. CODE ANN. § 14.07 (Vernon 1986) (same); UTAH CODE ANN. § 30-3-10 (Supp. 1988) (listing factors); VT. STAT. ANN. tit. 15, § 665 (Supp. 1988) (same); VA. CODE ANN. § 20-107.2 (Supp. 1988) (same); WIS. STAT. ANN. § 767.24 (West Supp. 1988) (same); WYO. STAT. § 20-2-113 (Supp. 1988) (without listing factors); *see also* UNIF. MARRIAGE & DIVORCE ACT § 402, 9A U.L.A. at 561 (1987) [hereinafter UNIFORM ACT].

[7] *See, e.g.,* Wolff v. Wolff, 349 N.W.2d 656, 658 (S.D. 1984).

[8] *See, e.g.,* Adams v. Adams, 357 So. 2d 881, 883 (La. Ct. App.), *cert. denied,* 359 So. 2d 1309 (La. 1978); *see also* Atkinson, *Criteria for Deciding Child Custody in the Trial and Appellate Courts,* 18 FAM. L.Q. 1, 39–40 (1984) (noting that only 18% of the reported custody appeals in 1982 resulted in reversal).

[9] *See infra* p. 121. *See generally* Sheppard, *Lesbian Mothers II: Long Night's Journey Into Day,* 8 Women's Rts. L. Rep. (Rutgers Univ.) 219, 228 (1985) (noting that a lesbian parent faces the risk that a court will find her unable to provide the right psychological environment for her child).

best interests standard to deny custody to gay and lesbian parents.[10] Statutory law in about half the states specifies the relevant factors in determining the child's best interests,[11] and many of these factors can be interpreted to permit consideration of the parent's sexual orientation.[12]

In some states, courts have created apparently irrebuttable presumptions against granting custody to gay or lesbian parents.[13] Other states have rebuttable presumptions that require a gay or lesbian parent to prove that his or her sexual orientation will not harm the child.[14] In contrast, at least ten states have explicitly rejected presumptions against awarding custody to gay and lesbian parents.[15] Courts in these states have held that they will not deny custody to a parent on the grounds of sexual orientation absent proof that the parent's orientation would adversely affect the child. In addition,

---

[10] *See* cases cited *infra* notes 13–14. *See generally* Note, *Custody Denials to Parents in Same-Sex Relationships: An Equal Protection Analysis*, 102 HARV. L. REV. 617 (1989) [hereinafter Note, *Custody Denials*] (arguing that the equal protection clause restricts a state's ability to deny custody due to a parent's same-sex relationship). Although in this decade gay men and lesbians are increasingly winning custody cases, *see* Harris, *Non-Nuclear Proliferation*, UTNE READER, Mar.-Apr. 1989, at 22–23, they are still frequently denied custody. *See id.*; Sheppard, *supra* note 9, at 232, 243.

[11] *See* statutes cited *supra* note 6. In Ohio, for example, courts must consider the following factors: (1) the wishes of the child's parents regarding custody; (2) the wishes of the child regarding custody if the child is age eleven or older; (3) the child's interaction and interrelationship with his or her parents, siblings and any other person who may significantly affect the child's best interests; (4) the child's adjustment to his or her home, school, and community; and (5) the mental and physical health of all persons involved. *See* OHIO REV. CODE ANN. § 3109.04(C)(1)–(5) (Anderson Supp. 1987).

[12] For example, factors such as the "moral fitness" of the parent, *see, e.g.*, ALA. CODE § 30-3-1 (1983); FLA. STAT. § 61.13(3)(f) (1988), and the "emotional environment" provided by the parent, *see, e.g.*, IND. CODE ANN. § 31-1-11.5-21(g) (Burns 1987), might be interpreted to permit consideration of the parent's sexual orientation.

[13] *See* G.A. v. D.A., 745 S.W.2d 726, 728 (Mo. Ct. App. 1987); *id.* (Lowenstein, J., dissenting) (criticizing the irrebuttable presumption against gay and lesbian parents and arguing for a presumption that could be rebutted by credible evidence that the parent's same-sex relationship will not harm the child); N.K.M. v. L.E.M., 606 S.W.2d 179, 186 (Mo. Ct. App. 1980); Roe v. Roe, 228 Va. 722, 723–24, 324 S.E.2d 691, 693–94 (1985).

[14] *See, e.g.*, Constant A. v. Paul C.A., 344 Pa. Super. 49, 58, 496 A.2d 1, 5 (1985).

[15] *See* S.N.E. v. R.L.B., 699 P.2d 875, 879 (Alaska 1985); *In re* Marriage of Birdsall, 197 Cal. App. 3d 1024, 1028, 243 Cal. Rptr. 287, 289 (1988); Nadler v. Superior Court, 255 Cal. App. 2d 523, 525, 63 Cal. Rptr. 352, 354 (1967); D.H. v. J.H., 418 N.E.2d 286, 293 (Ind. Ct. App. 1981); Doe v. Doe, 16 Mass. App. Ct. 499, 503, 452 N.E.2d 293, 296 (1983); *In re* J. S. & C., 129 N.J. Super. 486, 489, 324 A.2d 90, 92 (Ch. Div. 1974), *aff'd*, 142 N.J Super. 499, 362 A.2d 254 (1976); Guinan v. Guinan, 102 A.D.2d 963, 964, 477 N.Y.S.2d 830, 831 (1984); Stroman v. Williams, 291 S.C. 376, 379–80, 353 S.E.2d 704, 705–06 (Ct. App. 1987); Medeiros v. Medeiros, 8 Fam. L. Rep. (BNA) 2372 (Vt. Super. Ct. 1982); *In re* Marriage of Cabalquinto, 100 Wash. 2d 325, 329, 669 P.2d 886, 888 (1983); Rowsey v. Rowsey, 329 S.E.2d 57, 60–61 (W. Va. 1985); *see also In re* Jacinta M., 107 N.M. 769, 764 P.2d 1327 (Ct. App. 1988) (dictum) (stating that the homosexuality of the child's brother was not sufficient alone to deny him custody).

some courts make in-depth assessments of the purported ill effects of granting custody to an otherwise qualified parent involved in a same-sex relationship.[16]

The best interests of the child standard also governs visitation by noncustodial parents,[17] but courts presume that visitation is in the child's best interest.[18] Most states have a policy of assuring continued contact between the child and the noncustodial parent.[19] Courts will generally deny or restrict visitation only if there is evidence that visitation would harm the child.[20] Although courts often place restrictions on the gay or lesbian parent's visitation rights, courts have never completely denied such rights on the basis of sexual orientation.[21] Courts have, for example, prohibited gay and lesbian parents from having their children visit overnight[22] or from taking their children to the homes they share with their same-sex companions.[23] Such restrictions deny almost any chance for visits by parents who live far away from their children, because the child cannot stay at the parent's home and the parent may not be able to find or afford a place to stay in the child's hometown. Some courts have also required that the child not be taken to gay or lesbian gatherings,[24] or not be in the

---

[16] *See, e.g.,* M.P. v. S.P., 169 N.J. Super. 425, 438–39, 404 A.2d 1256, 1263 (1979) (noting that changing custody would not remove the source of the child's stigma and that keeping custody with the parent involved in a same-sex relationship would benefit the children by teaching them to define their values and overcome popular prejudice).

[17] *See, e.g.,* J.L.P.(H.) v. D.J.P., 643 S.W.2d 865, 870 (Mo. Ct. App. 1982); *J. S. & C.,* 129 N.J. Super. at 494, 324 A.2d at 95.

[18] *See, e.g., In re* Marriage of Matthews, 101 Cal. App. 3d 811, 818, 161 Cal. Rptr. 879, 883 (1980); Stewart v. Stewart, 521 N.E.2d 956, 962–63 (Ind. Ct. App. 1988). This presumption is consistent with psychological research suggesting that the child benefits from maintaining an ongoing relationship with both parents. *See* Wallerstein, *The Child in the Divorcing Family,* JUDGES' J., Winter, 1980, at 17–19, 40–43; Elkin, *Joint Custody: In the Best Interest of the Family,* in JOINT CUSTODY & SHARED PARENTING 13 (J. Folberg ed. 1984).

[19] *See, e.g.,* CAL. CIV. CODE § 4600(a) (West Supp. 1989); COLO. REV. STAT. § 14-10-129 (1987 & Supp. 1988); IND. CODE ANN. § 31-1-11.5-24 (Burns 1987); MICH. COMP. LAWS ANN. § 722.27 (West Supp. 1988); *see also* Conkel v. Conkel, 31 Ohio App. 3d 169, 170–71, 509 N.E.2d 983, 985 (1987) (stating that a child has an interest in a continued bond with the noncustodial parent).

[20] *See* ARIZ. REV. STAT. ANN. § 25-337 (Supp. 1988); COLO. REV. STAT. § 14-10-129 (1987 & Supp. 1988); WIS. STAT. ANN. § 767.245 (West 1981 & Supp. 1988); UNIFORM ACT, *supra* note 6, 9A U.L.A. at 612; *see also In re* Marriage of Birdsall, 197 Cal. App. 3d 1024, 1030, 243 Cal. Rptr. 287, 290 (1988); Stewart v. Stewart, 521 N.E.2d 956, 960 (Ind. Ct. App. 1988).

[21] *But cf.* Roberts v. Roberts, 22 Ohio App. 3d 127, 129, 489 N.E.2d 1067, 1070 (1985) (stating that the trial court might conclude that the only adequate way to protect the children from the effects of their father's "errant sexual behavior" would be to prohibit all visitation until the children were old enough not to be harmed or influenced by their father's lifestyle).

[22] *See, e.g.,* J.L.P.(H.) v. D.J.P., 643 S.W.2d at 871; *In re* Jane B., 85 Misc. 2d 515, 528, 380 N.Y.S.2d 848, 860 (1976).

[23] *See, e.g.,* Dailey v. Dailey, 635 S.W.2d 391, 396 (Tenn. Ct. App. 1981).

[24] *See In re* J. S. & C. 129 N.J. Super. 486, 498, 324 A.2d 90, 97 (1974), *aff'd,* 142 N.J. Super. 499, 362 A.2d 54 (1976); J.L.P.(H.) v. D.J.P., 643 S.W.2d 865, 870 (Mo. Ct. App. 1982)

presence of the parent's same-sex companion,[25] other "known homosexuals,"[26] or even any unrelated member of the parent's sex.[27]

In contrast, some courts have refused to infer that unrestricted visitation would be harmful from the mere fact that a parent is gay or lesbian.[28] In *Conkel v. Conkel*,[29] for example, the Ohio Court of Appeals affirmed a grant of overnight visitation privileges to a bisexual father living with his same-sex companion.[30] State appellate courts have struck down visitation restrictions that prevented parents from having their same-sex companions or other lesbians or gay men in their children's presence.[31]

In addition to cases determining the custody and visitation rights of parents involved in a divorce, a parent's sexual orientation is often relevant in cases brought to modify a previous custody or visitation order. Most states require that a parent seeking to modify a custody order prove that a substantial or material change in the living circumstances of the child warrants a change of custody.[32] Such a policy recognizes the importance of stability in a child's environment,[33] and prevents parents and children from being repeatedly subjected to the ordeal of custody litigation. Noncustodial parents often seek to change

---

(restricting the father from overnight visitation, and from taking his child to "gay activist social gatherings" or a gay church); Gottlieb v. Gottlieb, 108 A.D.2d 120, 121, 488 N.Y.S.2d 180, 181 (1985); *Jane B.*, 85 Misc. 2d at 528, 380 N.Y.S.2d at 861.

[25] *See, e.g.*, Irish v. Irish, 102 Mich. App. 75, 79–80, 300 N.W.2d 739, 741 (1980) (prohibiting overnight visitation if the parent's same-sex partner remained present); L. v. D., 630 S.W.2d 240, 245 (Mo. Ct. App. 1982); *J. S. & C.*, 129 N.J. Super. at 498, 324 A.2d at 97; DiStefano v. DiStefano, 60 A.D.2d 976, 977, 401 N.Y.S.2d 636, 638 (1978); *Jane B.*, 85 Misc. 2d at 528, 380 N.Y.S.2d at 860; Woodruff v. Woodruff, 44 N.C. App. 350, 352, 260 S.E.2d 775, 776 (1979); Dailey v. Dailey, 635 S.W.2d 391, 396 (Tenn. Ct. App. 1981). Some courts have also conditioned expanded visitation rights or custody grants on the parent's ceasing to cohabit with his or her same-sex companion. *See, e.g.*, *DiStefano*, 60 A.D.2d at 977, 401 N.Y.S.2d at 638; Schuster v. Schuster, 90 Wash. 2d 626, 585 P.2d 130 (1978).

[26] *See Jane B.*, 85 Misc. 2d at 528, 380 N.Y.S.2d at 861.

[27] *See* Roberts v. Roberts, 22 Ohio App. 3d 127, 128, 489 N.E.2d 1067, 1069 (1985).

[28] *See, e.g.*, *Birdsall*, 197 Cal. App. 3d at 1029–30, 243 Cal. Rptr. at 290–91; *J. S. & C.*, 129 N.J. Super. at 492, 324 A.2d at 94; *In re* Marriage of Cabalquinto, 100 Wash. 2d 325, 329, 669 P.2d 886, 888 (1983).

[29] 31 Ohio App. 3d 169, 509 N.E.2d 983 (1987).

[30] *Id.* at 170, 509 N.E.2d at 985.

[31] *See* Ashling v. Ashling, 42 Or. App. 47, 599 P.2d 475 (1979); *In re* Marriage of Cabalquinto, 43 Wash. App. 518, 718 P.2d 7 (1986).

[32] *See, e.g.*, COLO. REV. STAT. § 14-10-131 (1987); MO. REV. STAT. § 452.410 (1986); OHIO REV. CODE ANN. § 3109.04 (Anderson Supp. 1988); WASH. REV. CODE § 26.09.260 (Supp. 1985); *see also* UNIFORM ACT, *supra* note 6, § 409(b), 9A U.L.A. at 628. *See generally* A. HARALAMBIE, *supra* note 3, § 7.05, at 80. In contrast, parents seeking to modify a custody agreement may be entitled to a de novo hearing without a showing of a change in circumstances. *See id.* § 7.15, at 90–91.

[33] *See* Schuster v. Schuster, 90 Wash. 2d 626, 628, 585 P.2d 130, 132 (1978); *see also* Note, *In the "Best Interests of the Child" and the Lesbian Mother: A Proposal for Legislative Change in New York*, 48 ALBANY L. REV. 1021, 1030 (1984).

the custody order on the grounds that the sexual orientation of the custodial parent has changed, or, more often, that the court's awareness of the custodial parent's sexual orientation has changed.[34] Courts are divided on whether circumstances in existence but unknown to the court prior to the custody order amount to a material change,[35] but most courts have found that a change in a parent's sexual orientation or in the courts' knowledge of it is material.[36]

In many states it is easier to modify a prior visitation order than it is to change custody.[37] Generally the best interests of the child standard governs, and the party challenging the prior order need not establish a substantial or material change in circumstances.[38]

(b) Disputes Between Parents and Nonparents. — In a custody dispute between a parent and a third party,[39] courts consider both the child's interests and the interests of the natural parent in maintaining custody.[40] Most courts follow the traditional "parent's rights doctrine" and will award custody to a nonparent only if the parent is shown to be unfit.[41] In other jurisdictions, however, the nonparent need not prove unfitness but rather must make a strong showing that awarding custody to the natural parent will not be in the child's best interest.[42]

---

[34] *See, e.g., Schuster,* 90 Wash. 2d at 628, 585 P.2d at 132.

[35] *See* H. CLARK, *supra* note 4, § 19.9, at 838–39. If the parent seeking modification was aware of the other parent's homosexuality at the time of the original custody determination and did not raise the issue at that time, there is no change of circumstances, and the parent therefore will be unable to modify the custody order. *See, e.g.,* Stroman v. Williams, 291 S.C. 376, 353 S.E.2d 704 (Ct. App. 1987). *But see* Newsome v. Newsome, 42 N.C. App. 416, 424–25, 256 S.E.2d 849, 854 (1979) (holding that if a parent's sexuality was not disclosed to the court at the time of the original custody decision, the decree can be modified).

[36] *See, e.g., In re* Jane B., 85 Misc. 2d 515, 523, 380 N.Y.S.2d 848, 856 (1976) (finding that the unfitness of a parent is always a changed circumstance that would justify a change of custody; "the real issue" is whether the present environment is in the child's best interest); M.J.P. v. J.G.P., 640 P.2d 966 (Okla. 1982); Dailey v. Dailey, 635 S.W.2d 391, 393 (Tenn. Ct. App. 1981); *see also* Rivera, *Legal Issues in Gay and Lesbian Parenting,* in GAY AND LESBIAN PARENTS 203 (F. Bozett ed. 1987).

[37] *See* Irish v. Irish, 102 Mich. App. 75, 79–80, 300 N.W.2d 739, 741 (1981); L.L.T. v. P.A.T., 585 S.W.2d 157, 159 (Mo. Ct. App. 1979). *But see* Stewart v. Stewart, 521 N.E.2d 956, 963 (Ind. Ct. App. 1988).

[38] *See Irish,* 102 Mich. App. at 79–80, 300 N.W.2d at 741; *L.L.T.,* 585 S.W.2d at 159; Kallas v. Kallas, 614 P.2d 641, 643 (Utah 1980). *But see Stewart,* 521 N.E.2d at 963.

[39] The standing of third parties to bring a custody action varies by state. The Uniform Marriage and Divorce Act provides that third parties may not bring custody actions when the child is in the physical custody of the natural parent. *See* UNIFORM ACT, *supra* note 6, § 401(d)(2), 9A U.L.A. at 550.

[40] *See* H. CLARK, *supra* note 4, § 19.6, at 821.

[41] *See id.* § 19.6, at 823.

[42] *See, e.g.,* Matson v. Matson, 639 P.2d 298, 300 (Alaska 1982); R.A.D. v. M.E.Z., 414 A.2d 211, 212–13 (Del. Super. Ct. 1980); *In re* Guardianship of Sams, 256 N.W.2d 570, 572 (Iowa 1977); *In re* Weldon, 397 Mich. 225, 262, 244 N.W.2d 827, 837 (1976); Phillips v. Choplin, 65 N.C. App. 506, 511, 309 S.E.2d 716, 720 (1983); Albright v. Commonwealth *ex rel.* Fetters,

There are few cases in which courts have awarded custody to a nonparent because the parent was gay or lesbian,[43] and in those cases, the parent had voluntarily given up custody to the nonparent for some time prior to the custody determination.[44] Other courts have refused to grant custody to the nonparent, stressing the importance of maintaining the natural parent-child bond.[45]

(c) Termination of Parental Rights. — Neglect or dependency proceedings can result in permanent termination of parental rights. All states deprive a parent of custody of his or her child in such proceedings only upon a showing that the parent is unfit.[46] State neglect statutes usually define unfitness as requiring a finding of abandonment, abuse, or serious neglect of parental obligations.[47] Courts have held that "[u]nless the state can prove by clear and convincing evidence that a child is actually suffering or is likely to suffer physical and/or emotional harm, there is no reason to disturb the basic security of a family relationship."[48]

There are no reported dependency or neglect cases in which sexual orientation alone was found sufficient to terminate a natural parent's rights.[49] However, courts do sometimes mention the parent's sexual orientation as one of several factors leading to the termination of parental rights.[50]

---

491 Pa. 320, 323, 421 A.2d 157, 158 (1980) ("[T]he parent has a prima facie right to custody, which will be forfeited only if convincing reasons appear that the child's best interests will be served by an award to the third party.").

[43] *See* Chaffin v. Frye, 45 Cal. App. 3d 39, 119 Cal. Rptr. 22 (1975) (awarding custody to the maternal grandparents over the lesbian mother); Roberts v. Roberts, 25 N.C. App. 198, 212 S.E.2d 410 (1975) (awarding custody to maternal aunt and uncle over the lesbian mother).

[44] *See Chaffin*, 45 Cal. App. 3d at 42, 119 Cal. Rptr. at 22; *Roberts*, 25 N.C. App. at 199, 212 S.E.2d at 411–12.

[45] *See* Gerald & Margaret D. v. Peggy R., No. C-9104, Petition No. 79-12-143-CV (Del. Fam. Ct. Nov. 17, 1980) (LEXIS, States library, Delaware file); Bezio v. Patenaude, 381 Mass. 563, 576, 410 N.E.2d 1207, 1214 (1980).

[46] *See* H. CLARK, *supra* note 4, § 19.6, at 823. Although custody cases and cases terminating parental rights both use the word "unfitness," parental behavior that qualifies as unfit in the former cases may be insufficient in the latter. *Compare, e.g.*, Roe v. Roe, 228 Va. 722, 727, 324 S.E.2d 691, 693–94 (1985) (finding a father unfit based solely on his same-sex relationship) *with* Doe v. Doe, 222 Va. 736, 284 S.E.2d 799 (1981) (reversing the lower court's termination of parental rights of a mother living in an "open lesbian relationship").

[47] *See, e.g.*, CAL. WELF. & INST. CODE § 300 (West Supp. 1989); COLO. REV. STAT. § 19-3-102 (Supp. 1988); N.Y. SOC. SERV. LAW § 384-b (McKinney 1983 & Supp. 1989).

[48] *In re* Jonathan, 415 A.2d 1036, 1039 (R.I. 1980); *see also In re* William L., 477 Pa. 322, 333, 383 A.2d 1228, 1233 ("[A]gency officials [are] powerless to remove a child from parental care and control absent a clear showing that the child either has been subjected to abuse or suffered serious harm, or that the threat of such harm is real and substantial and cannot be alleviated by means less drastic than removal."), *cert. denied*, 439 U.S. 880 (1978).

[49] *But cf.* Daly v. Daly, 715 P.2d 56 (Nev. 1986) (terminating a transsexual's parental rights based largely on the risk of serious emotional injury to the child).

[50] *See, e.g., In re* Breisch, 290 Pa. Super. 404, 434 A.2d 815 (1981); *see also* Wallar, *A*

Parental rights can also be terminated by the adoption of the child by the other parent's spouse.[51] In *Doe v. Doe*,[52] for example, the natural parents had divorced; the father, who was the custodial parent, had remarried and the stepmother sought to adopt the child and terminate the natural mother's parental rights.[53] The Virginia Supreme Court held that the mother's interest could be terminated only if her continued relationship with the child "'would be detrimental to the child's welfare.'"[54] It refused to affirm the lower court's termination of the mother's parental rights based merely on the mother's involvement in a same-sex relationship, and declined to hold that every gay or lesbian parent is per se unfit.[55]

  2. *Statutory Limitations on Decisions Predicated on a Parent's Sexual Orientation.* — Custody denials and visitation restrictions premised on a parent's homosexuality are impermissible under state laws that require such decisions to be based on the child's best interests, because these decisions are either based on factually unsupported assumptions[56] or on factors that bear no relationship to the child's best interests.[57] The statutory and constitutional arguments that follow will focus on custody denials between natural parents. Due to the fundamental nature of the parent-child relationship, the arguments are even stronger in disputes between parents and nonparents, and in cases involving complete termination of parental rights.

  The fundamental problem with the decisions denying custody to and restricting visitation by gay and lesbian parents is that they treat the parent's sexual orientation as determinative despite the statutory requirement that custody decisions be based on the child's overall best

---

Functional Approach to the Representation of Parents and Children in Abuse and Neglect Proceedings, in FOSTER CHILDREN IN THE COURTS 39 (M. Hardin ed. 1983).

  [51] Four states and the District of Columbia allow a nonparent to adopt a child without the consent of both parents if a parent's refusal to consent is contrary to the best interests of the child. *See* J. AREEN, CASES AND MATERIALS ON FAMILY LAW 1357 (2d ed. 1985).

  [52] 222 Va. 736, 284 S.E.2d 799 (1981).

  [53] *See id.* at 739–40, 284 S.E.2d at 801.

  [54] *Id.* at 739, 284 S.E.2d at 800 (quoting Ward v. Faw, 219 Va. 1120, 1125, 253 S.E.2d 658, 661 (1979)).

  [55] *See id.* at 748, 284 S.E.2d at 806.

  [56] *See* Note, *supra* note 33, at 1038 (arguing that evidence of a parent's sexual preference should be excluded as irrelevant in the absence of proof of actual harm resulting to the child).

  [57] Studies have demonstrated that gay and lesbian parents are just as capable of good parenting as non-gay parents. *See, e.g.*, Harris & Turner, *Gay & Lesbian Parents*, 12 J. HOMOSEXUALITY 101, 103 (1985–1986); Kleber, Howell & Tibbits-Kleber, *The Impact of Parental Homosexuality in Child Custody Cases: A Review of the Literature*, 14 BULL. AM. ACAD. PSYCHIATRY & L. 81, 86 (1986); *see also* McCandlish, *Against All Odds: Lesbian Mother Family Dynamics*, in GAY AND LESBIAN PARENTS, *supra* note 36, at 24 (citing other sources); Note, *The Avowed Lesbian Mother and Her Right to Child Custody: A Constitutional Challenge That Can No Longer Be Denied*, 12 SAN DIEGO L. REV. 799, 860 (1975) [hereinafter Note, *Lesbian Mother*].

interests. In *Jacobson v. Jacobson*,[58] for example, the North Dakota Supreme Court reversed an award of custody to a lesbian mother on the grounds that the minor children might suffer from social disapproval and might be more likely to become gay or lesbian.[59] The court found these factors decisive, without considering the lower court's finding that awarding custody to the mother would be less disruptive to the children's schooling and their relationships with their parents, and that both parents were equally fit.[60] In *G.A. v. D.A.*,[61] a Missouri appellate court affirmed a grant of custody to the avowedly heterosexual father based solely on the mother's lesbianism,[62] despite evidence indicating that the mother would provide a better home environment.[63] In both these cases, the courts ignored the statutory requirement that they be guided only by the child's best interests. Instead of ruling out one parent as a potential custodian simply because of fears based on one of the rationales discussed below, courts should, as the statutes require, balance the advantages and disadvantages to the child of awarding custody to each parent.

Courts denying custody to or restricting visitation by gay or lesbian parents typically use one or more of five rationales to conclude that granting custody or unrestricted visitation to such a parent is not in the child's best interest.[64] First, courts fear that the child will be harassed or ostracized.[65] Second, they fear that the child may become

---

[58] 314 N.W.2d 78 (N.D. 1981).

[59] *See id.* at 81–82.

[60] *See id.* at 79.

[61] 745 S.W.2d 726 (Mo. Ct. App. 1987).

[62] *See id.* at 727–28; *see also id.* at 729 (Lowenstein, J., dissenting) ("To say it is in the best interests of this little boy to put him in the sole custody of the father, who was pictured leering at a girly magazine, solely on the basis of the mother's sexual preference would be and is a mistake.").

[63] *See id.* at 729 (Lowenstein, J., dissenting) (explaining that the mother provided "the child with his own room in a well kept house, [and] enroll[ed] him in a pre-school, ha[d] a steady nursing job, [and] care[d] about the child." By contrast, "the father has limited education, an income of $6500 and lives in basically a one room cabin containing a toilet surrounded by a curtain; the child sleeps in a foldup cot by a woodstove and plays in an area littered with Busch beer cans . . . .").

[64] *See* Note, *Custody Denials, supra* note 10, at 620–21 & nn.16–20. Recently, cases have arisen in which the fear of AIDS is mentioned. In an unreported case, a lesbian mother was ordered not to kiss her children or visit with them in her home, despite the fact that she did not have AIDS and despite the extremely low risk of a lesbian having AIDS. *See* Rivera, *supra* note 36, at 215. Other courts have been less willing to restrict visitation based on AIDS. *See* Conkel v. Conkel, 31 Ohio App. 3d 169, 173, 509 N.E.2d 983, 987 (1987) (refusing to deny overnight visitation to a gay father who did not have AIDS and had not tested positive for HIV, simply because the mother feared that the children might get AIDS); Stewart v. Stewart, 521 N.E.2d 956 (Ind. Ct. App. 1988) (refusing to deny all visitation rights to a father with AIDS); Jane W. v. John W., 137 Misc. 2d 24, 519 N.Y.S.2d 603 (1987) (same).

[65] *See, e.g.,* Jacobson v. Jacobson, 314 N.W.2d 78, 81 (N.D. 1981); M.J.P. v. J.G.P., 640 P.2d 966, 969 (Okla. 1982); Dailey v. Dailey, 635 S.W.2d 391, 394 (Tenn. Ct. App. 1981).

gay or lesbian.[66] Third, they believe that living or visiting with a gay or lesbian parent may harm the child's moral well-being.[67] Fourth, they worry that the child will be sexually molested.[68] Finally, they point to state sodomy statutes that they claim embody a state interest against homosexuality.[69]

None of these reasons are sufficiently related to the child's best interests to justify denying custody or restricting visitation to gay and lesbian parents. The fear that children will be harassed is rarely supported by evidence,[70] and, in fact, only one reported case has presented actual evidence of harassment.[71] Nonetheless, courts sometimes allow the risk of harassment and stigmatization to be decisive without any evidence proving that harassment has occurred or is likely to occur.[72] Courts should not assume that harassment will occur without supporting evidence. Moreover, they should recognize that community disapproval will not necessarily adversely affect children. Indeed, as at least two courts have recognized, being aware of some community disapproval may even strengthen a child's character.[73]

The concern that the child will become gay or lesbian is unsupported[74] and also not clearly related to the child's best interests.

---

[66] *See, e.g.*, J.L.P.(H.) v. D.J.P., 643 S.W.2d 865, 872 (Mo. Ct. App. 1982); *Dailey*, 635 S.W.2d at 394.

[67] *See, e.g.*, Chaffin v. Frye, 45 Cal. App. 3d 39, 47, 119 Cal. Rptr. 22, 26 (1975); Hall v. Hall, 95 Mich. App. 614, 615, 291 N.W.2d 143, 144 (1980); Roberts v. Roberts, 489 N.E.2d 1067, 1070 (Ohio Ct. App. 1985); M.J.P. v. J.G.P., 640 P.2d 966, 969 (Okla. 1982); Kallas v. Kallas, 614 P.2d 641, 643 (Utah 1980); Roe v. Roe, 228 Va. 722, 726–27, 324 S.E.2d 691, 693 (1985).

[68] *See* J.L.P.(H.) v. D.J.P., 643 S.W.2d 865, 867, 869 (Mo. Ct. App. 1982) (refusing to believe expert testimony that 95% of molestation is heterosexual: "Every trial judge . . . knows that the molestation of minor boys by adult males is not as uncommon as the psychological experts' testimony indicated."); Newsome v. Newsome, 42 N.C. App. 416, 419, 256 S.E.2d 849, 851 (1979).

[69] *See, e.g.*, L. v. D., 630 S.W.2d 240, 243 (Mo. Ct. App. 1982); *In re* J. S. & C., 129 N.J. Super. 486, 498, 324 A.2d 90, 97 (1974) (restricting visitation), *aff'd*, 142 N.J. Super. 499, 362 A.2d 54 (1976); Constant A. v. Paul C.A., 344 Pa. Super. 49, 57, 496 A.2d 1, 5 (1985) (claiming that the lesbian mother might be subject to arrest if she traveled to states with sodomy statutes).

[70] *See, e.g.*, Hitchens & Price, *Trial Strategy in Lesbian Mother Custody Cases: The Use of Expert Testimony*, 9 GOLDEN GATE U.L. REV. 451, 468–69 (1978–1979); Hotvedt & Mandel, *Children of Lesbian Mothers*, in HOMOSEXUALITY 282 (W. Paul, J. Weinrich, J. Gonsiorek & M. Hotvedt eds. 1982).

[71] *See* L. v. D., 630 S.W.2d at 244 (referring to evidence that the children were teased about the lesbian mother's lifestyle while in the custody of the non-gay father).

[72] *See, e.g.*, Thigpen v. Carpenter, 21 Ark. App. 194, 197–98, 730 S.W.2d 510, 514 (1987) (speculating that the child might be teased); Dailey v. Dailey, 635 S.W.2d 391, 394 (Tenn. Ct. App. 1981) (summarizing expert testimony about the theoretical possibility of social stigma).

[73] *See* M.A.B. v. R.B., 134 Misc. 2d 317, 320–21, 510 N.Y.S.2d 960, 963–65 (Sup. Ct. 1986); M.P. v. S.P., 169 N.J. Super. 425, 438, 404 A.2d 1256, 1262 (1979).

[74] *See, e.g.*, J.L.P.(H.) v. D.J.P., 643 S.W.2d 865, 866 (Mo. Ct. App. 1982).

Although the exact "cause" of homosexuality is not known,[75] studies have found that gay and lesbian parents are no more likely to have gay or lesbian children than are non-gay parents.[76] Moreover, to deny custody on this basis assumes that it is not in the child's best interest to be gay or lesbian. If this premise is not simply a reflection of irrational prejudice against gay men and lesbians, it must be based either on the conception of homosexuality as a disease — a view that every professional mental health organization has rejected[77] — or an unsupported assumption that gay men and lesbians are unhappier than their non-gay counterparts.[78]

The judge's view of the child's moral well-being may not be the same as the child's best interest. Because of the fluidity of the concept of moral well-being and the existence of radically differing viewpoints on homosexuality, it is impossible to state definitively what beliefs regarding sexual orientation are best for the child. In a pluralistic society, judges should avoid legislating their own sense of morality through custody decisions.[79]

The courts' fear that gay or lesbian parents will molest children is unfounded.[80] The vast majority of child molesters are heterosexual

---

[75] See Comment, *Assessing the Children's Best Interests When a Parent Is Gay or Lesbian: Toward a Rational Custody Standard*, 32 UCLA L. REV. 852, 882–83 & n.194 (1985).

[76] See, e.g., Golombok, Spencer & Rutter, *Children in Lesbian and Single-Parent Households: Psychosexual and Psychiatric Appraisal*, 24 J. CHILD PSYCHOLOGY & PSYCHIATRY 551, 568 (1983); Green, *The Best Interest of the Child with a Lesbian Mother*, 10 BULL. AM. ACAD. PSYCHIATRY & L. 7, 13 (1982); Green, Mandel, Hotvedt, Gray & Smith, *Lesbian Mothers and Their Children: A Comparison with Solo Parent Heterosexual Mothers and Their Children*, 15 ARCHIVES SEXUAL BEHAV. 167, 181 (1986); Kirkpatrick, Smith & Roy, *Lesbian Mothers and Their Children: A Comparative Survey*, 51 AM. J. ORTHOPSYCHIATRY 545, 551 (1981); see also Bozett, *Children of Gay Fathers*, in GAY AND LESBIAN PARENTS, *supra* note 36, at 47; Note, *Lesbian Mother*, *supra* note 57, at 860–61.

[77] See Law, *Homosexuality and the Social Meaning of Gender*, 1988 WIS. L. REV. 187, 214 & n.131.

[78] See, e.g., Gonsiorek, *Results of Psychological Testing on Homosexual Populations*, in HOMOSEXUALITY, *supra* note 70, at 72–79 (discussing psychological research that concludes that homosexuals and heterosexuals score similarly on psychological tests); Sang, *Lesbian Relationships: A Struggle Toward Partner Equality*, in WOMEN-IDENTIFIED WOMEN 55 (T. Darty & S. Potter eds. 1984) (summarizing studies indicating that lesbian relationships are "more emotionally satisfying" than heterosexual relationships).

[79] See, e.g., Bezio v. Patenaude, 381 Mass. 563, 579, 410 N.E.2d 1207, 1216 (1980). Unfortunately, judges in custody cases involving gay or lesbian parents too frequently base their decisions on their own personal views of homosexuality. See, e.g., M.J.P. v. J.G.P., 640 P.2d 966, 968 (Okla. 1982); Constant A. v. Paul C.A., 344 Pa. Super. 49, 53–54, 496 A.2d 1, 3 (1985); Kallas v. Kallas, 614 P.2d 641, 643 (Utah 1980).

[80] See cases cited *supra* note 68; Totenberg, *Morning Edition*, National Public Radio broadcast, Feb. 7, 1989 (recording lawyer/psychologist Brian Welch saying "gay men and lesbians are less likely to molest children or to commit crimes with children than are heterosexual men and women").

men.[81] Women, regardless of their sexual orientation, rarely molest children. If courts were making custody decisions based solely on the risk of molestation, therefore, they would award custody to the mother, whether or not she were a lesbian.

Finally, the state's desire to promote the policies underlying its sodomy statute is not a statutorily permissible predicate for a custody denial or visitation restriction because it is irrelevant to the child's best interests.[82] Furthermore, because most state sodomy statutes prohibit opposite-sex as well as same-sex sodomy,[83] these statutes cannot justify custody denials to only gay men and lesbians. Most courts denying custody to gay and lesbian parents have not heard evidence indicating that the gay or lesbian parent has violated the sodomy statutes, or that the non-gay parent has not.[84] Assumptions that gay and lesbian parents are more likely to engage in prohibited conduct,[85] or that they are likely to be arrested,[86] are without support.

3. Constitutional Limitations. — As discussed above, the five justifications for denying custody or visitation privileges to gay and lesbian parents violate statutory requirements that decisions be based on the child's best interests. Because the only statutorily permissible state interest is the child's best interests, the state cannot use other state interests to justify these decisions. Rational relationship review under the equal protection clause[87] therefore tracks the statutory analysis above; rational relationship review, however, generally requires a weaker connection to the child's best interests. Even if state courts view custody denials and visitation restrictions premised solely on sexual orientation as sufficient under a best interests standard, such decisions should still be invalidated because, as discussed in Part III

---

[81] *See* R. GEISER, HIDDEN VICTIMS: THE SEXUAL ABUSE OF CHILDREN 75 (1979); Bozett, *supra* note 76, at 47; Note, *supra* note 33, at 1036–37 & nn.87–89.

[82] *See* Note, *Custody Denials, supra* note 10, at 635 ("Surely, assuming that the child is not present during the sexual activity, the difference between the child's parent receiving sexual gratification through oral [as opposed to] manual stimulation will not affect the child's well-being.").

[83] *See* statutes cited in Part II, note 5, *supra* p. 10.

[84] *See* Note, *Custody Denials, supra* note 10, at 635 & n.96.

[85] Many lesbians rarely or never have oral sex, *see* P. BLUMSTEIN & P. SCHWARTZ, AMERICAN COUPLES 236 (1983), and, in response to the AIDS epidemic, many gay men no longer engage in sodomy. *See, e.g.,* Martin, *The Impact of AIDS on Gay Male Sexual Behavior Patterns in New York City,* 77 AM. J. PUB. HEALTH 578, 580 (1987). Most heterosexual couples have engaged in prohibited conduct. *See* P. BLUMSTEIN & P. SCHWARTZ, *supra,* at 236 (noting that 90% of heterosexual couples have engaged in fellatio, and 93% have engaged in cunnilingus); C. TAVRIS & S. SADD, THE REDBOOK REPORT ON FEMALE SEXUALITY 93 (1977) (reporting that 43% of women surveyed had tried anal sex).

[86] *See* Bowers v. Hardwick, 478 U.S. 186, 198 n.2 (1986) (Powell, J., concurring) (noting that there were no "reported decision[s] involving prosecution for private homosexual sodomy under [Georgia's sodomy] statute for several decades").

[87] *See supra* p. 47.

above, sexual orientation classifications should be considered suspect or quasi-suspect,[88] and because such decisions amount to gender discrimination.

In states that deny custody to parents in same-sex relationships, but not to parents with opposite-sex cohabitants,[89] decisions denying custody to gay and lesbian parents discriminate on the basis of gender.[90] A mother who is involved with another woman is denied custody or visitation, although a father who is involved with a woman is not; similarly, a father involved with a man is denied custody, although a mother involved with a man is not. The argument that classifications based on the fact that members of a couple are of the same gender constitute sex discrimination is explored in detail above.[91]

Because custody denials and visitation restrictions involving gay men and lesbians both burden a suspect or quasi-suspect class and discriminate on the basis of gender, and because they do not advance sufficiently strong governmental interests, they should be invalidated.[92] The state's interests in preventing the child from becoming gay or lesbian and in protecting the child's moral well-being are illegitimate because they depend directly or indirectly on animus toward a protected class.[93] Because state sodomy statutes also reflect animus toward gay men and lesbians,[94] the state's interest in promoting those statutes is similarly illegitimate. Insofar as these interests

---

[88] *See supra* pp. 55–60; *see also* Note, *Custody Denials, supra* note 10, at 623–25 (arguing that the combination of the suspect-like features of those in same-sex relationships and the important interest in intimate relationships at stake warrant heightened scrutiny).

[89] *Compare, e.g.,* Wilhelmsen v. Peck, 743 S.W.2d 88 (Mo. Ct. App. 1987) (finding a mother's opposite-sex cohabitation insufficient to justify a change of custody) *with* S.E.G. v. R.A.G., 735 S.W.2d 164 (Mo. Ct. App. 1987) (affirming the denial of custody to and restriction on visitation by a mother on the basis of her involvement in a same-sex relationship); Michael T.L. v. Marilyn J.L., 363 Pa. Super. 42, 525 A.2d 414 (1987) (finding opposite-sex relationships to be relevant only insofar as they have an adverse effect on the child) *with* Constant A. v. Paul C.A., 344 Pa. Super. 49, 496 A.2d 1 (1985) (holding that there exists a rebuttable presumption against custody or visitation awards to gay and lesbian parents).

[90] For a discussion of this argument, see Note, *Custody Denials, supra* note 10, at 626–30. *See also supra* pp. 17–18. Custody denials or visitation restrictions to gay and lesbian parents are almost always based on the existence of a same-sex relationship, rather than on the parent's sexual orientation standing alone. *See* Note, *Custody Denials, supra* note 10, at 618–19 & nn.9–11. That courts award custody to gay and lesbian parents as long as the child is not exposed to the parent's same-sex partner suggests that it is the same-sex relationship, rather than the parent's sexual orientation, that the court finds offensive. *See id.*

[91] *See supra* pp. 17–18.

[92] *See supra* p. 55.

[93] *Cf.* Loving v. Virginia, 388 U.S. 1, 11 (1967) (stating that statutes addressing a protected class "must be shown to be necessary to the accomplishment of some permissible state objective, independent of the . . . discrimination which it was the object of the Fourteenth Amendment to eliminate"); *see also* Note, *Custody Denials, supra* note 10, at 630–31; Note, *The Miscegenation Analogy: Sodomy Law as Sex Discrimination*, 98 YALE L.J. 145, 158–60 (1988).

[94] *See supra* p. 16.

reflect animus against women,[95] they constitute constitutionally impermissible gender discrimination as well.[96]

The state's interest in protecting children from harassment is insufficient to survive heightened scrutiny because it relies on and reinforces societal prejudice against a protected group. In *Palmore v. Sidoti*,[97] the Supreme Court held that denying a mother custody of her child because of a risk that the child would be stigmatized as a result of the mother's interracial marriage violated the equal protection clause. As the Court stated, "[t]he Constitution cannot control such prejudices but neither can it tolerate them."[98]

In addition to violating gay and lesbian parents' equal protection rights, irrebuttable presumptions against awarding custody to gay and lesbian parents and in favor of restricting their visitation rights violate the parents' procedural due process rights. The Supreme Court has found that statutes employing irrebuttable presumptions burdening protected interests deny due process because they do not give those affected an opportunity to be heard in a meaningful manner.[99] A parent's right to care and custody of his or her children is a constitutionally protected liberty interest.[100] As such, states with irrebuttable presumptions that preclude custody or visitation awards to gay and lesbian parents deny those parents procedural due process.[101]

B. Adoption and Foster Care

Adoption and foster care provide homes for children who do not have parents able and willing to care for them.[102] Adoption termi-

---

[95] *See supra* p. 18.

[96] The state's purported interest in protecting the child's moral well-being is also illegitimate because it violates the first amendment by trying to control a child's beliefs. *See* Note, *Custody Denials, supra* note 10, at 633. Moral beliefs can sometimes be used to justify laws that regulate conduct, *see, e.g.,* Bowers v. Hardwick, 478 U.S. 186, 196 (1986), but they are an impermissible basis for laws designed to regulate beliefs themselves. *See* Abood v. Detroit Bd. of Educ., 431 U.S. 209, 234–35 (1977) ("[A]t the heart of the First Amendment is the notion that an individual should be free to believe as he will, and that in a free society one's beliefs should be shaped by his mind and his conscience rather than coerced by the State.").

[97] 466 U.S. 429 (1984).

[98] *Id.* at 433; *see also* Note, *supra* note 33, at 1038.

[99] *See* Armstrong v. Manzo, 380 U.S. 545, 552 (1965); *see also* Cleveland Bd. of Educ. v. LaFleur, 414 U.S. 632 (1974) (striking down a statutory presumption that pregnant women are unfit to teach past the fourth month of pregnancy); Vlandis v. Kline, 412 U.S. 441 (1973) (striking down a statute creating an irrebuttable presumption of out-of-state residency).

[100] *See* Santosky v. Kramer, 455 U.S. 745, 753 (1982); Smith v. Organization of Foster Families, 431 U.S. 816, 845 (1977); Stanley v. Illinois, 405 U.S. 645, 651 (1972); Prince v. Massachusetts, 321 U.S. 158, 166 (1944); Meyer v. Nebraska, 262 U.S. 390, 399 (1923).

[101] *See* Stanley v. Illinois, 405 U.S. 645 (1972) (invalidating a law that presumed without a hearing that unwed fathers were unfit); Note, *Lesbian Mother, supra* note 57, at 830.

[102] For general discussions of gay men and lesbians adopting children and becoming foster parents, see Ricketts & Achtenberg, *The Adoptive and Foster Gay and Lesbian Parent,* in GAY

nates the rights and responsibilities of the natural parents and vests them in the adoptive parent or parents.[103] Adoptions take place either through public or state-licensed private agencies or through private placements.[104] A court, guided by the child's best interests, must review all adoption petitions;[105] in addition, the consent of the agency is required for agency adoptions[106] and in most states, judges hearing private adoption petitions must consider agency or social worker recommendations.[107] Foster care, by contrast, is intended to supply a temporary home until the child can be either returned to his or her natural parents or adopted.[108] Foster parents are state-licensed and are paid for caring for foster children; in general, foster parents are not licensed for a particular child but for whomever the agency decides to place with them.[109]

Although no statistical information is available, anecdotal reports suggest that adoptions and foster care by gay men and lesbians are not uncommon.[110] Only Florida and New Hampshire statutorily prohibit gay men and lesbians from adopting.[111] New Hampshire also prohibits placing foster children in homes with homosexuals,[112] and Massachusetts has regulations intended to prevent gay men and lesbians from becoming foster parents.[113] In other states, although many

---

AND LESBIAN PARENTS, cited above in note 36, at 89–94; H. CURRY & D. CLIFFORD, A LEGAL GUIDE FOR LESBIAN AND GAY COUPLES 7:18–7:30 (5th ed. 1988), which provides legal advice for nonpractioners; and J. SCHULENBURG, GAY PARENTING 97–104 (1985).

[103] See H. CLARK, supra note 4, § 20.2, at 855. Stepparent and co-parent adoptions only terminate one parent's rights. See infra p. 146.

[104] See H. CLARK, supra note 4, § 20.7, at 906.

[105] See, e.g., ALASKA STAT. § 25.23.120 (1983); IOWA CODE § 600.13(1) (1981); NEB. REV. STAT. § 43-109 (1988); S.C. CODE ANN. § 20-7-1760 (Law. Co-op. 1985); WIS. STAT. § 48.91(3) (1987).

[106] See A. HARALAMBIE, supra note 3, § 15.13, at 238. However, denial of agency consent does not preclude adoption in many states if the petitioner can convince the court that the adoption is in the child's best interests. See H. CLARK, supra note 4, § 20.4, at 881.

[107] See, e.g., GA. CODE ANN. §§ 19-8-11 to -8-12 (1982) (requiring an agency investigation); LA. REV. STAT. ANN. § 9:427 (West 1965) (same); H. CLARK, supra note 4, § 20.7, at 906.

[108] See A. HARALAMBIE, supra note 3, § 11.07, at 160–61.

[109] See I. ELLMAN, P. KURTZ & A. STANTON, FAMILY LAW 1176 (1986).

[110] See, e.g., Dullea, Gay Couples' Wish To Adopt Grows, Along with Increasing Resistance, N.Y. Times, Feb. 7, 1988, § 1, at 26, col. 1; Cummings, Homosexual Views Adoption Approval as Victory, N.Y. Times, Jan. 10, 1983, at A8, col. 2. See generally Ricketts & Achtenberg, supra note 102, at 89–94 (discussing the history and the growing numbers of gay and lesbian adoptive and foster parents).

[111] See FLA. STAT. ANN. § 63.042(3) (West 1985); N.H. REV. STAT. ANN. § 170-B:4 (Supp. 1988).

[112] See N.H. REV. STAT. ANN. § 161:2(IV) (Supp. 1988). In addition, North Dakota only permits married couples to be foster parents. See N.D. ADMIN. CODE § 75-03-14-04(1) (1984).

[113] See MASS. REGS. CODE tit. 110, § 7.103(3)(a) (1986) (requiring foster parent applicants to state sexual orientation); id. § 7.101 (ranking types of foster care homes so that gay men and lesbians have almost no chance of becoming foster parents). Although these regulations do not explicitly state that gay men and lesbians cannot be licensed as foster parents, they are generally

agencies or caseworkers are opposed to placements in gay or lesbian homes, such placements occur either when caseworkers are unaware of the applicant's sexual orientation or because they realize that the gay or lesbian applicant will provide a good home for the child.[114]

Restrictions on the ability of gay men and lesbians to provide foster or adoptive homes run counter to the welfare of the children needing such homes. Refusals to permit lesbians and gay men to adopt or become foster parents stems in part from a fear of appearing to accept gay people and same-sex relationships to any degree.[115] For example, an Ohio appeals court recently held that homosexuals are, as a matter of law, ineligible to adopt because "[i]t is not the business of the government to encourage homosexuality."[116] In the court's view, "[t]he so-called 'gay lifestyle' is patently incompatible with the manifest spirit, purpose and goals of adoption. Homosexuality negates procreation. Announced homosexuality defeats the goals of adoption."[117] When courts and agencies are guided by such fears, they

---

viewed as having that effect and intent. *See, e.g.,* Witcher, *Panel Recommends Change in Gay Foster Parents Policy,* Boston Globe, Dec. 18, 1986, at 45, col. 1. A special state commission recommended against allowing disqualifications based on sexual orientation, *see id.;* however, the policy is still in effect and was recently made a condition of the Department of Social Services' funding. *See* Fehrnstrom, *Sneak Hit at Gay-Fosters,* Boston Herald, July 28, 1988, at 1, col. 1. A challenge to these regulations is now pending in state court. *See* Babets v. Secretary of the Exec. Office of Human Serv., 403 Mass. 230, 526 N.E.2d 1261 (1988) (deciding a discovery issue).

[114] *See* Ricketts & Achtenberg, *supra* note 102, at 92–93. Agencies are particularly likely to allow gay men and lesbians to become foster parents to gay and lesbian teenagers. *See id.* at 93.

Lesbians and gay men generally apply to adopt as unmarried individuals, particularly if they do not wish to emphasize their same-sex relationships. However, adopting as a couple gives the child two legal parents and assures that the child will remain with the surviving parent if one dies and will be able to maintain contact with both if the couple separates. *See infra* p. 145. Courts in California have allowed joint adoptions by lesbian couples of children not related to either woman. *See* No. 17350 (Cal. Super. Ct., Alameda County, Apr. 8, 1986) (cited in Ricketts & Achtenberg, *supra* note 102, at 98); No. 17945 (Cal. Super Ct., San Francisco County, Feb. 24, 1986) (same). The issues raised by joint adoptions are very similar to those raised by co-parent adoptions. *See infra* pp. 145–47. In addition, however, statutes listing those eligible to adopt may be interpreted to bar adoptions by two individuals not married to each other. *See infra* note 192.

[115] *See, e.g., In re* Appeal in Pima County Juvenile Action B-10489, 151 Ariz. 335, 340, 727 P.2d 830, 835 (Ct. App. 1986); *In re* Adoption of Charles B., 1988 Ohio App. LEXIS 4435, No. CA-3382 (Oct. 28, 1988).

[116] *Charles B.,* 1988 Ohio App. LEXIS 4435, at 2. The court read the adoption statute to prohibit adoption by homosexuals, despite the complete lack of any statutory basis, because "the concepts of homosexuality and adoption are so inherently mutually exclusive and inconsistent, if not hostile, that the legislature never considered it necessary to enact an express ineligibility provision." *Id.* at 1–2.

[117] *Id.* at 5. The court's statement is factually incorrect in at least two ways. First, adoption is not limited to those who can procreate; indeed, it is often seen as a way for those unable to procreate to have families. *See, e.g.,* J. Thoburn, A. Murdoch & A. O'Brien, Permanence in Child Care 4 (1986). Second, homosexuals are as capable of procreating as heterosexuals.

put their adverse reactions to gay people above the welfare of the children affected.[118] From the viewpoint of a child needing an adoptive or foster home, whether or not the state is seen as encouraging homosexuality is irrelevant.

States' and agencies' refusals to place children with gay men and lesbians are also sometimes based on perceived potential harm to the children. Decisionmakers fear that the parent's sexual orientation will influence the child's,[119] that the child will be subject to peer harassment or ostracism,[120] or that the child will not be able to "pass" as the natural child of the same-sex couple.[121] As noted above, however, the concern for the child's sexual orientation is unsupported and the likelihood of peer harassment is small.[122] Although it is true that the child obviously cannot "pass" as the natural child of a same-sex couple, a child of similar racial and ethnic make-up could easily be perceived as the biological child of one of the partners. In addition, studies have repeatedly shown that no differences exist between the ability of heterosexuals and homosexuals to be good parents.[123]

More importantly, deciding whether a particular placement is in a child's best interests always involves balancing that placement against the available alternatives. The benefits from placing a child in a gay or lesbian home are especially clear-cut for "hard-to-place" children — those who are older, nonwhite, disabled, or emotionally disturbed. Most states currently have a shortage of foster or adoptive parents for such children[124] and many end up either in inappropriate settings,

---

Although a same-sex couple cannot produce a child within the relationship, individuals in same-sex relationships can and do produce children through sexual intercourse, artificial insemination, and other reproductive techniques. *See infra* notes 142–145 and accompanying text.

[118] For example, although the *Charles B.* court implicitly admitted that it would be in the seven-year-old leukemia victim's best interests to be adopted by his gay psychologist after a three-year futile search for a more traditional adoptive family, the court nevertheless refused to permit the adoption. *See Charles B.*, 1988 Ohio App. LEXIS 4435, at 12–14.

[119] *See* Opinion of the Justices, 129 N.H. 290, 296, 530 A.2d 21, 25 (1987).

[120] *See, e.g.*, Fehrnstrom, *supra* note 113, at 24, col. 4 (quoting the sponsor of anti-gay foster care legislation as stating that her motivation was "to remove . . . the 'stigma' that would be attached to a foster child who is raised in a gay or lesbian household").

[121] *See Charles B.*, 1988 Ohio App. LEXIS 4435, at 1.

[122] *See supra* pp. 127–29. If the adoptive or foster parent is not in a relationship, it is even less likely that the child's peers will learn that the parent is gay and tease the child. Similarly, if a court chooses to ignore evidence that children do not imitate their parents' sexual orientation, such imitation would be improbable if the child is not exposed to a relationship.

[123] *See* sources cited *supra* note 57.

[124] *See* NAT'L COMM. FOR ADOPTION, ADOPTION FACTBOOK 41 (1985); Jacobs, *The Fragile System of Foster Care*, Boston Globe, May 5, 1988, at 34, col. 5; Daley, *The Struggle To Recruit Foster Parents*, N.Y. Times, May 6, 1987, at B1, col. 2. Because of the severe shortage of adoptive parents for such children, Congress created an adoption assistance program that reimburses states for financial assistance to those adopting "special needs" children. *See* 42 U.S.C. § 673 (Supp. IV 1986).

In contrast, there is a large surplus of qualified potential parents seeking to adopt healthy

such as state-run diagnostic centers or child-care institutions,[125] or in a series of foster homes.[126] Because a permanent home is critical to a child's development,[127] gay and lesbian couples can provide a much-needed source of potential foster and adoptive parents for such children.[128]

Because refusals to allow gay men and lesbians to become adoptive or foster parents do not serve the affected children's best interests, they can in some instances be challenged in court on that basis. In all states other than Florida and New Hampshire, a would-be parent challenging a judge's refusal to grant a private placement adoption petition can argue that the denial does not serve the child's best interests. In other situations, however, such as a denial of a foster care license, or when an agency refuses to place gay and lesbian couples on its wait list, the would-be parent has no state law cause of action with which to challenge the denial. Such litigants can, however, bring constitutional challenges to state actions that assume

---

newborns. *See* Bernstein, *Couples Caught in Adoption Maze*, N.Y. Times, Oct. 13, 1985, § 11, at 24, col. 3 (Long Island ed.) (discussing the shortage of adoptable infants); Ranii, *Adoption: The Focus Shifts to Lawyers*, Nat'l L.J., Aug. 20, 1984, at 1, cols. 2–3 (stating that for each healthy white infant, there are forty couples who want to adopt; "there is no glut of healthy minority babies either").

[125] *See, e.g.*, Daley, *At Group Foster Home, the Hunger Is for Love*, N.Y. Times, Sept. 30, 1988, at B1, col. 2; Oreskes & Rimer, *Youths Languish in Diagnostic Centers*, N.Y. Times, Mar. 27, 1987, at B1, col. 2.

[126] *See, e.g.*, H. CLARK, *supra* note 4, § 20.1, at 854.

[127] *See, e.g.*, J. GOLDSTEIN, A. FREUD & A. SOLNIT, BEYOND THE BEST INTERESTS OF THE CHILD 31–34 (1973) ("Continuity of relationships, surroundings, and environmental influence are essential for a child's normal development."); Rosenberg, *The Techniques of Psychological Assessment as Applied to Children in Foster Care and Their Families*, in FOSTER CHILDREN IN THE COURTS, *supra* note 50, at 551.

The outlook for children without permanent homes is not promising. For example, studies have estimated that "between 25 percent and 50 percent of the young men in New York City's homeless shelters are former foster children." *See* Oreskes, *A System Overloaded: The Foster-Care Crisis*, N.Y. Times, Mar. 15, 1987, § 1, at 32, col. 6.

[128] Lesbian and gay foster and adoptive parents are viewed as especially appropriate for gay and lesbian adolescents, a group that is sometimes included among "special needs" children. *See, e.g.*, Oreskes, *supra* note 127, § 1, at 32, col. 4 ("'It's hard to find an agency that will handle a homosexual kid . . . .'" (quoting a city social worker)). However, one court refused to permit the Department of Social and Health Services to place a sixteen-year-old boy with "homosexual tendencies" with a gay male foster couple. Although numerous expert witnesses recommended the placement, and the department stated that it might have to institutionalize the boy if the placement were not approved, the court denied the placement, holding that the boy "should be encouraged to behave normally regardless of his sexual orientation." *In re* Davis, 1 Fam. L. Rep. (BNA) 2845, 2847 (Wash. Super. Ct. 1975).

Lesbians and gay men are also likely to be more willing to adopt a child who has AIDS or is HIV-positive. Due to the prevalence of AIDS in the gay community, gay men and lesbians are both more aware that the virus is not transmitted through casual contact and are less afraid of those with AIDS.

gay men and lesbians are per se unfit to adopt. These constitutional issues are most clearly presented by statutory or regulatory prohibitions against gay and lesbian foster or adoptive parents.

As noted above, Florida, New Hampshire, and Massachusetts have statutes or regulations intended to prevent gay men and lesbians from adopting children and/or becoming foster parents.[129] Although no court has yet ruled on the legality of such restrictions,[130] the New Hampshire Supreme Court, responding to the state legislature's request for an advisory opinion, concluded that the subsequently enacted bill was constitutional.[131] The court applied only rational basis equal protection review, asserting without citation that sexual orientation is neither a suspect nor a quasi-suspect classification.[132] It found the exclusion rationally related to the bill's purpose of providing appropriate role models because of "the reasonable possibility of environmental influences" affecting a child's future sexual orientation.[133]

This equal protection holding rests on shaky assumptions.[134] First, the court assumed without discussion that gay men and lesbians do not constitute a suspect or quasi-suspect class, despite the persuasive arguments to the contrary.[135] Moreover, the court did not consider

---

[129] *See* FLA. STAT. ANN. § 63.042(3) (West 1985); MASS. REG. CODE tit. 10, §§ 7.101, 7.103(3)(a) (1986); N.H. REV. STAT. ANN. § 170-B:4 (Supp. 1988).

[130] A challenge to the Massachusetts policy is pending. *See* Babets v. Secretary of the Exec. Office of Human Serv., 403 Mass. 230, 526 N.E.2d 1261 (1988) (deciding a discovery issue).

[131] *See* Opinion of the Justices, 129 N.H. 290, 530 A.2d 21 (1987). The bill defined a "homosexual" as "'any person who performs or submits to any sexual act involving the sex organs of one person and the mouth or anus of another person of the same gender.'" *Id.* at 294, 530 A.2d at 24 (quoting N.H. House Resolution 32). *But cf. supra* p. 1521 (noting that homosexuality is not equivalent to participation in sodomy). The court found that the bill's foster care restrictions, as applied only to prospective applicants, did not violate equal protection, due process, right to privacy, or freedom of association under either the federal or state constitution. *See id.* at 295–300, 530 A.2d at 24–27.

[132] *See id.* at 295, 530 A.2d at 24.

[133] *See id.* at 296, 530 A.2d at 25. In contrast, the court did find that the bill's proposed prohibition on homosexual day care operators lacked a rational basis because of the "noncontinuous nature of the provision of many day care services" and the state's reduced responsibility in regulating day care as compared to foster care and adoption. *See id.* at 297, 530 A.2d at 25.

[134] In addition to violating the equal protection clause, discriminatory adoption and foster care policies may violate statutory and constitutional privacy guarantees by requiring disclosure of highly personal information that is not necessary to assess an applicant's qualifications, for example, when a celibate foster care applicant is forced to disclose his or her sexual orientation. *See* Plaintiffs' Memorandum of Law in Opposition to Defendants' Motion to Dismiss, Babets v. Dukakis, No. 81083 (Mass. Super. Ct. filed Jan. 30, 1986).

[135] *See supra* pp. 55–60. Although no federal courts had held that sexual orientation was suspect or quasi-suspect at the time *Opinion of the Justices* was handed down, three courts have since so held. *See* Watkins v. United States Army, 847 F.2d 1329 (9th Cir), *reh'g granted en banc*, 847 F.2d 1362 (9th Cir. 1988); High Tech Gays v. Defense Indus. Sec. Clearance

the gender classification inherent in disadvantaging an individual based solely on the fact that the members of a couple are of the same gender.[136]

Even under rational basis review, the statute's validity is questionable. According to the dissent, "[t]he legislature received no meaningful evidence to show that homosexual parents endanger their children's development of sexual preference, gender role identity, or general physical and psychological health any more than heterosexual parents" because "the overwhelming weight of professional study . . . concludes" that children raised by homosexual parents are no different from their peers.[137] Under the weakest formulation of the rational basis test, the legislature can arguably enact legislation unsupported by scientific evidence unless "the legislative facts on which the classification is apparently based could not reasonably be conceived to be true by the governmental decisionmaker."[138] Although the legislature conceivably could have believed that gay men or lesbians would not be appropriate role models for children, its tenacity in persisting in this belief in the face of "the overwhelming weight" of professional research to the contrary is strong evidence that the true motivation for this legislation was "irrational prejudice"[139] rather than concern for children's welfare. Under this analysis, the legislation is unconstitutional.[140]

C. Procreation and Parenting

"[H]omosexuals are as capable of procreation as are bisexuals or heterosexuals."[141] Today, many gay men and women, especially les-

---

Office, 668 F. Supp. 1361 (N.D. Cal. 1987); benShalom v. Marsh, 703 F. Supp. 1372 (E.D. Wis. 1989).

[136] *See supra* pp. 17–18; *see also* Note, *Custody Denials, supra* note 10, at 626–30; *supra* p. 1641. Because the statute defines "homosexual" by participation in same-sex oral/genital or anal/genital contact, it punishes precisely that behavior criminalized in sodomy statutes. *See* Part II, note 2, *supra* p. 9. Thus the gender discrimination argument made above in connection with sodomy statutes applies equally here. Interestingly, New Hampshire does not criminalize sodomy. *See* Opinion of the Justices, 129 N.H. 290, 300, 530 A.2d 21, 28 (1987) (Batchelder, J., concurring in part and dissenting in part).

[137] 129 N.H. at 301, 530 A.2d at 28 (Batchelder, J., concurring in part and dissenting in part). In addition, the assumption that becoming gay is harmful to the child is questionable. *See supra* pp. 128–29.

[138] Vance v. Bradley, 440 U.S. 93, 111 (1979).

[139] *Cf.* City of Cleburne v. Cleburne Living Center, Inc., 473 U.S. 432, 450 (1985) (invalidating state action that "appear[ed] . . . to rest on an irrational prejudice").

[140] *Cf.* United States Dep't of Agric. v. Moreno, 413 U.S. 528, 534 (1973) (holding that "a bare . . . desire to harm a politically unpopular group cannot constitute a *legitimate* governmental interest"); *supra* p. 53.

[141] J. MONEY, GAY, STRAIGHT, AND IN-BETWEEN: THE SEXOLOGY OF EROTIC ORIENTATION 54 (1988).

bian couples, are choosing to have children.[142] However, gay and lesbian parenting is frustrated by a number of legal barriers. First, lesbians and gay men may be denied access to necessary reproductive techniques such as artificial insemination,[143] in vitro fertilization,[144] or surrogate motherhood.[145] Second, once they have children, gay and lesbian parents face further problems in defining the legal relationships both between the child and the second biological parent, and between the child and the "co-parent" — the nonbiological parent in a same-sex couple.

   1. Access to Reproductive Techniques. — (a) Issues Faced by Lesbians. — Most lesbians wishing to become pregnant can do so through either artificial insemination or sexual intercourse.[146] Both techniques are simple procedures easily done at home.[147] Thus, although some states have fornication statutes[148] and/or statutes that can be interpreted as prohibiting the artificial insemination of unmarried women,[149] states cannot easily prevent access to either technique.[150] In the case of artificial insemination, however, such statutes may inhibit physicians from performing artificial insemination on unmarried women.[151] Denial of access to physician-performed artificial

---

[142] *See* Adams, *Gay Couples Begin a Baby Boom*, Boston Globe, Feb. 6, 1989, at 2, col. 2; Kolata, *Lesbian Partners Find Means To Be Parents*, N.Y. Times, Jan. 30, 1989, at A13, col. 1; *see also Editor's Note*, N.Y. Times, Feb. 3, 1989, at A3, col. 1 (correcting certain inaccurate anti-lesbian statements in the above article).

[143] In artificial insemination, semen is introduced into a woman's uterus or vagina by means other than sexual intercourse.

[144] Women who cannot conceive due to fallopian tube disorders use this technique, in which an egg is fertilized outside a woman's body and then implanted in her uterus. *See* Note, *Reproductive Technology and the Procreation Rights of the Unmarried*, 98 HARV. L. REV. 669, 669 n.2 (1985) [hereinafter Note, *Reproductive Technology*].

[145] In surrogacy, a woman agrees to be artificially inseminated and to surrender the resulting child to the father or the father and his wife, usually for a fee. *See id.* at 669 n.4.

[146] Some lesbians who cannot conceive through either of these techniques may be able to become pregnant through in vitro fertilization. *See supra* note 144.

[147] *See* Note, *The Lesbian Family: Rights in Conflict Under the California Uniform Parentage Act*, 10 GOLDEN GATE U.L. REV. 1007, 1009 n.11 (1980) (stating that a woman can artificially inseminate herself "with a needleless syringe, turkey baster, or eyedropper").

[148] Fornication statutes generally criminalize sexual intercourse between unmarried persons. *See, e.g.,* IDAHO CODE § 18-6603 (1987); MINN. STAT. § 609.34 (1988) (criminalizing intercourse between any man and a single woman); N.C. GEN. STAT. § 14-184 (1987); R.I. GEN. LAWS § 11-6-3 (1981); VA. CODE ANN. § 18.2-344 (1986); W. VA. CODE § 61-8-3 (1989).

[149] *See, e.g.,* CONN. GEN. STAT. § 45-69g(b) (1989) (requiring the consent of both the husband and wife for artificial insemination); IDAHO CODE § 39-5403 (1987) (requiring the consent of the woman's husband); OKLA. STAT. ANN. tit. 10, § 551 (West 1987). One might, however, interpret these statutes as requiring the husband's consent only if the woman is married. *See* Kritchevsky, *The Unmarried Woman's Right to Artificial Insemination: A Call for an Expanded Definition of Family*, 4 HARV. WOMEN'S L.J. 1, 19 (1981).

[150] *See, e.g.,* Doe v. Duling, 782 F.2d 1202, 1206 (4th Cir. 1986) (dismissing a constitutional challenge to Virginia's fornication statute because the threat of prosecution was too remote to give standing).

[151] In addition, physicians may refuse to artificially inseminate unmarried women or lesbians

insemination is a serious concern in part because the parental rights
of the donor may turn on whether a physician performed the procedure.[152]

Statutes that prohibit the artificial insemination of or fornication
by unmarried women should be invalidated as an unconstitutional
restriction of the right to procreate.[153] The Supreme Court has repeatedly recognized constitutional protection for the "decision whether
to bear or beget a child."[154] Although almost all of these cases involve
the right of access to techniques that prevent procreation,[155] the procreation right also requires a compelling justification for legislation
limiting access to reproductive techniques.[156] Prohibiting both artifi-

---

because of moral or religious objections. *See, e.g.,* Strong & Schinfeld, *The Single Woman and
Artificial Insemination by Donor,* 29 J. REPRODUCTIVE MED. 293, 297–99 (1984) (discussing
ethical objections to the artificial insemination of single women and lesbians); Perkoff, *Artificial
Insemination in a Lesbian: A Case Analysis,* 145 ARCHIVES INTERNAL MED. 527, 528 (1985)
(discussing religious objections to artificial insemination).

[152] *See infra* pp. 143–44. Women who do not use physicians can decrease the risk of a
custody battle by using sperm from more than one donor or by having a third party act as an
intermediary to prevent the donor from learning her identity. *See* Note, *Family Law in a Brave
New World: Private Ordering of Parental Rights and Responsibilities for Donor Insemination,*
1 BERKELEY WOMEN'S L.J. 140, 143 (1985) [hereinafter Note, *Private Ordering*]. *See generally*
Note, *The Fourteenth Amendment's Protection of a Woman's Right To Be a Single Parent
Through Artificial Insemination by Donor,* 7 Women's Rts. L. Rep. (Rutgers Univ.) 251, 253–
57 (1982) [hereinafter Note, *Single Parent*] (discussing the advantages and disadvantages of using
sperm banks, third-party intermediaries, and known donors). Denial of physician-performed
artificial insemination also harms women by making access to and screening of potential donors
more difficult.

[153] *See* Skinner v. Oklahoma, 316 U.S. 535, 541 (1942) (stating that procreation is a "basic
civil right[] of man"); *see also* Bowers v. Hardwick, 478 U.S. 186, 190–91 (1986) (dictum)
(formulating the right to privacy as extending to procreation and procreation decisions). *See
generally* Note, *Reproductive Technology, supra* note 144, at 674–84 (arguing that restricting
unmarried persons' access to reproductive techniques may violate the right to procreate and the
equal protection clause); Note, *Single Parent, supra* note 152, at 259–83 (same). At least one
fornication statute has been held unconstitutional on privacy grounds. *See* State v. Saunders,
75 N.J. 200, 210–20, 381 A.2d 333, 337–43 (1977).

[154] Eisenstadt v. Baird, 405 U.S. 438, 453 (1972); *accord Hardwick,* 478 U.S. at 190; Carey
v. Population Servs. Int'l, 431 U.S. 678, 685 (1977) (quoting *Eisenstadt*). The right to procreate
is not limited to married couples. Privacy rights inhere in the individual rather than in a
marriage or family relationship. *See, e.g., Eisenstadt,* 405 U.S. at 453; *see also* Robertson,
Embryos, Families, and Procreative Liberty: The Legal Structure of the New Reproduction, 59
S. CAL. L. REV. 939, 962–64 (1986) (discussing arguments for and against recognizing a right
of unmarried persons to procreate). Robertson believes that the Court may differentiate between
unmarried persons' right to contraception and abortion and their right to procreate on the
grounds that the denial of the former "interferes with bodily integrity." *Id.* at 963. However,
privacy cases explicitly place abortion and contraception rights in the context of the procreative
decision. *See, e.g., Hardwick,* 478 U.S. at 190.

[155] *See, e.g.,* Roe v. Wade, 410 U.S. 113 (1973) (abortion); Griswold v. Connecticut, 381
U.S. 479 (1965) (contraception). *But see* Skinner v. Oklahoma, 316 U.S. 535, 541 (1942) (holding
unconstitutional a statute authorizing sterilization of certain types of criminals).

[156] *See, e.g.,* Note, *Reproductive Technology, supra* note 144, at 674–84; Donovan, *The*

cial insemination and fornication completely denies an unmarried woman the ability to procreate. Denying access to either form of procreation, furthermore, hinders the procreation decision as severely as prohibitions on either contraception or abortion alone. The Court has held that strict scrutiny is required for legislation that limits access to contraception or abortion even if it does not entirely prohibit access.[157] Similarly, prohibiting access only to artificial insemination burdens the right to choose to procreate even though procreation through sexual intercourse may still be available.

The state interests served by prohibitions against artificial insemination or fornication insufficiently justify the burdens they impose on the fundamental right to procreate. The major state interests in prohibiting these practices are in discouraging single-parent families and in encouraging marriage. The former is most likely based on a belief that children are better off in "traditional" two-parent households but is not sufficiently served by these restrictions. It is overinclusive in that many children conceived by unmarried women will be raised by two adults; it is underinclusive since many children born to married women are raised by only one parent.[158] Furthermore, recent studies belie the assumption that children are better off in two-parent families.[159]

The state interest in promoting marriage is likewise insufficient to justify limiting the right to procreate. First, as discussed above,[160] this state interest is not compelling enough to justify burdening a fundamental right. Moreover, restrictions on only either artificial insemination or fornication are insufficiently related to the state's goal. It is improbable that women who otherwise would remain single would choose to marry simply because they could not be artificially inseminated.

(b) Issues Faced by Gay Men. — The major difficulty encountered by gay men wishing to become fathers is not in access to reproductive methods but in ensuring parental rights. Gay men, like lesbians, can use either artificial insemination or sexual intercourse to produce their

---

Uniform Parentage Act and Nonmarital Motherhood-by-Choice, 11 N.Y.U. REV. L. & SOC. CHANGE 193, 222–25 (1983); Robertson, *supra* note 154, at 964–67.

[157] *See* Carey v. Population Servs. Int'l, 431 U.S. 678, 688 (1977).

[158] Approximately half of first marriages are expected to end in divorce; the more children a woman has, the less likely she is to remarry. *See* P. BLUMSTEIN & P. SCHWARTZ, *supra* note 85, at 33.

[159] *See* McGuire & Alexander, *Artifical Insemination of Single Women*, 43 FERTILITY & STERILITY 182, 182–83 (1985) (citing studies); *see also* Golombok & Rust, *The Warnock Report and Single Women: What About the Children?*, 12 J. MED. ETHICS 182, 182 (1986) (noting that previous studies showing higher rates of emotional and behavioral problems for children raised in fatherless families failed to control for effects of mothers' divorces, smaller incomes, and greater social isolation).

[160] *See supra* p. 100 (arguing that promoting traditional values is an uncompelling state interest).

children. Because the restrictions on access to artificial insemination depend solely on the woman's marital status, gay men in every state can legally father children by donating semen to artificially inseminate married women.[161] However, a man wishing to raise the child he sires wants more than a role in conception. Such a man must, like all men who want to raise their natural children, find a woman willing to bear the child for him and allow him to share in parenting responsibilities. Defining both of their legal rights and responsibilities poses the major obstacle to parenting by gay men.

2. Legally Defining Rights and Responsibilities. — Gay men and lesbians who do have children may face difficulties in legally defining two relationships with the child. First, they may be unable to control the extent of the other biological parent's rights and responsibilities. Some lesbian and gay parents want the second biological parent to have no contact with the child, while others may wish to share custody and responsibility.[162] Second, they may be unable to ensure that the parent's same-sex partner, or "co-parent," has the legal rights of a parent, including the rights to give consent on behalf of the child or to custody or visitation if the couple separates or the biological parent dies.

(a) Rights of the Other Biological Parent. — Unless a child is adopted, his or her natural mother is a legal parent. Whether the father is a legal parent is more complicated and depends on the mother's marital status, the reproductive technique used, and applicable statutes.[163] Both natural parents' rights can be terminated by adoption and can sometimes be limited or terminated by an agreement between the parents.

Assuming the mother is unmarried, if the child is conceived through sexual intercourse and paternity is established, the father generally has equal rights and responsibilities.[164] If the child is conceived through artificial insemination, the donor's status depends on whether the state has a statute that regulates artificial insemination

---

[161] In states with fornication statutes, sexual intercourse to produce the child is illegal if the man is not married to the child's mother. *See supra* note 148 and accompanying text.

[162] *See* J. SCHULENBURG, *supra* note 102, at 90.

[163] The following discussion assumes that the parents are not married to each other. However, sometimes a lesbian and a gay man who choose to have a child together will marry each other to simplify the legal relationships. *See, e.g.,* J. SCHULENBURG, *supra* note 102, at 98 (discussing a gay man and a lesbian who are married to each other and raising three adopted children).

[164] *See* A. HARALAMBIE, *supra* note 3, § 2.07, at 15. If the mother is married, there is a presumption that her husband is the father. *See, e.g.,* CAL. CIV. CODE § 7004(a)(1) (West 1983); MD. EST. & TRUSTS CODE ANN. § 1-206 (1974). This presumption may be effectively irrebuttable when challenged by a putative father seeking parental rights due to provisions permitting only the mother or her husband to bring an action to determine paternity. *See, e.g.,* CAL. EVID. CODE § 621(c), (d) (West 1966 & Supp. 1989).

of unmarried women. Of the twenty-eight states with artificial insemination statutes,[165] only seven have statutes that facially apply to the paternity of an unmarried woman's child.[166] In five of these states, a donor of semen for physician-performed insemination will not be the legal father, but these statutes do not cover at-home inseminations.[167] The other two states eliminate donor paternity regardless of a physician's participation.[168]

If the state has no applicable statute, it is unclear whether the legal status of the natural father of a child born to an unmarried woman differs depending on the method of conception.[169] Only two reported cases have decided whether a sperm donor is a legal parent when the woman is unmarried; both treated the child conceived via at-home insemination as the natural child of the donor.[170] In both cases, however, the donor was known and he expected to play a role in the child's life.[171] If the donor is eager to be a father to the child and the court believes it is important for the child to have a legal father,[172] or if there is a statute that denies donors paternity rights in other situations but is silent as to the particular situation at issue,[173] courts may be more likely to consider the donor the legal father. On the other hand, if attempts were made to make the donation anony-

---

[165] See Note, *Artificial Insemination: Donor Rights in Situations Involving Unmarried Women*, 26 J. FAM. L. 793, 795 n.14 (1987–1988) (citing statutes).

[166] See CAL. CIV. CODE § 7005(b) (West 1983); COLO. REV. STAT. § 19-4-106(2) (Supp. 1988); N.J. REV. STAT. § 9:17-44 (Supp. 1988); OR. REV. STAT. ANN. § 109.239 (1987); TEX. FAM. CODE ANN. § 12.03(b) (Vernon 1986); WASH. REV. CODE § 26.26.050(2) (1985); WYO. STAT. § 14-2-103(b) (1986).

The other 21 statutes refer only to married women. *See, e.g.*, ALA. CODE § 26-17-21 (1986); ALASKA STAT. § 25.20.045 (1987); MINN. STAT. § 257.56(2) (1988); MONT. CODE ANN. § 40-6-106(2) (1987); VA. CODE ANN. § 64.1-7.1 (1987).

[167] See CAL. CIV. CODE § 7005(b) (West 1983); COLO. REV. STAT. § 19-4-106(2) (Supp. 1988); N.J. REV. STAT. § 9:17-44 (Supp. 1988); WASH. REV. CODE § 26.26.050(2) (1985); WYO. STAT. § 14-2-103(b) (1986). By making the donor's legal status hinge on a doctor's participation, these statutes give the medical profession an unjustifiable power to determine who will and will not have access to artificial insemination without the threat of paternity claims.

[168] See OR. REV. STAT. ANN. § 109.239 (1987); TEX. FAM. CODE ANN. § 12.03(b) (Vernon 1986).

[169] See Donovan, *supra* note 156, at 220.

[170] See Jhordan C. v. Mary K., 179 Cal. App. 3d 386, 224 Cal. Rptr. 530 (1986) (awarding visitation rights to the donor of semen used in an at-home insemination); C.M. v. C.C., 152 N.J. Super. 160, 377 A.2d 821 (Juvenile & Dom. Rel. Ct. 1977) (same).

[171] See *Jhordan C.*, 179 Cal. App. 3d at 389, 179 Cal. Rptr. at 532; *C.M.*, 152 N.J. Super. at 161, 377 A.2d at 821–22.

[172] See *C.M.*, 152 N.J. Super. at 167, 377 A.2d at 824–25. If the mother intends to raise the child with her same-sex partner or another adult, the fact that "[i]t is in a child's best interests to have two parents whenever possible," *id.*, 377 A.2d at 825, should not affect whether the donor is the legal father.

[173] For example, in *Jhordan C.*, the statute denied the donor paternity rights if the donation was "provided to a licensed physician." *See Jhordan C.*, 179 Cal. App. 3d at 389, 224 Cal. Rptr. at 531 (quoting CAL. CIV. CODE § 7005(b) (West 1983)).

mous or if the donor should not have expected that he would have contact with the child, courts may be more likely to follow cases holding that, in the insemination of a married woman, the donor "is no more responsible for the use made of his sperm than is the donor of blood or a kidney."[174]

Regardless of the technique used or the state statutory scheme, a natural parent's rights and responsibilities under certain circumstances may be terminated or limited by agreement. A parent can consent to termination of his or her rights by consenting to adoption of the child[175] or, in some states, by agreeing to relinquish parental rights independent of an adoption.[176] However, such agreements are always revocable before the birth of the child.[177] Although parents cannot apportion custody and visitation rights to the detriment of the child's best interests, agreements as to custody and visitation may affect future court decisions.[178]

Denying a woman the ability to eliminate contractually a man's parental rights and responsibilities burdens her right to procreate. Otherwise, women who wish to procreate are forced to find a man willing to risk being legally obligated to support a child financially.[179] The state has no countervailing interest that justifies this burden on a woman's right to procreate. As long as the woman is willing to accept full responsibility for financially supporting the child, eliminating the burden on the woman's procreation right will not force the state to support additional children. The state might defend schemes that do not permit unmarried women to agree with potential fathers to eliminate their parental rights and responsibilities as necessary to ensure that the child has a legally-established father. However, this justification is insufficiently related to the state action. Most men who

---

[174] People v. Sorenson, 68 Cal. 2d 280, 284, 437 P.2d 495, 498, 66 Cal. Rptr. 7, 10 (1968).

[175] *See* A. HARALAMBIE, *supra* note 3, § 13.17, at 210. Termination of parental rights via adoption can also occur without consent under specified circumstances. *See, e.g.*, HAW. REV. STAT. § 578-2(c) (1988) (stating that consent is not required from a parent who, although able to do so, has failed to communicate with or to provide support and care for the child for at least one year); IND. CODE § 31-3-1-6(g)(1) (1976) (stating that consent is not required from a parent who abandoned the child for the preceding six months).

[176] *See, e.g.*, ARK. STAT. ANN. § 9-9-220(b) (1987). Generally, termination of parental rights occurs in connection with either adoption or state-initiated neglect proceedings. *See* 3 L. WARDLE, C. BLAKESLEY & J. PARKER, CONTEMPORARY FAMILY LAW § 28.01, at 2 (1988).

[177] *See* M. FIELD, SURROGATE MOTHERHOOD 84 (1988).

[178] *See, e.g.*, Raddish v. Raddish, 652 S.W.2d 668, 670 (Ky. Ct. App. 1983) (stating that "free and voluntary agreements" between parents may impact child custody orders); Masitto v. Masitto, 22 Ohio. St. 3d 63, 67, 488 N.E.2d 857, 861 (1986) (holding that voluntary relinquishment can be the basis for a custody award to a nonparent).

[179] *See* Donovan, *supra* note 156, at 226–27; Robertson, *Procreative Liberty and the Control of Conception, Pregnancy and Childbirth*, 69 VA. L. REV. 405, 436 (1983) (arguing that "[t]he right to noncoital, collaborative reproduction . . . includes the right of the parties to agree how they should allocate their obligations and entitlements with respect to the child").

would agree to terminate their paternal rights would not want to help raise a child. Because of the possibility of financial obligation, however, if pre-conception contracts to terminate parental rights are unenforceable, these men may be unwilling to father children.

Surrogacy arrangements — in which a man or a couple pays a woman to bear the man's child and terminate her parental rights — raise additional issues about the validity of contracts to terminate parental rights.[180] Some states have enacted legislation making compensated surrogacy arrangements unenforceable or illegal;[181] in other states, courts have refused to enforce surrogacy contracts, holding that they violate baby-selling laws.[182]

(b) Rights of the Co-Parent. — When a gay or lesbian couple chooses to have a child, only the biological parent is automatically the child's legal parent. If that parent dies, the surviving partner, or "co-parent," may lose custody to either the child's other biological parent or other relatives of the child. In addition, if the couple breaks up, the legal parent may be able to prohibit any contact between the co-parent and the child.

Same-sex couples can attempt to avoid these difficulties in several ways. First, adoption of the child by the co-parent, if permitted without extinguishing the legal parent's rights, ensures that both partners will have equal legal rights and responsibilities with respect to the child.[183] Second, the natural parent can appoint the co-parent as testamentary guardian in case of death. Finally, if the couple separates or the natural parent dies, the co-parent can claim custody or visitation rights under a "psychological parent" theory.[184]

---

[180] For a comprehensive treatment of all the statutory, constitutional, and policy issues raised by surrogacy, see M. FIELD, cited above in note 177; and *Surrogate Motherhood*, 16 LAW, MED. & HEALTH CARE 5 (1988), which presents a collection of articles on surrogacy.

[181] *See* FLA. STAT. § 63.212(1)(i) (Supp. 1987) (making compensated surrogacy arrangements illegal); LA. REV. STAT. ANN. § 9:2713 (West Supp. 1989) (declaring compensated surrogacy contracts null and void); 1988 Mich. Legis. Serv., Pub. Act. No. 199 (West) (to be codified as MICH. COMP. LAWS § 722.855) (declaring surrogate parenting contracts void and unenforceable); *id.* (to be codified as MICH. COMP. LAWS § 722.859) (declaring participation in a surrogacy arrangement a misdemeanor).

[182] *See, e.g., In re* Baby M., 109 N.J. 396, 537 A.2d 1227 (1988) (finding surrogacy contract illegal under baby-selling prohibitions).

[183] *See generally* Note, *Second Parent Adoption: When Crossing the Marital Barrier Is in a Child's Best Interests*, 3 BERKELEY WOMEN'S L.J. 96 (1987) [hereinafter, Note, *Crossing the Barrier*]; Note, *Private Ordering, supra* note 152; Comment, *Second Parent Adoption for Lesbian-Parented Families: Legal Recognition of the Other Mother*, 19 U.C. DAVIS. L. REV. 729 (1986).

Joint guardianship of the child by the parent and his or her partner, if state law permits two unmarried persons to be joint guardians, will achieve a similar result but with less permanence. *See, e.g.,* CONN. GEN. STAT. § 45-45 (1989) (permitting appointment of "coguardians").

[184] A psychological parent is an adult who, regardless of biological relationship to the child, "on a continuing day-to-day basis . . . fulfills the child's psychological needs for a parent, as

In at least three states, courts have permitted a parent's same-sex partner to adopt a child without terminating the parent's rights.[185] This type of adoption is effectively identical to a stepparent adoption in which a child is adopted by the new spouse of a remarried parent without affecting the latter's parental rights.[186] Stepparent adoptions, however, are often covered by special statutory provisions that do not provide for adoption by partners in a nonmarital relationship.[187] Whether courts will permit co-parent adoptions therefore depends on the requirements of the rest of the state adoption statute and on the court's analysis of the child's best interests.

Depending on the state, there are at least two potential statutory roadblocks to co-parent adoptions.[188] First, statutes provide that adoption terminates both natural parents' rights and obligations.[189] In states without explicit exceptions for stepparent adoptions,[190] however, couples can argue that such provisions are not meant to apply to situations in which a natural parent plans to raise the child jointly with the adoptive parent. In other states, couples can argue that the court should waive the termination provision,[191] or they can attempt to present the adoption as a joint adoption between the parent and co-parent.[192]

---

well as the child's physical needs." J. GOLDSTEIN, A. FREUD & A. SOLNIT, *supra* note 127, at 98.

[185] *See* Note, *Crossing the Barrier, supra* note 183, at 98 (citing *In re* Adoption Petition of N., No. 18086 (Cal. Super. Ct., San Francisco County, filed Mar. 11, 1986); *In re* Adoption of a Minor Child, No. 1-JU-86-73 (Alaska Super. Ct. Feb. 6, 1987); and *In re* Adoption of M.M.S.A., No. D-8503-61930 (Or. Cir. Ct., Multnomah County, Sept. 4, 1985)). The Lesbian Rights Project, 1370 Mission Street, Fourth Floor, San Francisco, CA 94103, has additional information on co-parent adoptions.

[186] *See* H. CLARK, *supra* note 4, § 20.10, at 928 (stating that stepparent adoptions are an exception to the general rule of termination of both parents' rights).

[187] *See, e.g.,* ALASKA STAT. § 25.23.130 (1983); VA. CODE ANN. § 63.1-233 (1987).

[188] Florida and New Hampshire both prohibit adoption by homosexuals. *See* FLA. STAT. ANN. § 63.042(3) (West 1985); N.H. REV. STAT. ANN. § 170-B:4 (Supp. 1988). The co-parent will probably be unable to adopt the child in these states.

[189] *See, e.g.,* ARIZ. REV. STAT. ANN. § 8-117(B) (1974); COLO. REV. STAT. § 19-4-113(2) (1986); N.Y. DOM. REL. LAW § 117(a) (McKinney 1988); N.C. GEN. STAT. § 48-23(2) (1984).

[190] *See, e.g.,* MASS. GEN. L. ch. 210, § 6 (1987).

[191] *See, e.g., In re* Adoption of a Minor Child, No. 1-JU-86-73, slip op at 4 (Alaska Super. Ct. Feb. 6, 1987) (permitting waiver in a co-parent adoption).

[192] There are two potential difficulties with the latter approach. First, statutes in many states that specify who is eligible to adopt could be interpreted to bar adoptions by two persons not married to each other because the statute does not explicitly authorize such adoptions. *See, e.g.,* HAW. REV. STAT. ANN. § 578-1 (1988) (permitting any unmarried adult, any spouse of a legal parent, or a husband and wife to petition to adopt); N.D. CENT. CODE § 14-15-03 (1981); VT. STAT. ANN. tit. 15, § 431 (1974) (permitting "a person or husband and wife together" to adopt). Second, some states may not permit a parent to adopt his or her own child, particularly if the effect of the adoption is to terminate the other biological parent's rights. *See* H. CLARK, *supra* note 4, § 20.7, at 910.

Second, some state laws severely limit private placement adoptions by requiring all adoptions other than by stepparents or blood relatives to be placed through an agency.[193] Because this gives the agency discretion in placing the child, such a provision could effectively prevent co-parent adoptions. Couples can also argue that the agency placement requirement, which was meant to prevent baby-selling,[194] should be waived as the parent is not relinquishing his or her parental rights.

As in child custody determinations, state law stipulates that a primary consideration in adoption cases is the child's best interests. Even if co-parent adoptions do not fit exactly within the statutory framework, courts should grant such petitions because they would further the children's best interests.[195] Because the child will be raised in a gay or lesbian household whether or not the adoption is granted, the effect of a co-parent's orientation on a child is of little significance.[196] Rather, the major effect of granting the adoption is to give the child the benefit and additional security of having two legal parents willing to assume responsibilitites. After such an adoption, the child not only has two adults obligated to support him or her, and able to consent to medical care and otherwise peform legal parental duties, but the relationship between the child and the co-parent cannot be disrupted absent a good cause. Because continuity of relationships is extremely important to a child's psychological well-being,[197] formalizing this relationship may in fact be the most important benefit from co-parent adoptions.

If the co-parent does not adopt the child, there are other, albeit less effective, ways to ensure that his or her relationship with the child continues if the parent dies or the couple separates. First, the parent, in drawing up his or her will, can nominate the co-parent to

---

[193] *See* CONN. GEN. STAT. § 45-63(3) (1989); DEL. CODE ANN. tit. 13, § 904 (Supp. 1988); *see also* N.M. STAT. ANN. § 40-7-34 (1986) (requiring a minor to be placed in the home of proposed adopting parents by a licensed child placement agency unless the adopter is a blood relative, a stepparent, or a sponsor at a baptism or confirmation). Many other states require agency investigations or recommendations for private placement adoptions other than stepparent adoptions. *See, e.g.,* IDAHO CODE § 16-1506 (1979); KAN. STAT. ANN. § 59-2278 (1979); MASS. GEN. L. ch. 210, § 2A (1987).

[194] *See* H. CLARK, *supra* note 4, § 20.1, at 852–53.

[195] In some states, provisions state that the child's best interests are the "paramount consideration in the construction and interpretation" of the adoption statutes. *See, e.g.,* ILL. REV. STAT. ch. 40, para. 1525 (1987). Furthermore, because it is unlikely that those who enacted the current adoption statutes considered whether to permit co-parent adoptions, the legislative intent to further the child's best interests should take precedence over the technical provisions with which these adoptions may not comply. *See* Note, *Crossing the Barrier, supra* note 183, at 113–14.

[196] As discussed in section VI.A above, courts should not assume that being raised by a gay or lesbian parent is not in a child's best interests. *See supra* pp. 127–29.

[197] *See* J. GOLDSTEIN, A. FREUD & A. SOLNIT, *supra* note 127, at 31–34.

be the testamentary guardian of the child.[198] Generally, in the event
of the natural parent's death or incapacitation, the court will appoint
the person nominated as guardian unless there is another surviving
legal parent.[199]

Second, if the legal parent dies or the couple separates, the co-
parent can argue that he or she is a psychological parent of the child
and therefore entitled to custody or at least visitation rights.[200] If the
biological parent dies, the co-parent's chances of obtaining legal custody depend on whether the other biological parent is a legal parent
and petitions for custody.[201] All states have a presumption favoring
a biological parent in custody cases against a nonparent.[202] In some
states, the parent prevails unless the nonparent proves that the parent
is unfit or that the child's welfare requires that the nonparent be
awarded custody.[203] In other states, however, a nonparent can prevail
even if the parent is fit, if custody with the nonparent is clearly in
the child's best interests.[204] In several cases in which a child has
lived with and formed an attachment to a nonparent, courts have
awarded the nonparent custody based explicitly or implicitly on a
determination that the nonparent is the child's psychological parent.[205]

---

[198] *See, e.g.*, ALA. CODE § 26-2A-71 (Supp. 1988); MD. EST. & TRUSTS CODE ANN. § 13-
701 (1974); R.I. GEN. LAWS § 33-5-4 (1984).

[199] *See, e.g.*, DEL. CODE ANN. tit. 12, § 3904 (1987) (providing that the guardian named by
the sole surviving parent "shall be appointed, if there is no just cause to the contrary"); OKLA.
STAT. tit. 30, § 6 (1976); TEX. PROB. CODE ANN. § 117 (Vernon 1980) (stating that a surviving
parent can appoint "any qualified person"). In many states, however, a child above a certain
age can challenge the appointment. *See, e.g.*, ALASKA STAT. § 13.26.040 (1985) (minor over
fourteen); CONN. GEN. STAT. § 45-51(b) (1987) (ward over the age of twelve); N.M. STAT.
ANN. § 45-5-203 (1978) (over age fourteen).

[200] *See, e.g.*, *In re* Hatzopoulos, 4 Fam. L. Rep. (BNA) 2075 (Colo. Juvenile Ct. 1977)
(granting custody to mother's ex-lover after mother's death based implicitly on the psychological
parent theory).

[201] Of course, if the other biological parent is unaware of the child's identity he or she cannot
request custody.

[202] *See supra* p. 124.

[203] *See, e.g.*, Turner v. Pannick, 540 P.2d 1051 (Alaska 1975); Pape v. Pape, 444 So. 2d
1058 (Fla. Ct. App. 1984); Paquette v. Paquette, 146 Vt. 83, 92, 499 A.2d 23, 30 (1985).

[204] In a custody dispute involving a third party, courts generally use a stricter test than the
best interests standard applied in custody cases between parents. *See, e.g.*, Cebrzynski v.
Cebrzynski, 63 Ill. App. 3d 66, 379 N.E.2d 713 (1978) (awarding a stepmother custody despite
the mother's fitness because change could be detrimental to the children's psychological well-
being); Hoy v. Willis, 165 N.J. Super. 265, 398 A.2d 109 (1978); Husack v. Husack, 273 Pa.
Super. 192, 417 A.2d 233 (1979); Bailes v. Sours, 231 Va. 96, 340 S.E.2d 824 (1986); *In re
Marriage of Allen*, 28 Wash. App. 637, 645–46, 626 P.2d 16, 21 (1981); *see also* R.A.D. v.
M.E.Z., 414 A.2d 211 (Del. Super. Ct. 1980) (awarding a grandmother custody on a best
interests test).

[205] *See, e.g.*, Gorman v. Gorman, 400 So. 2d 75, 78 (Fla. Ct. App. 1981); *Cebrzynski*, 63
Ill. App. 3d 66, 379 N.E.2d 713 (1978); *Husack*, 273 Pa. Super. 192, 417 A.2d 233; *Bailes*, 231
Va. 96, 340 S.E.2d 824. *But see In re* Custody of Krause, 111 Ill. App. 3d 604, 444 N.E.2d
644 (1982) (awarding custody to the natural parent where the child had lived with his stepparent
most of his life and preferred the stepparent).

Although none of these cases involved children raised by a gay or lesbian couple, the psychological parent theory is equally applicable in such a case.

In disputes between the co-parent and a nonparent relative of the child, the parties begin on an equal footing.[206] Courts generally view the wishes of the deceased parent or parents as a relevant factor.[207] A co-parent with whom the child has lived and to whom the child has formed ties should therefore have a very strong argument for custody over a nonparent relative.[208]

If the couple separates, the co-parent in many states does not have standing to petition for custody or visitation.[209] If the co-parent does have standing, visitation will probably be granted;[210] however, only in exceptional circumstances will the co-parent be able to override the presumption favoring custody by the parent. Unlike disputes between the co-parent and the other biological parent following the custodial parent's death, both litigants in these disputes will have lived with and formed ties to the child. Therefore, it is less likely that the co-parent can argue for custody on a psychological parent theory. However, in unusual situations courts have awarded custody to a stepparent upon the divorce of the stepparent and the parent.[211]

D. Conclusion

Today, gay men and lesbians are raising children in a variety of circumstances. Some are children from former marriages or nonmarital heterosexual relationships, others are adopted or foster children, and a growing number are children gay and lesbians couples and individuals choose to have. Regardless of the circumstances of the

---

[206] See H. CLARK, supra note 4, § 19.8, at 833–34 (stating that the burden between nonparents is equally divided).

[207] See id. at 834.

[208] See In re Hatzopoulos, 4 Fam. L. Rep. (BNA) 2075 (Colo. Juvenile Ct. 1977) (granting custody to mother's former lover over child's aunt and uncle because of the strong ties between the ex-lover and the child).

[209] Many state statutes allow nonparents to petition for custody only if the child is not in the physical custody of a parent. See, e.g., ARIZ. REV. STAT. ANN. § 25-331(B)(2) (Supp. 1988); see also WASH. REV. CODE § 26.09.180(1)(b) (1985) (permitting a nonparent to bring a custody petition if it "alleges that neither parent is a suitable custodian"). California courts, in contrast, have given standing to nonparents on a psychological parent theory. See In re B.G., 11 Cal. 3d 679, 692–93, 523 P.2d 244, 253–54, 114 Cal. Rptr. 444, 453–54 (1974); Shapiro & Schultz, Single-Sex Families: The Impact of Birth Innovations upon Traditional Family Notions, 24 J. FAM. L. 271, 271–73 (discussing Loftin v. Flournoy, No. 569630-7 (Cal. Super. Ct. Sept. 4, 1984), which awarded a co-parent visitation rights to her ex-lover's child).

[210] Courts are often willing to award a stepparent visitation rights when the stepparent is in loco parentis if the visitation is in the child's best interests. See, e.g., Bryan v. Bryan, 132 Ariz. 353, 645 P.2d 1267 (Ct. App. 1982); Collins v. Gilbreath, 403 N.E.2d 921 (Ind. Ct. App. 1980).

[211] See, e.g., In re Marriage of Allen, 28 Wash. App. 637, 648, 626 P.2d 16, 23 (1981).

child's birth, the legal treatment of the parent/child relationship should not turn solely on the parent's sexual orientation. Rather than promoting prejudice by basing decisions on false stereotypes or perceived community intolerance, courts and legislatures should instead further the children's welfare by focusing on their need for stable and supportive home environments. As this Part has argued, because sexual orientation alone is irrelevant to parenting ability, gay men and lesbians should not be denied custody of or visitation with their children, or the possibility of becoming adoptive or foster parents. Similarly, rather than burdening the choice of lesbians and gay men to become parents by limiting access to reproductive techniques, the state should help ensure continuity of care by recognizing the co-parent's role through permitting co-parent adoptions.

VII. OTHER DISCRIMINATION ISSUES

In recent years, the growing public awareness that gay men and lesbians constitute a discrete social group[1] has contributed to discrimination on the basis of sexual orientation in a variety of diverse areas. This section explores several areas in which sexual orientation discrimination has emerged as a basis for litigation.[2]

A. Immigration and Deportation

The legal status of aliens[3] is in jeopardy at all stages of the immigration and naturalization process. Working together, the Immigration and Naturalization Service (INS)[4] and the Public Health Service (PHS)[5] may deny aliens a visa or entry into the country, may re-evaluate and deny aliens re-entry should they leave the country and then wish to return, may deport aliens, or may deny aliens permanent citizenship.

---

[1] *See supra* p. 5.

[2] These areas are for the most part new to the courts, and have not been clearly defined. The incidence of discrimination in these areas is also difficult to assess because many cases of alleged discrimination do not reach the courts but are instead brought to the attention of human rights commissions or other similar entitites. *See, e.g.,* BOSTON, MA., CODE tit. 12, ch. 16, § 411 (1984) (establishing procedures for filing complaints of sexual orientation discrimination with the Boston Human Rights Commission).

[3] An "alien" is "any person not a citizen or national of the United States." 8 U.S.C. § 1101(a)(3) (1982).

[4] The INS is responsible for performing general inspection procedures on immigrants. *See id.* § 1225(a).

[5] The PHS is responsible for performing medical examinations on immigrants. *See id.* § 1224.

Gay and lesbian aliens have been particularly affected by section 212(a) of the Immigration and Nationality Act (INA).[6] Subsection 1182(a)(4) denies entry into the United States to persons "afflicted with psychopathic personality, or sexual deviation,"[7] and subsection 1182(a)(9) provides that "[a]liens who have been convicted of a crime involving moral turpitude" may not be admitted.[8]

Generally, gay men and lesbians have been disqualified as "psychopaths" under subsection 1182(a)(4). In *Boutilier v. Immigration & Naturalization Service*,[9] the Supreme Court ruled that Congress, in adopting the INA, intended to exclude all homosexuals from admission under the category of "psychopathic personality." In so ruling, the Court relied heavily not only on the act's legislative history but also on the Public Health Service's determination that "psychopathic personality" is a broad term that encompasses homosexuality. Although subsection 1182(a)(4) also excludes "sexual deviates," the Court regarded homosexuality as a psychopathic disorder rather than a sexual deviation.[10]

Subsequent to the Court's ruling in *Boutilier*, federal courts and the medical community have differed over whether and in what manner determinations about an alien's psychological state should be made. In 1979, the Department of Health, Education, and Welfare ordered that, in accordance with prevailing psychiatric and medical theories, the PHS could no longer certify that an alien suffered from a medical condition requiring exclusion solely because he or she was a homosexual.[11] The change in this practice of issuing "Class A" certificates significantly restricted the INS's ability to exclude gay and lesbian applicants.

Despite the administrative mandate, federal courts have continued to rely upon medical certification, albeit to differing degrees. In *Hill v. United States Immigration & Naturalization Service*,[12] the Ninth Circuit prohibited the INS from excluding an alien unless he or she

---

[6] Pub. L. No. 82-414, 66 Stat. 163 (1952) (codified as amended at 8 U.S.C. §§ 1101–1503 (1982)).

[7] 8 U.S.C. § 1182(a)(4) (1982).

[8] *Id.* § 1182(a)(9).

[9] 387 U.S. 118 (1967).

[10] *See id.* at 122; *see also* Note, *The Propriety of Denying Entry to Homosexual Aliens: Examining the Public Health Service's Authority over Medical Exclusions*, 17 J. L. REFORM 331 (1984) (pointing out that current U.S. immigration policy is ill-defined and largely contingent on a determination of the PHS's role in defining medical states and disorders for the purposes of exclusion under the INA).

[11] *See* Memorandum from Julius Richmond, Assistant Secretary for Health, United States Department of Health, Education, and Welfare, to William Foege, Director, CDC, and George Lythcott, Administrator, HSA (Aug. 2, 1979), *reprinted in* 56 INTERPRETER RELEASES 398–99 (1979).

[12] 714 F.2d 1470 (9th Cir. 1983).

has received a Class A certification. The court argued that excluding an alien on the basis of any other information, such as the testimony of the applicant or any other lay person, would be contrary to judicial precedent, administrative custom, legislative intent, and the language of the act.[13] However, in *In re Longstaff*,[14] the Fifth Circuit held that a medical certificate was a mere formality and that personal testimony from the applicant about his or her sexual preferences was dispositive in determining whether he or she was a "psychopath" for purposes of the INA.[15]

An alien may also be excluded under the INA if he or she admits to having solicited homosexual acts, whether or not he or she was ever arrested or convicted for that conduct. In *Ganduxe y Marino v. Murff*,[16] for example, the Fifth Circuit Court of Appeals ordered the deportation of a gay alien for failing to report in his entry application that he had pled guilty to engaging in "disorderly conduct" for loitering with the purpose of inducing men to commit homosexual acts. Had the plaintiff reported the incident at the time of his entry, however, he could have been rejected as a "psychopath." Under *Ganduxe*, gay and lesbian aliens are thus caught in a dilemma: exclusion could result from either acknowledging the prior conviction or failing to report it.

Naturalization applicants face different hurdles. In order to become a naturalized citizen, an applicant must have been lawfully admitted into the country and must establish that he or she was "of good moral character" during the statutory waiting period.[17] In *Nemetz v. Immigration & Naturalization Service*,[18] the Fourth Circuit held that Congress did not intend to include sexual orientation in its requirement of "good moral character."[19] The court concluded that homosexual acts, so long as they are private, consensual, and harmless to the public, do not offend the congressional definition of good moral character.[20]

---

[13] *See id.* at 1480.

[14] 716 F.2d 1439 (5th Cir. 1983), *cert. denied*, 467 U.S. 1219 (1984).

[15] *See id.* at 1448. *See generally* Fowler & Graff, *Gay Aliens and Immigration: Resolving the Conflict Between* Hill *and* Longstaff, 10 U. DAYTON L. REV. 621, 638 (1985) (arguing that *Hill*, which adheres to the procedure prescribed in the INA, is more persuasive than *Longstaff*).

[16] 183 F. Supp. 565 (S.D.N.Y. 1959), *aff'd sub nom.* Ganduxe y Marino v. Esperdy, 278 F.2d 330 (2d Cir.), *cert. denied*, 364 U.S. 824 (1960).

[17] *See* § 8 U.S.C. § 1427 (a)(1), (3) (1982). *But see* Immigration Reform and Control Act of 1986, Pub. L. 99-603, 100 Stat. 3359 (codified in scattered sections of 7, 8, 20, 29 & 42 U.S.C.) (granting legal status to those aliens who have continuously resided in the United States since January 1, 1982 and who have complied with the laws of this country).

[18] 647 F.2d 432 (4th Cir. 1981).

[19] *See id.* at 436–37.

[20] *See id.* at 437; Kovacs v. United States, 476 F.2d 843, 845 (2d Cir. 1973) (denying naturalization application on the grounds of perjury, but stating that private sexual life would not have been grounds for denial); *In re* Brodie, 394 F. Supp. 1208 (D. Or. 1975); *In re* Labady, 326 F. Supp. 924 (S.D.N.Y. 1971).

Finally, gay and lesbian aliens who are partners of American citizens face unique hurdles in seeking citizenship or entry. In order to qualify as an immediate relative for the purpose of expediting immigration, the partner must be a legal spouse under both state law and the INA. In *Adams v. Howerton*,[21] the Ninth Circuit held that Congress has plenary power to exclude aliens, and has not included gay and lesbian partners in its definition of "spouse."[22] The court therefore affirmed the Board of Immigration Appeals' denial of an alien gay partner's petition for classification as an immediate family member of an American citizen.

Given the current legal standards, gay and lesbian aliens are likely to continue to be denied visas, entrance, and naturalization. Because the PHS is an expert body relied upon consistently by Congress in formulating medical definitions under the INA,[23] the INS and the courts should follow the PHS's current policy of not classifying gay and lesbian aliens as "psychopaths." In addition, the INS should grant gay and lesbian life-partners immigration and naturalization privileges, for the same fairness reasons that courts and legislatures should grant same-sex couples private law entitlements.[24]

B. Insurance

The tremendous impact of AIDS on the insurance industry[25] has adversely affected gay men trying to purchase life and health insurance. Because gay men constitute seventy-three percent of the known AIDS cases in the United States,[26] sexual orientation has emerged as a potential factor in the risk classification process of insurance under-

---

[21] 673 F.2d 1036 (9th Cir.), *cert. denied*, 458 U.S. 1111 (1982).

[22] *See id.* at 1040–41.

[23] *See* Note, *supra* note 10, at 359.

[24] *See supra* pp. 118–19.

[25] By 1991, up to 270,000 Americans will develop AIDS. *See* U.S. Public Health Service, Public Health Service Plan for the Prevention and Control of AIDS and the AIDS Virus 5 (Report of the Coolfont Planning Conference, June 4–6, 1986) (on file at Harvard Law School Library). Because the estimated cost of caring for a single AIDS patient is as high as $147,000, AIDS presents obvious economic dilemmas to the insurance industry. *See* Hardy, Rauch, Echenberg, Morgan & Curran, *The Economic Impact of the First 10,000 Cases of Acquired Immunodeficiency Syndrome in the United States*, 255 J. A.M.A. 209, 210 (1986); *see also* Clifford & Iuculano, *AIDS and Insurance: The Rationale for AIDS-Related Testing*, 100 HARV. L. REV. 1806, 1817–21 (1987) (noting that the long latency period of AIDS prevents insurance companies from protecting themselves against adverse selection because policies cannot normally be challenged after the four-year latency period under the incontestability clause required by most states).

[26] *See* U.S. PUB. HEALTH SERVICE, AIDS INFORMATION BULLETIN — THE PUBLIC HEALTH SERVICE RESPONSE TO AIDS (1985). This figure includes both gay and bisexual men.

writing.[27] The high incidence of AIDS among gay men places obvious pressure on the insurance industry to classify gay men in a unique category in order to avoid both paying the high costs associated with the treatment of AIDS and over-charging those policy holders at lower risk for AIDS.

Insurers may attempt to reduce the number of AIDS cases among their personal insurance policyholders at the application stage by several means, most of which are not directly linked to sexual orientation. The most direct and least controversial method is classification according to actual medical or scientific evidence volunteered by the applicant or obtained through medical records supplied in the application process.

More problematic, however, are other classification methods in which sexual orientation plays a prominent role. For example, although the insurance industry claims that sexual orientation does not constitute grounds for denying insurance applications,[28] the medical information that does constitute grounds for denial is often requested only from those applicants who fit within an "AIDS profile."[29] An insurance company may, for example, target male applicants who live in particular geographic areas, are unmarried, are employed in stereotypically gay professions, live with unrelated individuals of the same sex, or name unrelated men as beneficiaries.[30] Whether or not

---

[27] *See* Schatz, *The AIDS Insurance Crisis: Underwriting or Overreaching?*, 100 HARV. L. REV. 1782, 1786–92 (1987). In issuing personal insurance policies, the industry looks to such factors as past history of disease, weight, smoking habits, alcohol consumption, and certain genetic predispositions. Premiums for group policies, on the other hand, are determined according to the insurer's experience with the specific group. Group insurance can absorb high risk individuals by spreading the costs over the larger group. *See* Hammond & Shapiro, *AIDS and the Limits of Insurability*, 64 (Supp. 1) MILBANK Q. 143, 162–64 (1986). Gay men may nonetheless be discriminated against in group policies. Employers and other group sponsors may fear that any incidence of AIDS will drastically and disproportionately affect their premiums. *See* Oppenheimer & Padgug, *AIDS: The Risk to Insurers, the Threat to Equity*, HASTINGS CENTER REP., Oct. 1986, at 18, 20–21.

[28] *See* Clifford & Iuculano, *supra* note 25, at 1816 (asserting that guidelines supported by the Health Insurance Association of America and the American Council of Life Insurance barring the use of sexual orientation in the underwriting process refutes any contention that such factors are used and endorsed by the industry).

[29] *See* Myers, *The Impact of AIDS: A Survey of Large Life and Health Insurers*, J. AM. SOC. C.L.U. & CH. F.C., May 1987, at 72, 74, 76 (noting that AIDS testing is requested based on a variety of medical reasons or because of the "designation of an unrelated male beneficiary without a business need for the insurance," and that heightened scrutiny may be given to applications from gay men, residents of high risk areas, or other high risk groups).

[30] The use of such stereotypical generalizations raises obvious nonlegal problems, mainly the perpetuation of stereotypes and the encouragement of gay men to disguise their sexual preference. *See* Schatz, *supra* note 27, at 1786–88 (arguing that an "AIDS profile" presents dangers of employment discrimination, places economic burdens on men within the profile, and most importantly, condones "stereotyping at its worst").

medical information is the ultimate basis for denying an application, the possibility remains that insurance companies scrutinize those engaging in stereotypically gay occupations or living in largely gay areas to a much greater degree than the population at large. Thus the distinction between "medical evidence" and nonscientific stereotyping blurs.

Use of these nonscientific factors in underwriting could be challenged under various regulations. All fifty states and the District of Columbia have enacted some type of unfair trade practices act.[31] These statutes define "unfair" discrimination as categorizations that are without persuasive actuarial justification, and require that risk classifications be neither unreasonably underinclusive nor overinclusive. Under these regulations, classifications may be challenged if stereotypes are used to identify a high-risk group.[32]

Moreover, insurers' policies may be directly regulated under state law.[33] Insurance companies may be barred from conducting or requesting the results of past AIDS tests.[34] Finally, actuarially unsound classifications may be challenged under the Civil Rights Act of 1871 or under the fourteenth amendment, if insurers' actions constitute state action.[35]

On the other hand, given the correlation between the incidence of AIDS and male homosexuality, current law effectively permits insurers

---

[31] *See* Hoffman & Kincaid, *AIDS: The Challenge to Life and Health Insurers' Freedom of Contract*, 35 DRAKE L. REV. 709, 718 n.60 (1986–1987).

[32] Insurance companies may, however, argue that state legislation prohibiting unfair trade practices mandates a positive duty on the part of the insurer to separate applicants with identified health risks (notably those testing positive for the AIDS antibody) from those who do not. *See* Clifford & Iuculano, *supra* note 25, at 1811–12.

[33] For example, the District of Columbia bars the use of sexual orientation in determining the conditions of insurance coverage or in accepting or rejecting an applicant. *See* D.C. CODE ANN. § 35-223(b)(1) (Supp. 1987).

[34] *See* CAL. HEALTH & SAFETY CODE § 199.21(f) (West Supp. 1988) (effective Apr. 4, 1985) (barring the use of AIDS antibody test results in underwriting); D.C. CODE ANN. §§ 35-221 to -229 (Supp. 1987); WIS. STAT. ANN. § 631.90 (West Supp. 1988) (same). Similarly, Florida authorizes the Department of Health to conduct serologic testing when a threat of infectious disease exists, with the proviso that such test results cannot be released or used to discriminate in insurance or employment applications. *See* FLA. STAT. ANN. § 381.606 (West 1986); *see also* American Council of Life Ins. v. District of Columbia, 645 F. Supp. 84, 88 (D.D.C. 1986) (upholding a local ordinance barring the use of AIDS test results in underwriting). Without consistent nationwide regulation, these regulations only substitute one problem for another by effectively eliminating the availability of insurance within certain jurisdictions.

[35] Courts have divided as to whether life and health insurers are sufficiently regulated to constitute state actors. *Compare* Life Ins. Co. of N. Am. v. Reichardt, 591 F.2d 499, 502 (9th Cir. 1979) (holding that California's regulation of insurance companies was an insufficient ground for finding that the Insurance Commissioner's activities constituted state action for the purposes of 42 U.S.C. § 1983 (1982)) *with* Stern v. Massachusetts Indem. & Life Ins. Co., 365 F. Supp. 433, 438 (E.D. Pa. 1973) (holding that "pervasive control" by the Commonwealth of Pennsylvania rendered a private insurance company's conduct state action).

to classify gay men as a separate category, requiring tests for the AIDS virus.[36] Using gay men as a proxy for those at risk for AIDS both feeds on and furthers popular prejudice against gay men.[37] Distinguishing gay men for the purposes of insurance underwriting can exacerbate common misconceptions that all gay men are AIDS carriers or that only gay men can contract the virus. These misconceptions are harmful to both gay men and the population at large. First, they engender hostility toward gay men as the "cause" of the AIDS epidemic.[38] Second, they further the common stereotype that gay men are promiscuous and therefore run uniformly high risks of contracting the AIDS virus. Finally, segregating gay men from the general population's insurance pool facilitates the dangerous misconception among women and heterosexual men that they are not at risk for AIDS. This state interest will become increasingly compelling as public health education regarding AIDS prompts a decline in the percentage of new cases in the gay population.[39]

C. Incorporation and Tax Exemption

Organizations promoting gay people's interests have in some states encountered governmental resistance to their incorporation. For example, the Ohio Secretary of State, with the approval of the Ohio courts, refused to accept the articles of incorporation for a gay organization on the ground that "promotion of homosexuality as a valid life style is contrary to the public policy of the state,"[40] despite the fact that Ohio had revoked its law outlawing sodomy.[41] Gay organizations in New York have encountered similar resistance, although they were eventually allowed to incorporate.[42]

---

[36] *See* Hoffman & Kincaid, *supra* note 31, at 741–47.

[37] *See* Oppenheimer & Padgug, *supra* note 27, at 21 (arguing that popular prejudice against gay men may lead to discrimination in the insurance industry). The states have largely accepted a similar argument regarding racial discrimination in insurance underwriting and redlining. *See* DeWolfe, Squires & DeWolfe, *Civil Rights Implications of Insurance Redlining*, 29 DePaul L. Rev. 315 (1979) (noting that redlining practices have underlying racially discriminatory intent and should therefore be prohibited).

[38] *Cf.* Triantafillou & Withers, *AIDS and the Law: Blaming the Victim*, Boston B.J., May/June 1986, at 7 (noting that the "association of AIDS with homosexuality in particular has lent cover to basic homophobia and prejudice").

[39] *See* Langone, *How to Block a Killer's Path*, Time, Jan. 30, 1989, at 61 (discussing the dramatic drop in new cases of AIDS in the gay population and noting expert testimony that "'[t]he epidemic is all but over with gay men'"); Part II, note 74, *supra* p. 19.

[40] *See* State v. Brown, 39 Ohio St. 2d 112, 113–14, 313 N.E.2d 847, 848 (1974).

[41] *See id.*

[42] *See, e.g.*, *In re* Thom for Incorporation of Lambda Legal Defense and Education Fund, Inc., 33 N.Y.2d 609, 301 N.E.2d 542, 347 N.Y.S.2d 571 (1973) (allowing the formation of Lambda Legal Defense and Education Fund, Inc., as a legal assistance organization under New York law); Gay Activists Alliance v. Lomenzo, 31 N.Y.2d 965, 293 N.E.2d 255, 341 N.Y.S.2d 108 (1973) (allowing a gay organization to incorporate).

Although gay corporations may encounter similar public policy arguments in attaining tax-exempt status under I.R.C. section 501(c)(3), the Court of Appeals for the District of Columbia Circuit struck down a regulation that gave the Commissioner the discretion to deny exempt status to controversial corporations. In *Big Mama Rag, Inc. v. United States*,[43] the court held that the Internal Revenue Service may not withhold tax exemption under section 501(c)(3) based on the "content and quality of an applicant's views and goals."[44] In so holding, the court struck down a Treasury regulation[45] that provided that an educational organization may advocate a particular viewpoint so long as it presented a "sufficiently full and fair exposition of the pertinent facts as to permit an individual or the public to form an independent opinion or conclusion."[46] Noting that the IRS had applied the "full and fair exposition" requirement only to those organizations advocating controversial positions,[47] the court held that such arbitrary enforcement rendered the statute unconstitutionally vague and therefore impermissibly restricted the first amendment rights of controversial organizations.[48] Under *Big Mama Rag*, the IRS may not restrict the first amendment rights of organizations on the basis of their viewpoints regarding sexual orientation.

D. Local Legislation

Unfortunately, very little legislation protects gay men and lesbians from discrimination in the private sector. No federal statute bars discrimination by private citizens or organizations on the basis of sexual orientation. Nor do the states provide such protection: only Wisconsin has a comprehensive statute barring such discrimination in employment.[49] Moreover, few state courts have interpreted state civil rights statutes to bar discrimination on the basis of sexual orienta-

---

[43] 631 F.2d 1030 (D.C. Cir. 1980).

[44] *Id.* at 1040. *Big Mama Rag* involved a denial of tax-exempt status to a women's organization on the ground that it was not an educational organization for the puposes of 26 U.S.C. § 501(c)(3) (1976). *See* 631 F.2d at 1032–33. The IRS National Office affirmed the District Director's denial of Big Mama Rag's application, citing the commercial nature of the paper, its political commentary, and its published articles promoting lesbianism. *See id.* at 1033.

[45] Treas. Reg. § 1.501(c)(3)-1(d)(3)(i) (1959).

[46] *See Big Mama Rag*, 631 F.2d at 1039–40.

[47] *See id.* at 1036.

[48] *See id.* at 1040.

[49] *See* WIS. STAT. ANN. §§ 111.31–.395 (West 1988). Other states regulate certain forms of sexual orientation discrimination. *See, e.g.*, CAL. CIVIL CODE § 51.7 (West 1984) (barring violence based on sexual orientation against persons or property); MICH. COMP. LAWS ANN. § 333.20201(2)(a) (West 1984) (barring the denial of care in health facilities on the basis of sexual orientation). Alternatively, executive orders prohibit discrimination in some states. *See, e.g.*, N.Y. COMP. CODES R. & REGS. tit. 4, § 28 (1983) (barring sexual orientation discrimination in state employment or in the provision of state services and benefits).

tion.[50] In response to the dearth of protection at the national and state level, some localities have adopted measures to prohibit discrimination on the basis of sexual orientation by private citizens and organizations.[51] Indeed, the vast majority of the regulations aimed at eradicating sexual orientation discrimination are local ordinances and citywide executive orders, which tend to prohibit discrimination in employment, housing, or public accommodations.[52]

Local attempts to address these forms of discrimination are nonetheless limited in several respects. Executive orders, for example, are subject to rescission by referendum and to judicial invalidation.[53] Furthermore, such measures cannot be enforced where enforcement would interfere with congressional policies or conflict with constitutional limitations.[54]

Gay Rights Coalition of Georgetown University Law Center v. Georgetown University[55] presented one such conflict when a local anti-

---

[50] In California, for example, the state courts have found that although gay people are not listed explicitly as a protected group in the Unruh Civil Rights Act, gay men and lesbians are protected under the Act. *See* Rolon v. Kulwitzky, 153 Cal. App. 3d 289, 200 Cal. Rptr. 217 (Ct. App. 1984); Hubert v. Williams, 133 Cal. App. 3d Supp. 1, 184 Cal. Rptr. 161 (App. Dep't Super. Ct. 1982) (applying the Act to housing discrimination).

[51] According to the Lambda Legal Defense and Education Fund, Inc., the following cities and counties have enacted some form of anti-discrimination regulation: Tucson (Arizona); Berkeley, Cupertino, Davis, Laguna Beach, Los Angeles, Mountain View, Oakland, Sacramento, San Francisco, San Jose, Santa Barbara, Santa Cruz, and West Hollywood (California); Aspen and Boulder (Colorado); Hartford (Connecticut); District of Columbia; Atlanta (Georgia); Honolulu (Hawaii); Champaign, Chicago, Evanston, and Urbana (Illinois); Iowa City (Iowa); Baltimore, and Montgomery County (Maryland); Amherst, Boston, and Malden (Massachusetts); Ann Arbor, Detroit, East Lansing, Ingham County, Lansing, and Saginaw (Michigan); Hennepin County, Minneapolis, and Mankato (Minnesota); Alfred, Buffalo, Ithaca, New York City, Rochester, and Troy (New York); Chapel Hill, Durham, and Raleigh (North Carolina); Columbus, Cuyahoga, and Yellow Springs (Ohio); Portland (Oregon); Harrisburg and Philadelphia (Pennsylvania); Austin (Texas); Clallam County, King County, Olympia, Pullman, and Seattle (Washington); Dane County, Madison, and Milwaukee (Wisconsin). *See* Letter from Paula L. Ettelbrick, Legal Director, Lambda Legal Defense and Education Fund, Inc., to Anne Seidel (Mar. 7, 1989).

[52] *See, e.g.*, BOSTON, MA., CODE tit. 12, ch. 16, § 400–407 (1984) (barring discrimination in employment, labor organizations, credit transactions, insurance, education, and public accommodations).

[53] *See, e.g.*, Under 21 v. City of New York, 65 N.Y.2d 344, 482 N.E.2d 1, 492 N.Y.S.2d 522 (Ct. App. 1985) (invalidating a New York City executive order barring city contractors from discriminating on the basis of sexual orientation because the mayor, as the chief executive officer of the city, could not create a remedy; only the legislature was empowered to do so).

[54] *See, e.g.*, United States v. City of Philadelphia, 798 F.2d 81 (3d Cir. 1986) (holding that the Philadelphia Fair Practices Ordinance, PHILADELPHIA, PA., CODE §§ 9-1101 to -1110 (1982), which prohibited discrimination on the basis of sexual orientation, could not be enforced to ban congressionally approved policies of military recruitment on university campuses, even though military hiring practices barred employment of gay men and lesbians).

[55] 536 A.2d 1 (D.C. 1987).

discrimination ordinance conflicted with the free exercise clause of the first amendment. In *Georgetown*, a group of gay and lesbian students at Georgetown University argued that school authorities had violated a District of Columbia anti-discrimination ordinance[56] by refusing to grant official recognition to a gay student organization. The university contended that requiring recognition of a gay organization would violate its free exercise rights as a Catholic institution.[57]

Noting traditional Catholic teaching that homosexuality is sinful,[58] the court found that the university, as a Catholic institution, could not be compelled to recognize the organization.[59] Mandatory endorsement, according to the court, would be tantamount to "compelled expression in violation of the first amendment."[60] Thus, the student groups were entitled to equal access to the tangible facilities afforded other organizations, but not to university recognition.[61]

The *Georgetown* decision does not resolve several ambiguities regarding the tension between anti-discrimination ordinances and the free exercise clause. First, the court held that a university's "recognition" of a student organization constitutes endorsement of the organization's beliefs.[62] This conception of "recognition" is inconsistent with the common meaning of "endorsement." Instead of viewing university "recognition" as an endorsement of the beliefs espoused by an organization, an outside observer is more likely to view such university action as a recognition of the organization's right to exist and promulgate those beliefs.[63] Requiring a large institution to provide forums for all of its students, regardless of the viewpoints ex-

---

[56] This section of the District of Columbia Human Rights Ordinance, D.C. CODE ANN. §§ 1-2501 to -2557 (1981), provided that it is unlawful for an educational institution:

> [To] deny, restrict, or to abridge or condition the use of, or access to, any of its facilities and services to any person otherwise qualified, wholly or partially, for a discriminatory reason, based upon the race, color, religion, national origin, sex, age, marital status, personal appearance, sexual orientation, family responsibilities, political affiliation, source of income or physical handicap of any individual.

Id. § 1-2520(1).

[57] *Georgetown*, 536 A.2d at 11.

[58] *See id.* at 22–23.

[59] *See id.* at 21–22.

[60] *Id.* at 25.

[61] The court found that the compelling government interest in eliminating discrimination on the basis of sexual orientation outweighed the very limited burden such equal access would place on the university's free exercise. The court emphasized that requiring that the students be given access to university facilities was not a burden precisely because the Human Rights Act does not require "endorsement" in the form of university recognition. *See id.* at 38.

[62] *See id.* at 21.

[63] *Cf.* Widmar v. Vincent, 454 U.S. 263, 274 n.14, 277 (1981) (requiring a public university to allow an officially recognized student religious group to use campus facilities, and noting that university students, as young adults, could not reasonably infer university support from the "mere fact of a campus meeting place").

pressed, does not mandate endorsement of the students' beliefs. Such requirements are less burdensome than requiring an institution to voice the various viewpoints itself.[64]

Furthermore, the court's definition of "equal treatment" leaves open the possibility that religious institutions may differentiate on the basis of sexual orientation, so long as no material, quantifiable disparities result. This definition fails to recognize that the denial of official recognition may harm gay and lesbian student groups by differentiating and stigmatizing them for their "unrecognized" status.[65] The *Georgetown* decision may thus help perpetuate the unfounded belief that gay and lesbian students are unacceptable to campus life, and further divide students on the basis of sexual orientation. Because the Supreme Court has declined to define homosexuality as a suspect classification,[66] such discrimination may continue under current law.

Conflicts between the free exercise clause and anti-discrimination ordinances cannot be easily resolved; the *Georgetown* case indicates that the balancing of interests in future litigation depends on an ill-defined standard of "harm" that may vary from case to case. Local legislators are free to exempt religious organizations from any anti-discrimination ordinances they enact.[67] Most importantly, absent heightened scrutiny of sexual orientation discrimination, the state interest in eradicating prejudice will not be a sufficiently compelling justification for restricting the right to free exercise of one's religion. Because of such limitations, local legislation, although the most prevalent means of barring anti-gay discrimination, cannot sufficiently protect gay men and lesbians in the private sector.

E. Public Accommodations

Private operators of service organizations have the right to regulate the use of their facilities and property within reasonable limits. They can, for example, maintain dress codes, regulate the decency and noise levels of their patrons, and otherwise regulate their customers' behavior in order to maintain a desirable atmosphere for themselves and

---

[64] *See Georgetown*, 556 A.2d at 53 (Ferren, J., concurring in part in the result and dissenting in part); *cf.* PruneYard Shopping Center v. Robins, 447 U.S. 74 (1980) (requiring a privately owned shopping center to allow leaflet distribution on its premises).

[65] *See Georgetown*, 556 A.2d at 49–50 (Ferren, J., concurring in part in the result and dissenting in part) (arguing that the court's decision allows "'separate but equal'" treatment that is "an obvious affront to human dignity, amounting to a form of discrimination at least as intolerable as the denial of tangible facilities and services").

[66] *See supra* p. 55.

[67] *See* Clarke v. United States, 57 U.S.L.W. 2379 (D.D.C. Dec. 13, 1988) (holding that Congress could not require the District of Columbia City Council to exempt religious institutions on first amendment grounds, but leaving open the possibility that Congress itself could enact such a provision).

their clientele.[68] Such regulations cannot, however, discriminate against classes of individuals protected by federal or local law.[69] Thus, local regulations may prohibit businesses deemed "public accommodations"[70] from discriminating on the basis of sexual orientation.[71] Furthermore, because private businesses do not enjoy the freedom of association as do private social groups and individuals, a business' attempts to defend discriminatory practices under the first amendment are unlikely to succeed.[72]

F. Conclusion

Discrimination on the basis of sexual orientation affects gay men and lesbians in a wide range of contexts in both the public and private sectors. Although, as illustrated in this section, a number of local jurisdictions have taken affirmative steps to protect gay men and lesbians from discrimination, the piecemeal coverage that results from relying solely on local legislation to protect gay men and lesbians is inadequate to protect them consistently. Absent increased legislative and judicial action, gay men and lesbians will remain unable to conduct their lives free from discrimination.

---

[68] *See, e.g.*, Moolenaar v. Atlas Motor Inns, Inc., 616 F.2d 87 (3d Cir. 1980) (noting that a hotel manager could, under a state statute, evict a patron for violating hotel dress codes).

[69] *See, e.g.*, Garrity v. Gallen, 522 F. Supp. 171 (D.N.H. 1981) (barring discrimination against handicapped people by service organizations under a New Hampshire statute). *But see* Moose Lodge No. 107 v. Irvis, 407 U.S. 163 (1972) (refusing to bar a discriminatory service policy by a private club even though the club was regulated under state liquor license requirements).

[70] "Public accommodations" have been variously defined. *See* Big Bros., Inc. v. Minneapolis Comm'n on Civil Rights, 284 N.W.2d 823 (Minn. 1979) (holding that a "Big Brother" program is a public accommodation and subject to the Minneapolis civil rights law barring sexual orientation discrimination).

[71] California, for example, has interpreted its Civil Rights Act to provide this kind of protection. *See* Rolon v. Kulwitzky, 153 Cal. App. 3d 288, 200 Cal. Rptr. 217 (Dist. Ct. App. 1984) (holding that under the Act a restaurant could not legally refuse to seat a same-sex couple in a private booth reserved for "couples only," and noting that a restauranteur's right to regulate within reasonable levels a patron's conduct does not include the right to bar admission to gay and lesbian couples).

[72] *See* Blanding v. Sports & Health Club, Inc., 373 N.W.2d 784 (Minn. Ct. App. 1985) (upholding a city anti-discrimination ordinance against a challenge under the first amendment free exercise clause), *aff'd*, 389 N.W.2d 205 (1986). In *Blanding*, the court rejected the club owner's free exercise claim that mandating admission of gay patrons would interfere with his practice of his fundamentalist Christian beliefs. The court held that the corporate club did not have standing to make such a claim, because the free exercise clause was intended solely for the benefit of individuals. *See id.* at 790. Moreover, the court noted that admission of the plaintiff to the club would not be a burden on the club owner's free exercise rights. *See id.* at 791.

AFTERWORD

Since this study first appeared in the May 1989 issue of the *Harvard Law Review*, there have been a number of significant legal developments regarding the rights of lesbian and gay people. This afterword summarizes those recent developments and offers some concluding observations on the future of gay and lesbian legal rights. As further developments will undoubtedly occur after this book goes to press, this afterword should be viewed not as a definitive summary of the current state of the law, but rather as a capsule summary of emerging legal trends.

I. RECENT DEVELOPMENTS

A. Family Law

The most significant recent development in the area of family law is the New York Court of Appeals' decision in *Braschi v. Stahl Associates, Co.*[1] In *Braschi*, the court held that unmarried cohabitants, including gay and lesbian couples, will in some cases constitute "families" under the state's rent-control law.[2] These provisions bar eviction of family members of deceased tenants;[3] therefore, if a gay or lesbian couple qualifies as a family, the surviving domestic partner can remain in a rent-controlled apartment upon the death of the partner who was the tenant.

Braschi is the first case in which a state's highest court held that a gay or lesbian couple may constitute a family under the law. Writing for the court, Judge Titone presented a very broad conception of "family":

> The intended protection against sudden eviction should not rest on fictitious legal distinctions or genetic history, but instead should find its foundation in the reality of family life. In the context of eviction, a more realistic, and certainly equally valid, view of a family includes two adult lifetime partners whose relationship is long-term and characterized by an emotional and financial commitment and interdependence. This view comports both with our society's traditional concept

---

[1] No. 108 (N.Y. July 6, 1989) (1989 N.Y. LEXIS 877); *see also supra* p. 104 (discussing the lower court opinions in *Braschi*).

[2] New York City Rent Control Law §§ 26-401 to -415, N.Y. UNCONSOL. LAW § 8617 (McKinney 1987).

[3] *See* New York City Rent and Eviction Regulations § 2204.6(d), N.Y. UNCONSOL. LAW § 8597 (McKinney 1987) ("No occupant of housing accommodations shall be evicted . . . where the occupant is either the surviving spouse of the deceased tenant or some other member of the deceased tenant's family who has been living with the tenant.").

of 'family' and with the expectations of individuals who live in such nuclear units.[4]

Based on this definition, the court set forth objective guidelines for determining whether a particular relationship qualifies as a family under the statute.[5] Although the *Braschi* court carefully restricted its holding to the definition of family under the rent-control statute, its recognition that "fictitious legal distinctions or genetic history" are not the essence of familial relationships establishes a significant precedent for further legal recognition of lesbian and gay families.

In addition to the *Braschi* decision, two recent local laws have extended partial legal protection to gay and lesbian couples. In May 1989, the San Francisco Board of Supervisors adopted an ordinance extending legal recognition to "domestic partnerships," including both same- and opposite-sex couples.[6] Domestic partners would be entitled to spousal visitation rights in hospitals, and, if employed by the city government, would be entitled to bereavement leave upon the death of one partner.[7] Under the ordinance, moreover, future public policies cannot differentiate between domestic partnerships and marriages.[8]

In New York City, Mayor Edward Koch issued an executive order that grants partial legal recognition to domestic partnerships of city employees, including gay and lesbian couples.[9] Under the order, city employees may obtain bereavement leave upon the death of their domestic partners or a member of the partner's immediate family. This policy may herald the extension of other spousal benefits to unmarried couples in New York City.[10]

---

[4] *Braschi*, slip op. at 9–10 (1989 N.Y. LEXIS 877, *11–*12).

[5] *See id.* at 12 (1989 N.Y. LEXIS 877, *15) (listing as relevant factors the "exclusivity and longevity of the relationship, the level of emotional and financial commitment, the manner in which the parties have conducted their everyday lives and held themselves out to society, and the reliance upon one another for daily family services").

[6] *See* Bishop, *San Francisco Grants Recognition to Partnerships of Single People*, N.Y. Times, May 31, 1989, at 17, col. 1. Under the ordinance, persons who are not married to any third parties, who "have chosen to share one another's lives in an intimate and committed relationship," and who share responsibilities for all expenses, may file a declaration of domestic partnership with the county clerk. *See id.*

[7] In addition, a committee is investigating the possibility of including domestic partners in city health insurance policies. *See id.*

[8] *See id.* Opponents of the ordinance have, however, temporarily blocked its enforcement pending a public referendum on the November ballot. Observers are confident that the ordinance will survive; according to a poll conducted by the office of City Supervisor Harry Britt, the author of the ordinance, 60% of the city's population currently supports the legislation. *See* Basheda, *Domestic Partnership Ordinance Stalls; Conservative Foes File Petition Urging Vote To Block San Francisco Measure*, L.A. Times, July 7, 1989, at 3, col. 1.

[9] *See* Dunlap, *Koch Grants Paid Leave to Unmarried Couples*, N.Y. Times, Aug. 8, 1989, at B3, col. 1.

[10] *See* Bohlen, *Koch Widens City's Policy on "Family,"* N.Y. Times, July 10, 1989, at B1, col. 5. For other developments concerning the recognition of gay and lesbian relationships, see

In contrast to these expansions of the legal recognition of same-sex couples, a recent Missouri decision drastically restricts the legal rights of lesbian and gay family members. In *J.P. v. P.W.*,[11] an intermediate court of appeals modified a trial court's custody decree to restrict visitation by a gay father to visitation in the mother's presence. More significantly, the court suggested that the possibility that the child might discover that the father is gay could be a sufficient reason to terminate the father's visitation rights entirely.[12] No other reported decision suggests this possibility as a basis for termination of visitation rights.[13]

B. Gay Men and Lesbians in the Military

Two recent decisions have called into question the continued viability of equal protection challenges to the armed services' anti-gay policies.[14] In *Watkins v. United States Army*,[15] the Court of Appeals for the Ninth Circuit, sitting en banc, held that the Army could not refuse to reenlist Sgt. Perry Watkins on the basis of his homosexuality, but declined to adopt the panel's determination that sexual orientation is a suspect classification under the equal protection clause.[16] For a six judge majority, Judge Pregerson wrote that, because the Army, "with full knowledge of [Watkins'] homosexuality, had repeatedly permitted him to reenlist,"[17] the Army was equitably estopped from barring his reenlistment on the basis of his sexual orientation.[18] Thus, the court found it unnecessary to reach the equal protection issues raised in the panel decision.[19]

T.W.A. Broadens Use of "Frequent Flier" Tickets, N.Y. Times, July 16, 1989, at 19, col. 1, which notes that, in response to a lawsuit filed by Lambda Legal Defense and Education Fund, TWA has adopted a policy permitting the use of "frequent flier" miles by the purchaser's same- or opposite-sex partner; and *American Lawyers To Test Danish Gay Marriage Law*, Au Courant, Aug. 7, 1989, at 3, col. 3, which reports the legalization of same-sex marriages in Denmark, and notes that a United States court might recognize a marriage, contracted in Denmark, by an American-Danish same-sex couple.

[11] Nos. 15937, 15981 (Mo. Ct. App. May 5, 1989) (1989 Mo. App. LEXIS 619).

[12] *See id.* at 17–19 (1989 Mo. App. LEXIS 619, *25–*27).

[13] *Cf.* J.L.P.(H.) v. D.J.P., 643 S.W.2d 865, 872 (Mo. Ct. App. 1982) (implying that the court might terminate the gay father's visitation rights "[i]f the father persists in his vehement espousal to the child of the 'desirability' of his chosen lifestyle . . . and that [persistence] results in harm to the child"). *See generally supra* pp. 122–23 (discussing the restrictions placed on gay and lesbian parents' visitation rights).

[14] For a discussion of equal protection challenges to anti-gay discrimination by the military and other public employers, see pp. 54–61 above.

[15] 875 F.2d 699 (9th Cir. 1989) (en banc).

[16] *See supra* pp. 56–57 (discussing the panel decision in *Watkins*).

[17] *Watkins*, 875 F.2d at 701.

[18] *See id.* at 704–05.

[19] *See id.* at 705. Judge Norris, concurring in the judgment, reiterated the equal protection arguments he had presented in the panel's earlier ruling. *See id.* at 711 (Norris, J., concurring in the judgment). Judge Canby joined both the majority opinion and Judge Norris' concurrence.

The en banc decision in *Watkins* greatly expands the rights of gay and lesbian servicepersons. Most notably, the court's specific finding that Watkins' sexual orientation had no adverse impact on his military performance[20] belies the Army's contention that "[h]omosexuality is incompatible with military service,"[21] and may therefore provide the basis for other successful fact-specific challenges to the military's policy of discrimination. Nonetheless, the court's refusal to reach the panel's broad equal protection arguments represents a setback for gay and lesbian rights, because, in withdrawing the panel decision, the court removed the only circuit court decision to hold that sexual orientation is a suspect classification.

Shortly after the *Watkins* decision, the Seventh Circuit, in *benShalom v. Marsh*,[22] removed a district court injunction[23] that barred the Army from considering Sgt. Miriam benShalom's sexual orientation as an adverse factor in her application for reenlistment in the service. The Seventh Circuit first rejected the lower court's finding that the dismissal of benShalom solely on the basis of her declaration of a same-sex sexual orientation violated her first amendment right to free speech.[24] Noting the Supreme Court's policy of granting wide latitude to military regulation of speech-related activities,[25] the court asserted that "the Army does not have to take the risk that an admitted homosexual will not commit homosexual acts which may be detrimental to its assigned mission."[26] Moreover, in language not specifically limited to the circumstances of military life, the court noted that benShalom's declaration of her lesbianism, "[a]lthough . . . in some sense speech," is primarily an act of identification and is therefore entitled to less protection under the first amendment.[27]

In addition to its first amendment holding, the *benShalom III* court also rejected the district court's determination that the Army's

---

[20] In upholding Watkins' right to reenlist in the Army, the court stated that "Sgt. Watkins has greatly benefitted the Army, and therefore the country, by his military service" and that "Watkin's [sic] homosexuality clearly has not hurt the Army in any way." *Id.* at 709.

[21] 32 C.F.R. pt. 41, app. A, pt. 1.H.1.a (1988).

[22] Nos. 88-2771, 89-213 (7th Cir. Aug. 7, 1989) (1989 U.S. App. LEXIS 11807) [hereinafter *benShalom III*].

[23] *See* benShalom v. Marsh, 703 F. Supp. 1372 (E.D. Wis. 1989) [hereinafter *benShalom II*]; *see also* benShalom v. Secretary of the Army, 489 F. Supp. 964 (E.D. Wis. 1980) [hereinafter *benShalom I*] (ordering the Army to reinstate benShalom for the remaining eleven months of her enlistment); *supra* p. 62 (discussing *benShalom I* and *benShalom II*).

[24] *See benShalom III*, slip op. at 9–10 (1989 U.S. App. LEXIS 11807, *13–*15). For a discussion of the first amendment argument in *benShalom I* and *benShalom II*, see pp. 61–63 above.

[25] The court relied heavily on Brown v. Glines, 444 U.S. 348 (1980), which upheld the Air Force's disciplining of an Air Force officer for circulating a petition on an Air Force base without obtaining the prior approval of the base commander. *See benShalom III*, slip op. at 9–10 (1989 U.S. App. LEXIS 11807, *13–*17).

[26] *See benShalom III*, slip op. at 11 (1989 U.S. App. LEXIS 11807, *17–*18).

[27] *See id.* at 13–14 (1989 U.S. App. LEXIS 11807, *22).

anti-gay regulations violate the equal protection clause.[28] Arguing that benShalom's sexual orientation "is compelling evidence that [she] has in the past and is likely to again engage in [homosexual] conduct,"[29] the court concluded that "the regulation does not classify plaintiff based merely upon her status as a lesbian, but upon reasonable inferences about her probable conduct in the past and in the future."[30] Because the Army does not classify people on the basis of "mere status," the court reasoned, the district court was wrong to accord heightened scrutiny to the classification.[31] Moreover, the court specifically found that *Bowers v. Hardwick*,[32] which upheld against a substantive due process challenge a state sodomy law as applied to same-sex sodomy, compels the conclusion that sexual orientation is not a suspect classification.[33] The Seventh Circuit's opinion in *benShalom III*, combined with the withdrawal of the panel decision in *Watkins*, leaves the future of equal protection challenges to the military's anti-gay policy in, at best, a state of confusion.[34]

---

[28] Following the panel decision in *Watkins*, *benShalom II* had held that sexual orientation is a suspect classification under the equal protection clause. *See* 703 F. Supp. 1372, 1379–80 (E.D. Wis. 1989).

[29] *benShalom III*, slip op. at 18 (1989 U.S. App. LEXIS 11807, *29).

[30] *Id.*

[31] *See id.* at 17 (1989 U.S. App. LEXIS 11807, *28–*29).

[32] 478 U.S. 186 (1986).

[33] *See benShalom III*, slip op. at 18–19 (1989 U.S. App. LEXIS 11807, *30–*31) ("If homosexual conduct may constitutionally be criminalized, then homosexuals do not constitute a suspect or quasi-suspect class entitled to greater than rational basis scrutiny for equal protection purposes."). In contrast to the *benShalom III* court's broad reading of *Hardwick*, at least one court recently confronted with the question of opposite-sex sodomy has adopted a more narrow interpretation of the *Hardwick* decision. In Hinkle v. State, 771 P.2d 232 (Okla. Crim. App. 1989), an Oklahoma state court held that a prior decision, Post v. State, 715 P.2d 1105 (Okla. Crim. App.), *cert. denied*, 479 U.S. 890 (1986), which relied on federal constitutional law to include heterosexual sodomy within the protection offered by the right to privacy, survives the Supreme Court's decision in *Hardwick*. *See Hinkle*, 771 P.2d at 233 & n.1.

[34] Gay men and lesbians continue to challenge the military's anti-gay policies. For example, a former midshipman has sued for reinstatement to the United States Naval Academy after being forced to resign because he was gay. *See* Steffan v. Cheney, No. 88-3669-oG (D.D.C. July 21, 1989) (1989 U.S. Dist. LEXIS 8347) (upholding Steffan's right to maintain an action in federal court against the Naval Academy). Under Naval Academy regulations, gay men and lesbians are separated from the Academy on the basis of their "insufficient aptitude." *See id.* (1989 U.S. Dist. LEXIS 8347, *3). Because the Academy's policy focuses on "aptitude" rather than on discipline and order, the military cases discussed above, *see supra* pp. 51–53, will provide no support for the Academy's discriminatory policy. Indeed, cases such as *Watkins* that explicitly recognize the outstanding service records of some gay or lesbian servicepersons, *see* 875 F.2d at 709, directly undermine the Academy's argument.

In addition, a military Board of Review has set aside a lower board's recommendation that Captain Judy Meade receive an other than honorable discharge for associating with a "known" lesbian. The Board of Review based its decision on the lack of evidence against Meade. *See* McKnight, *Marine Escapes Lesbian "Witchhunt,"* Gay Community News, July 16–22, 1989, at 1, col. 3; *see also supra* p. 45, note 9 (discussing the charges against Meade).

C. Congressional Activity

The Hate Crime Statistics Act, which has been introduced in Congress every year since 1984, would authorize the Attorney General to collect data relating to crimes manifesting prejudice based on the victim's race, religion, homosexuality or heterosexuality, or ethnicity.[35] In 1989, congressional controversy over whether to include sexual orientation as a category in the Act once again blocked its passage. In the House of Representatives, Representative William Dannemeyer of California and others led an effort to amend the bill to exclude anti-gay crimes.[36] In his remarks on the floor of the House, Representative Dannemeyer expressed strongly anti-gay sentiments; he lamented the progress of the gay rights movement and the repeal of many state sodomy laws,[37] and warned against "enshrin[ing] homosexuality on a pedestal alongside race and religion as the primary focus of our civil rights laws."[38] Senator Jesse Helms of North Carolina sponsored similar efforts in the Senate to exclude sexual orientation from the categories of biases warranting investigation; he attempted to amend the bill by adding anti-gay language that urged the enforcement of sodomy statutes, and depicted homosexuality as a threat to families.[39] Although the Act recently passed in the House,[40] the Senate failed to act on the bill before adjourning.[41]

Sexual orientation has also become a major issue in congressional appropriations. The Senate recently passed an amendment to its appropriations bill for the National Endowment for the Arts that would bar the use of federal funds to "promote" or depict "obscene or indecent materials," including materials that depict homoerotic subjects.[42]

[35] See Moore, Hate Crimes, 21 NAT'L J. 1604 (1989); supra pp. 38–39.

[36] See 135 CONG. REC. H3138 (daily ed. June 27, 1989) (statement of Rep. Dannemeyer); see also Stewart, Dannemeyer Suggests White House Policy Encourages Homosexuality, L.A. Times, July 1, 1989, at 28, col. 1 (discussing Dannemeyer's criticism that the Act is a "subtle affirmation of homosexuality").

[37] See 135 CONG. REC. H3183 (daily ed. June 27, 1989) (statement of Rep. Dannemeyer).

[38] Id. at H3138.

[39] See Moore, Hate Crimes, 21 NAT'L J. 1604 (1989).

[40] See 135 CONG. REC. H3238 (daily ed. June 27, 1989).

[41] In state legislatures, legislation against anti-gay crime may suffer a similar fate. In the New York state legislature, the Republican leadership in the Senate allowed a bill mandating tougher penalties for crimes motivated by biases based on race, creed, color, national origin, sex, disability, or sexual orientation, to die in committee. See Sultan, About Politics: This Bias Won't Speak Its Name, Newsday, June 19, 1989, at 46. Commentators have attributed the death of the bill — which was passed by the Democrat-controlled Assembly — to the Senate's reluctance to establish special legal protection for gay men and lesbians. See id. The prospects for a similar bill in New Jersey, passed by the state's Senate, appear equally dim, as the Speaker of the Assembly has authored an alternative bill that does not include penalties for anti-gay acts. See Kelly, States News Serv., June 7, 1989 (available on NEXIS).

[42] See 136 CONG. REC. S8806 (daily ed. July 26, 1989). The amendment bars the use of

Although the language of the amendment is extremely broad and would affect a vast range of material, the amendment's sponsor, Senator Helms, was responding to two exhibits that included anti-religious and homoerotic works.[43] The recent attempt to restrict the availability of funding for artwork associated with homosexuality follows previous congressional attempts to restrict appropriations as a result of anti-gay sentiments.[44]

II. Conclusion

The material presented in this book suggests a number of tentative conclusions regarding the viability of legal theories supporting the rights of lesbians and gay men. First, recent holdings under the equal protection clause demonstrate that, despite powerful arguments to the contrary,[45] judges equate homosexuality with sodomy,[46] and on that basis find that *Hardwick* precludes the application of heightened scrutiny to sexual orientation classifications.[47] These developments indicate that future equal protection challenges to anti-gay policies are unlikely to be successful.[48] In particular, the courts' interpretation of

---

public funds to "promote, disseminate or produce obscene or indecent materials, including but not limited to depictions of sadomasochism, homoeroticism, the exploitation of children, or individuals engaged in sex acts; or material which denigrates the objects or beliefs of the adherents of a particular religion or nonreligion." Oreskes, *Senate Votes To Bar U.S. Support of "Obscene or Indecent" Artwork*, N.Y. Times, July 27, 1989, at 1, col. 2.

[43] Senator Helms introduced the amendment in response to federal sponsorship of two artists, Andres Serrano and Robert Mapplethorpe. One of Serrano's works depicts a crucifix immersed in the artist's urine, while Mapplethorpe's photographs include homoerotic subjects. The amendment would cut off all funds for the two arts groups that sponsored the Serrano and Mapplethorpe exhibits. *See* Oreskes, *supra* note 42, at C19, col. 1. Even though the amendment may not become law, the Senate's approval of its broad language establishes a precedent for regulation of the arts by politicians. *See* Kimmelman, *Helms Bill, Whatever Its Outcome, Could Leave Mark on Arts Grants*, N.Y. Times, July 30, 1989, at 1, col. 1.

[44] The Senate previously restricted its appropriation for AIDS education, treatment, and research to exclude funding of programs that "provide educational, informational or risk-reduction materials or activities to promote or encourage, directly or indirectly, homosexual activity." Molotsky, *Programs To Fight AIDS Cleared By Senate; House's Approval Is Seen*, N.Y. Times, Apr. 29, 1988, at B4, col. 1; *see also Sex Education Manual Prompts Moral Outrage*, N.Y. Times, Apr. 24, 1988, at 39, col. 5 (describing a county's temporary withdrawal of public funds for a family planning clinic until the clinic agreed to recall all copies of a sex-education manual describing homosexuality as normal and healthy).

[45] *See, e.g., supra* pp. 56–60.

[46] *See, e.g.,* cases cited in Part III, notes 76–77, *supra* p. 55; *benShalom v. Marsh*, Nos. 88-2771, 89-1213, slip op. at 20 (7th Cir. Aug 7, 1989) (1989 U.S. App. LEXIS 11807, *33).

[47] *See, e.g., benShalom III*, slip op. at 20 (1989 U.S. App. LEXIS 11807, *33); Woodward v. United States, 871 F.2d 1068, 1076 (Fed. Cir. 1989) ("After *Hardwick*, it cannot logically be asserted that discrimination against homosexuals is constitutionally infirm.").

[48] Moreover, the Supreme Court's movement to cut back on the scope of existing substantive due process rights, *see, e.g.,* Webster v. Reproductive Health Servs., 109 S. Ct. 3040 (1989) (plurality opinion) (modifying *Roe v. Wade* by permitting states to regulate second trimester

Hardwick as precluding suspect class status even for classifications based explicitly on the status of sexual orientation[49] raises serious doubts that courts will uphold the application of heightened scrutiny in equal protection challenges to sodomy statutes, which classify solely according to conduct.[50]

Second, the relative success of gay and lesbian plaintiffs who have challenged discriminatory practices under the first amendment indicates that such challenges provide the strongest constitutional protection against discrimination on the basis of sexual orientation. Students in the public schools have successfully argued that public expression regarding sexual orientation and the freedom of gay and lesbian students to associate are protected by the first amendment.[51] The courts' recognition of the political and educational value of such speech in this context provides significant precedent for gay men and lesbians to assert that declarations of sexual orientation in other arenas constitute speech and are protected by the first amendment.[52]

Finally, given the lack of any comprehensive federal structure extending protection to gay and lesbian rights beyond the realm of the first amendment, the most viable means of legal protection is the adoption of state and local laws, and the enforcement of those laws by local agencies and state courts.[53] Local ordinances and executive

---

abortions to promote the state's interest in protecting potential life); Bowers v. Hardwick, 478 U.S. 186 (1986) (refusing to recognize a fundamental right under the due process clause to engage in same-sex sodomy), suggests that arguments for gay and lesbian rights premised on that portion of the Constitution will probably not fare well either.

[49] *See* cases cited *supra* note 47.

[50] *See supra* pp. 9–10. However, holdings by some courts that *Hardwick* precludes suspect class status for sexual orientation classifications per se do not compel the conclusion that the equal protection clause cannot be invoked to challenge discrimination against lesbians and gay men. As discussed above, discrimination against gay men and lesbians is a form of gender discrimination, as it is based on sexually stereotypical conceptions of male and female roles. *See supra* pp. 17–18; 70–71; 131; 137–38; *cf.* Price Waterhouse v. Hopkins, 109 S. Ct. 1775, 1791 (1989) (plurality opinion) (noting, in a title VII case, that, "[a]s for the legal relevance of sex stereotyping, we are beyond the day when an employer could evaluate employees by assuming or insisting that they matched the stereotype associated with their group").

[51] *See supra* pp. 74–85.

[52] Although the court in *benShalom III* rejected Miriam benShalom's first amendment argument, its holding was specific to the context of the armed services. The court was careful to note that the Army's policy did not address "speech per se," and that, in benShalom's case, it was her "act of identification" of herself as a lesbian, and hence a person ineligible for military employment, that resulted in her dismissal. *See benShalom III*, slip op. at 13–14 (1989 U.S. App. LEXIS 11807, *22–*23). Because the court couched its holding in the context of the military's substantial interest in maintaining its forces as it deems necessary, and because the court was careful to distinguish benShalom's declaration from "speech per se," the holding does not affect the validity of the cases protecting the first amendment rights of students.

[53] *See generally* A. LEONARD, GAY & LESBIAN RIGHTS PROTECTIONS IN THE U.S. (1989) (available from the National Gay & Lesbian Task Force) (describing various local protections and listing ninety-four areas which provide some form of protection against sexual orientation discrimination).

orders that specifically address gay and lesbian legal concerns provide the most effective protection against anti-gay discrimination,[54] but cases such as *Braschi* suggest that state and local statutes of more general applicability can also be used to frame successful legal challenges.

Despite some improvement, discrimination on the basis of sexual orientation persists throughout American society and the American legal system. This situation is unlikely to change until anti-gay discrimination is recognized as a legitimate issue and lesbian and gay concerns enter mainstream legal discourse. Without discussion and debate, difference will remain threatening, commonality unappreciated. It is hoped that, by reviewing and analyzing the current state of the law, this book will foster the development of that essential dialogue.

---

[54] *See supra* pp. 72–73. Such protection is, of course, drastically limited by an ordinance's subject matter and jurisdiction.